Advance p...
Larry Dixon and *Whe...*

"Not struggling with temptation and sin? Then this book is not for you. If you live in the real world, Dr. Dixon gives biblical, practical, relevant answers for fighting the two enemies of our souls."

Dr. Bill Jones, President,
Columbia International University

"Larry Dixon has done what not many others can do: He has taken a very serious and weighty subject (one that most of us cringe to hear mentioned) and has turned it into an honest, heartfelt and down-to-earth discussion of the practical ways we can find victory over temptation.

His use of humor, his poignant illustrations and his solid grasp of theology make for an easy but enlightening read. For a culture swept away by the lures of sin, this book could not have come at a better time."

David Henderson M.D.,
The Meier Clinics, Dallas, TX

"Larry Dixon has done it again. In a refreshing and insightful way, he has dealt with the hard stuff. This biblical and practical book won't make you perfect, but it'll make you better. Read this book."

Steve Brown, author,
seminary professor and host of the nationally
syndicated radio show "Steve Brown Etc."

"Dr. Larry Dixon takes on a subject that many have steered away from and does a great job answering some of the toughest questions about our struggle against sin. Drawing from Scripture, history and personal experience, he carefully reveals the perspective and plan we need in this fight. This book will teach, inspire and challenge you to understand the battle and the victory over temptation."

Jeremy Kingsley,
author of "Be Last—Descending to Greatness"

"Not many subjects remain taboo today, but Larry Dixon takes an unblinking look at one of the most taboo: the concept of sin. His description of the depth and extent of the problem is matched by his wise guidance amid the dangers, toils and snares."

Marshall Shelley
editor in chief, Leadership Media Group
vice president, Christianity Today International

WHEN
TEMPTATION
STRIKES

Gaining Victory Over Sin

Larry Dixon

CLC
PUBLICATIONS

Fort Washington, PA 19034

Published by CLC Publications

U.S.A.
P.O. Box 1449, Fort Washington, PA 19034

GREAT BRITAIN
51 The Dean, Alresford, Hants, SO24 9BJ

AUSTRALIA
P.O. Box 2299, Strathpine, QLD 4500

NEW ZEALAND
10 MacArthur Street, Feilding

ISBN: 978-0-87508-987-4

*This work is fondly dedicated
to my colleague and friend,*

Dr. Allan McKechnie.

*Thank you for modeling
a life of caring in light of heaven.*

Contents

Foreword

Jesus taught us more than two thousand years ago that if we obey one commandment, the Great Commandment, we will automatically avoid all other sins. The Great Commandment is, of course, to love God, love others and love ourselves in a spiritually healthy way. God loves us and wants what is best for us. He wants us to avoid all sins because all sins hurt somebody. Do you want to hurt people? Do you want to hurt yourself? If not, then why sin?

And yet we are all human and are clearly taught by the Scriptures that we all fail in many ways. There has only been one sinless person and that is Jesus. Thinking yourself sinless would be one of the greatest of sins—an arrogant attitude of spiritual superiority, which Solomon lists in Proverbs 6 as the number one sin God hates.

The Apostle Paul taught us that, as believers, there is absolutely no condemnation for our sins (Rom. 8:1). When we sin, it grieves God because He wants what is best for us and those we love (and those He loves), and our sins prevent us from experiencing His very best for us. He wants us to learn from our sins, but continues to love us unconditionally regardless of our level of obedience.

My goal in life is to learn more and more each day how to deeply love and be loved by God, others and myself—the Great Commandment. I don't avoid a sin merely because it is "against the rules." I avoid sin as much as possible because I want to be a genuine lover of people and of God, like Jesus was and forever will be.

As a psychiatrist, I have been listening to the deepest secrets of my clients for over 33 years now. I know from this experience that sins truly do destroy lives. Temptations tear people apart. Understanding how temptations and sins trick us into unloving acts that harm others and ourselves is therefore very important if we are to truly become happy, fulfilled people filled with love. That is why I am so delighted that Dr. Larry Dixon teaches us a great deal about these matters in his excellent book, *When Temptation Strikes*.

With ample doses of humor, Dr. Dixon faithfully reflects God's concern for our brokenness and recommends practical steps each of us can take to combat these constant threats to our lives. He is transparent about his own struggles (his appendix entitled "My Sin" is a case in point) and inspires us to trust him and his careful research into God's Word and his insights into life.

Biblical disciplines are clearly explained for those who want to grow in grace and not groan in disgrace. Healthy Christians practice biblical disciplines because we want to—because they assist us in leading lives of love. Those who do them "because they are supposed to" become legalists who are proud of their "super-spirituality" and false sense of humility.

This text is no mere mental exercise. Practical "Action Points" are provided at the end of each chapter for those who want to get serious in the battle. Dixon's discussion of the seven deadly mistakes we make about the Seven Deadly Sins I found to be particularly helpful and insightful. If "habit is broken by habit," then the development of holy, loving habits is a key to living out the victorious Christian life.

I am deeply concerned about the role of the church in helping people deal with temptation and sin. What Dixon suggests about the church, if followed, would revolutionize church-as-usual for most of us. He presents a balanced perspective on the need for professional counselors. Understanding why we are attracted to particular sins because of root problems enables us to figure out ways to meet our needs in loving and holy ways rather than making failed attempts at meeting those same needs through such sins as the lust of the flesh, the lust of the eyes and the pride of life (popularly known as unloving and selfish abuses of sex, power and money). God wants us to have sex, power and money, but in the correct, loving context and perspective. Sin misuses these wonderful creations of God.

Studying and applying the valuable lessons of this book will not turn you into an isolated monk who separates himself from society, walking miles daily to get his food and water so he can take pride in his false sense of spirituality. This book will help you turn into a lover of God, self and others, one who has meaning and purpose in life. That is why I recommend it so highly.

Paul Meier, M.D.
Founder of the National Chain of Meier Clinics,
Non-Profit Christian Counseling Centers
www.paulmeiermd.com

Introduction

This is a book about temptation and sin. It was not an easy book to write; I had to interview a lot of people for research. Telemarketers and used car salesmen have been especially helpful. Politicians, I discovered, were able to give me a great deal of useful material on these topics.

You see, I am a Bible teacher, a seminary professor and a former missionary. I've been reading the Bible since I became a Christian about forty years ago. If it weren't for a few sick days, I would have a string of perfect church attendance pins the length of a church aisle. Thus the necessity of all those interviews. After all, what would I know about temptation and sin?

The answer, unfortunately, is plenty. My privileged place of ministry hasn't made me immune from these two enemies of my soul. In fact, greater responsibility often comes with more subtle temptations, enticements to transgressions which receive a greater condemnation. I know. I've had numerous interviews with an expert in temptation and sin—myself.

Occasionally I get to teach research and writing to graduate students, and I tell them, "Write on something you know well." I am taking my own advice in this book. It's not too much to say that I've earned my share of credits toward a graduate degree in godlessness. Left to myself, I'm well on my way to a master's in missing God's mark. I know temptation and sin all too well.

I may not always recognize temptation or acknowledge sin as sin, but I've been a close associate of both since I was a wee lad. Temptation has been mostly winning in my life since childhood. I have willingly caved in to allurements to go my own way, plod my own path, make my own choices.

As I reflect on my past, I can vividly recall—and give specific examples of—fits of jealousy, bouts of envy, occasions of selfishness and acts of unkindness before I learned to shave. Pride, anger, hatred, prejudice, laziness, self-will, disrespect—all these had a place in my adolescent heart, and occasionally broke out into reality. (I'm not at all sure, by the way, that any of us ever really "grows out of" certain sins.)

I remember particular traits being modeled before me by other transgressors, whether friends, family or strangers. Outbursts of temper, impatience, lust, malice, unforgiveness, bitterness—the list could go on and on of living object lessons of temptation and sin's equal opportunity policy toward the people I knew growing up. I am not engaging in the culture of victimhood here. Both nature and nurture may help to explain my weaknesses and failings, but neither excuses me. Nor, may I say it delicately, are you off the hook because of family background or cultural environment. We each come into this world with what one writer calls "a curvature of the soul."

But if God is real and the Bible is true, we don't have to wallow in our sins. We do not have to live consistently failing Christian lives. God wants us to experience victory in His Son. And that's what this book is about.

Let me give a silly illustration. I've recently gotten into trying to solve a logical puzzle called Sudoku.© My daughter-in-law (whom I thought cared about me) introduced me to it.

Sudoku is played on a 9x9 grid, divided into 3x3 sub-grids called "regions." Some of the grid cells are already filled in with numbers (see illustration). The object of Sudoku is to fill in the empty cells with numbers between 1 and 9 (one number only in each cell) according to the following guidelines: (1) The number can appear only once in each row; (2) The number can appear only once in each column and (3) The number can appear only once in each region. The fewer the numbers originally provided in a Sudoku puzzle, the more difficult the puzzle.

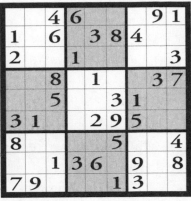

For many of us, temptation and sin are like trying to solve a Sudoku puzzle with no numbers at all! Or to put it another way, we all enter the world having to solve our own personal Sudoku puzzle, and the only number we're given to start with is ourselves! (I told you it was a silly illustration.)

I believe the Bible helps us solve life's puzzle of temptation and sin. But instead of starting with ourselves ("1") in the center, we must begin with Jesus Christ and His Word.

Some of the Bible's solutions are surprisingly straightforward. For example, we learn from the life of Joseph a very simple strategy to overcome temptation and avoid sin. You remember the story: Joseph had risen to a position of enormous power in Pharaoh's kingdom and worked for Potiphar, one of Pharaoh's officials. Joseph could have anything he wanted, with the exception of Potiphar's wife. But she wanted Joseph.

The biblical text tells us that her sexual solicitation of Joseph was a daily event: "And though she spoke to Joseph day after day, he refused to go to bed with her or even be with her" (Gen. 39:10). When she pulled out all the stops, got Joseph alone and started dropping her clothes, Joseph demonstrated a brilliant strategy for resisting temptation and turning away from sin: he ran away! Intellectual arguments about the sanctity of marriage or the current state of family values in Egypt were not Joseph's first resort. He laced up his sneakers and bolted!

Resisting temptation does not always merit the praise of others, and for his trouble Joseph got charged with attempted rape and thrown into jail. But we read,

> While Joseph was there in the prison, the LORD was with him; he showed him kindness and granted him favor in the eyes of the prison warden. So the warden put Joseph in charge of all those held in the prison, and he was made responsible for all that was done there. The warden paid no attention to anything under Joseph's care, because the LORD was with Joseph and gave him success in whatever he did. (39:20–23).

If you're at all like me, you need practical steps you can take to turn away from temptation and to say no to sin. Joseph illustrates the real-life nature of the Bible. He was a handsome guy; Potiphar's wife was probably the best-looking woman that Pharaoh's right-hand man could find. She throws herself at Joseph, but he refuses to play catch. He runs.

Other Bible passages tell us to hit the road, such as Paul's advice to the Corinthians: "Flee from sexual immorality" (1 Cor. 6:18), and "Flee from idolatry" (10:14). First Timothy 6:11, after discussing the love of money, financial contentment, and spiritual shipwreck, says, "But you, man of God, flee from all this, and pursue righteousness, godliness, faith, love, endurance and gentleness." And Second Timothy 2:22 also gives us our fleeing orders: "Flee the evil desires of youth, and pursue righteousness, faith, love and peace, along with those who call on the Lord out of a pure heart."

In the early twentieth century, The *Times of London* invited several eminent authors to write essays on the theme "What's Wrong with the World?" G.K. Chesterton (1874–1936), a Catholic scholar and novelist, sent this brief but pointed response:

> Dear Sirs,
> I am.
> Sincerely yours,
> G. K. Chesterton[1]

If you're prepared to agree with Chesterton, and want to learn biblical strategies for resisting temptation and sin, then lace on your sneaks and let's get running.

1

Chapter One

Shhhh! We're Going to Talk about the "S" Word!

Our problem is that we treat sin like a
creampuff, instead of like a rattlesnake. Billy Sunday

If you do what is right, will you not be accepted?
But if you do not do what is right, sin is crouching at your door;
it desires to have you, but you must master it. Genesis 4:7

There's an enemy out there, waiting to bring us down. Actually, "out there" doesn't really describe its location. It's a traitor in our midst, posing as an ally as it deceives and attacks us, opposing all that is good. It promises what it cannot deliver; it knows our weaknesses and shows us no mercy. We cannot fight this enemy on our own. It will drag us down to defeat and despair unless we recognize it and are equipped to oppose it.

Perhaps a better metaphor for this enemy would be a disease. This sickness has infected our very being. Like a cancerous tumor, it is invasive, progressive and lethal. Outside treatment, even of a radical nature, will not help. Without an inner healing, we are helpless and doomed to debilitation, decay and death.

This enemy can also be thought of as a massive debt, a drain on the economy of our lives. Spiritual bankruptcy is too weak an expression to describe its impact. We are victims of a monetary disaster far greater than that produced by a gang of scam artists with Internet access. Our bottom line is worse than a maxed-out credit card or a house in foreclosure. We can't even begin to pay down this debt. Worse yet, the amount we owe is multiplying at an alarming rate, compounding interest upon interest. How will it ever be paid?

This enemy could even be seen as a defilement, a contamination greater than a million Chernobyls. We have all received a lethal dose of its radiation—it lodges in our bones. And we have no one to blame but ourselves for our contaminated condition. We daily choose to be exposed to the bombardment of its invisible but destructive rays. Its pollution far outstrips the worst chemical landfill. We have been rendered unclean, filthier than a pig wallowing in its own excrement. This moral poisoning begins at birth and continues throughout life, hounding us to the grave—unless a kind of cleansing takes place. Without a wholesale decontamination, this defilement will cause us to become the eternal refuse of the universe.

We are, of course, talking about sin—and its diabolical forerunner, temptation. Sin is an enemy, the enemy of our souls. Yet most of us are unaware of the battle going on; we think we are at peace with the world, at peace with ourselves, at peace with whatever spiritual forces may be out there.

Sin has infected each of us, down to our very bone marrow. The tests have come back, they've checked the results twice, and it's bad news. The disease is malignant and progressive; it's only a matter of time. "There is no known medical treatment," the doctor says. "I'm sorry. Now is the time to put your affairs in order. I can recommend a good attorney if you need one."

We are woefully overdrawn on our spiritual bank account. There are no human resources available to consolidate our debt. Our bottom line is bleeding red ink, and we have no rich relatives to come to our aid. Spiritually speaking, the tow truck is outside, our car is being repossessed, and the bank has foreclosed on our life's mortgage. Sin has depleted our resources, and no one will extend us a line of credit— they won't even return our phone calls.

Because of sin we are defiled before a holy God. He has every right to point at us and cry out, as the Old Testament Jews did when approached by a leper, "Unclean! Unclean!"

Now, aren't you glad you bought this book?

Can We Talk?

Why don't we talk more about sin and temptation? Are they enemies in the past, no longer "crouching at our door" waiting to "have" us (Gen. 4:7)? Have sin and temptation ceased to be issues for us? Now that we know salvation in Christ, are we immune to sin's enticement?

I'm not sure what world you're living in, but no such miracle has taken place in my life! Have we become so calloused against sin that we no longer recognize its appetizer—temptation— and no longer grieve our giving in? Have we put down the menu of life, saying to the waiter, "The usual, please"?

Reasons for Our Silence: Definition

There are many reasons for silence among the saints about sin. One may be an issue of definition. Perhaps we're no longer sure what qualifies as sin. Our glossary has become worldly, our definitions degenerated to the level of personal opinion. We rely more on Gallup polls than God's Word in specifying sin and naming it as God names it.

> *"How I define a temptation and the resulting sin makes all the difference. If I define them in terms of human weakness, I can often find an excuse to justify them. If I define them in terms of offending God, it's much harder to find an excuse."*
> *(Dr. Lindsay Hislop, linguist)*

Someone has rightly warned us to beware of modern editors, for the moral dictionaries of our world are always being revised, updated, sanitized. What was a psychological disorder in a past generation is now looked at as an "alternative lifestyle." *Whatever Became of Sin?* is more than a book title. Is anyone even asking such a question anymore? A relativistic culture disdains dogmatic definitions, especially when they condemn all thoughts and actions which fail to conform to God's perfect standard.

A "Farside" cartoon in my files shows a goofy-looking man standing in his front yard. You can see that he has painted in big, bold, black letters the words "THE TREE" on a tree, "THE HOUSE" on the house, "THE DOOR" on his front door, "PANTS" on his pants, "THE DOG" on a mangy-looking dog in front of him, "THE CAT" on a disgusted cat crouched on the sidewalk, and the word "SHIRT" on the t-shirt he's wearing. With paintbrush in hand, and a bucket of paint in his other hand, he says, "Now! . . . That should clear up a few things around here!" It's important to name things—and avoiding definitions will not help us overcome temptation and sin.

Reasons for Our Silence: Denial

Perhaps our problem is denial. We don't want to admit the massive gap between God's glory and our performance. We want to soften sin, call it something other than what it is, give it a better name, a less offensive moniker.

We are guilty of what C.S. Lewis calls "chronological snobbery." We consider "sin" an old-fashioned, outdated term, the moral equivalent of a butter churn or a buggy whip. We think of our time as the brightest and most enlightened; ancient terms like "sin," "transgression" or "iniquity" belong to a primitive, sacrificial vocabulary of penance and propitiation, but seem out of place in our modern, or post-modern, context.

We euphemize sin, substituting less confrontive words like "I goofed," "I blew it" or "I slipped" to describe our actions. We employ expressions like "a mistake," "a bad call" or "a poor choice" to characterize what we have done, resorting even to color-coding our conduct: "After all," we say, "it was only a little white lie!"

Reasons for Our Silence: Defense

Maybe our problem is defense. We play the "blame game," citing circumstances, other people's behavior and life's challenges as reasons for our wickedness.

I have a confession to make (this book seems like a great place for confessions): I am addicted to "Calvin and Hobbes" cartoons. Because I sometimes co-teach a course on theology and counseling, I love the cartoon which has Calvin saying to Hobbes, "Nothing I do is my fault. My family is dysfunctional and my parents won't empower me! Consequently, I'm not self-actualized! My behavior is addictive functioning in a disease process of toxic co-dependency! I need holistic healing and wellness before I'll accept any responsibility for my actions!" Hobbes gives Calvin a bewildered look and says, "One of us needs to stick his head in a bucket of ice water." Then Calvin says, "I love the culture of victimhood."

We all seem to love the culture of victimhood. We compare ourselves to others, blithely thinking of God as a butcher who has our deeds on His scale in heaven, hoping against hope that His thumb is resting on the side of the scale that is weighing our good works.[1]

Some move from defense to offense. They look at the suffering of this world and feel little inclination to defend themselves. They think that God owes the world an explanation for all the suffering He has allowed to take place in His universe. Rather than Jonathan Edwards' "Sinners in the Hands of an Angry God," many think in terms of "God in the Hands of Angry Sinners." The novelist John Updike put it this way:

> We have become, in our Protestantism, more virtuous than the myths that taught us virtue; we judge them barbaric. We resist the bloody legalities of the Redemption; we face Judgment Day, in our hearts, much as young radicals face the mundane courts—convinced that acquittal is the one just verdict.

We judge our Judge . . . incidentally reducing his ancient foe to the dimensions of a bad comic strip.[2]

How shocked many will be on Judgment Day when they realize, to their eternal shame, that acquittal will not be granted to anyone apart from the blood of Christ!

We've redefined, denied and defended ourselves into spiritual confusion, not sure what sin and temptation are, or what prevention or remedy may be available to us. And in some ways the clearinghouse of sin, the church, has only made things worse. But more on that later.

> *"No one in the church admits to struggling with anything! And I'm certainly not going to start the discussion!" (Caroline, young mother)*

Imagine a Church

What would life be like if we could really be honest with one another in our churches? What if I had the freedom to ask for prayer concerning a particular temptation that seemed to be tightening its bony grip around my throat? What if I could acknowledge my sins to another brother or sister in Christ and receive, not judgmental shock or legalistic rejection, but exactly what I need from God—through them? If I am minimizing my sin, they would bring truth and clarity, wrapped in the embrace of tough love. If I am overwhelmed by the guilt of my sin, they would remind me of the promise of First John 1:9: "If we confess our sins, he is faithful and just and will forgive us our sins and purify us from all unrighteousness."

I have another confession to make. Are you ready? I am slightly envious of my Roman Catholic friends. You know why? Because they have a confessional booth where they can go and acknowledge their sins to a priest who will listen to them, absolve them and give them specific religious duties to perform to make up for their transgressions.

Confession is expected, at least once a year, in the Catholic community. People know they are sinners, and the machinery is in place for them to do something about it. We Protestants don't even have a dark little room where we can tell the truth about ourselves.

But what I have in being an evangelical Protestant (don't tell my Catholic friends this) far exceeds the cold, anonymous, works-oriented confessional booth in a Roman Catholic church. We have the community of God's people. We read in James 5:16, "Therefore confess your sins to each other and pray for each other so that you may be healed. The prayer of a righteous man is powerful and effective."

It is interesting that James says we are to confess to "each other." According to Scripture, every believer in Christ is a priest (see Rev. 1:6, 5:10 and 20:6) to whom others can confess their sins. But do we serve as priests? Have you recently heard a confession? Every believer in Christ can "bind and loose" sins (Matt. 16:19), which means declaring forgiven or unforgiven a person's transgressions. When was the last time you did that? Every believer in Christ can pour out the promises of God to one who has fallen and remind him or her that God has said, "as far as the east is from the west, so far has he removed our transgressions from us" (Ps. 103:12). Have you used Psalm 103:12 lately with another believer? Each of us can declare with God's authority that "everyone who believes in him receives forgiveness of sins through his name" (Acts 10:43). We can boldly proclaim to each other that "in him we have redemption through his blood, the forgiveness of sins, in accordance with the riches of God's grace" (Eph. 1:7). Forgiveness is a big deal with God. The term "forgive" is used numerous times in the Word of God. When was the last time you needed to remind another believer of their forgiveness in Jesus? Is it that we never question our cleansing in Christ? Do we take it for granted? Or do we keep our sins and our doubts to ourselves?

I'll say it again: What if we could really be honest with one another in church? Does such a church even exist? Not too long ago I spoke in a church on the topic of sin and confession. As the forty or so members came into that midweek prayer meeting, I handed each a 3x5 index card. After our season of prayer, it was my turn to preach the Word. I said, "Please take out the index card I gave you. Now, don't write your name on it, or the nature of your sin. I only want you to write down the date of your last known confession of sin. Ready? Go!"

When I collected the cards, I was not at all surprised to read some that said, "My last known sin I confessed was when I trusted Jesus as my Savior in 1934." Or, "My last known sin I confessed was twenty years ago when my first wife ran off with a local vacuum cleaner salesman." Hmmm. Last time I looked, Matthew 6:11-13 said, "Give us today our daily bread. Forgive us our debts, as we also have forgiven our debtors. And lead us not into temptation, but deliver us from the evil one." Just as we trust God for our daily bread, we are to confess to Him our daily need for forgiveness of our sins ("debts") and our daily need not to be led into temptation. Some Christians, it seems, change the word daily to decades!

Is There Hope?

The answer is yes! This enemy can be defeated. We can be trained and equipped to recognize this enemy and to withstand it. But make no mistake. We will never "come to terms with" sin or reach a truce with temptation. They will never change sides; they will always be enemies, never allies.

"It seems that weakness is the ultimate evil. We won't admit our struggles. In the church it's really the survival of the most dishonest!" (David, father of two)

Temptation and sin are to be fought with every fiber of our being. As the evangelist Billy Sunday once said, "I'm against sin. I'll kick it as long as I have a foot. I'll fight it as long as I have a fist. I'll butt it as long as I have a head. I'll bite it as long as I've got a tooth. And when I'm old and fistless and footless and toothless, I'll gum it till I go home to Glory and it goes home to perdition."

This disease has been cured. The Son of God took this disease upon Himself and bore it on His cross. Isaiah reminds us that "Surely he took up our infirmities and carried our sorrows . . . he was pierced for our transgressions, he was crushed for our iniquities; the punishment that brought us peace was upon him, and by his wounds we are healed" (Isa. 53:4–5). He stands ready to help us oppose any new outbreak of the illness.

What about our debt? We owed God a debt we could never repay. In fact, only God Himself could pay that debt, but God did not owe the debt to Himself. So God the Son became human so that He could die and pay our debt! It is as if we have received our credit card bill and it is marked across the top "PAID IN FULL!" Picture God, match in hand, burning the mortgage on our lives. We owe nothing. If we tried to pay for a gift, we'd insult the giver, wouldn't we?

Colossians 2:14 says that Jesus "cancelled the written code, with its regulations, that was against us and that stood opposed to us; he took it away, nailing it to the cross." Wow! Jesus crucified sin by the sacrifice of Himself. The Carpenter from Nazareth did some nailing of His own at Calvary.

But what about our defilement? How is our contamination taken away? There is an account of a supposed conversation between the great Rabbi Joshua ben Levi and the prophet Elijah. The rabbi asks, "When will the Messiah come?" and "By what sign may I recognize him?" Elijah tells the rabbi to go to the city's gates where he will find the Messiah sitting among the poor lepers. The prophet says that the Messiah sits there, bandaging his leprous sores one at a time, unlike the other lepers who bandage them all at once. When asked why, Elijah says that the Messiah might be needed at any time and would not want to be delayed. Elijah then says that the Messiah will come, "Today, if you listen to his voice."[3]

Another Jewish legend says that one of the names for the Messiah would be "the leper." We read in Sanhedrin 98b, "The Messiah—what is his name? . . . The Rabbis say, The Leper Scholar, as it is said, 'surely he has borne our griefs and carried our sorrows: yet we did esteem him a leper, smitten of God and afflicted . . .'"

The Baal Shem Tov (b. 1698), the founder of the Hasidic movement, was riding one day with a young student. He stopped his wagon at the hut of an old leper, horribly affected by the disease. The rabbi climbed down and spent a great deal of time with the poor man. When he returned to the wagon and recommenced his journey, the puzzled student asked the rabbi who it was that the rabbi had visited with. The rabbi replied that in every generation there is a Messiah who will reveal himself if the generation is worthy. The leper he had been meeting with was that Messiah, but the generation was not worthy, so the Messiah would depart.[4]

Where did this "Leper Messiah" idea come from? HaDaVar, a Messianic ministry, responds to the Jewish charge that Jesus could not have been the Messiah because He defiled Himself by touching a leper (Matt. 8:3). "The fact that Yeshua touched a leper—an unclean body—does not disqualify Him from Messiahship. This is especially true in light of the rabbinic doctrine concerning the 'Leper Messiah,' taken from Isaiah 53. Contact with 'leprosy' was a requirement for being the Messiah, an authenticating qualification, rather than a disqualification. According to Raphael Pata in *The Messiah Texts*, the name of the Messiah connected to Isaiah 53:4 is 'The Leprous of the House of Study.'"[5]

HaDaVar goes on to explain that the rabbis struggled with Isaiah 53, for they either saw the Messiah's sufferings as leprosy or split the Messiah in two, one a sufferer and one a conqueror. The Hebrew words in Isaiah 53:4, "stricken" (*nagua*) and "smitten" (*mukkay*) are interpreted as referring to a leprous condition. Either word can refer to being stricken with a disease, yet they need not be understood in that way, just as our English word "stricken" may or may not refer to disease.

Either way, Jesus was stricken. He was certainly made sick by the Roman floggings and beatings and the tortuous ordeal of crucifixion. He was certainly stricken with the Roman lash. As a leper was despised and rejected of men, so also was the Messiah despised and rejected. And still today there are many who see Jesus as being as repugnant as leprosy and his followers as those who should be isolated and shunned. To the followers of the Suffering One, His afflictions described in Isaiah 53 are the agonies of One dying to provide atonement. The lamb being led to slaughter envisioned by Isaiah is described as one punished in the place of his people. Jesus, the true Messiah, came as the "Lamb of God who takes away the sin of the world." His crucifixion provided a substitutionary sacrifice adequate to fulfill the punishment we all deserve.[6]

> *"Opportunity may knock once, but temptation bangs on your front door forever."*
> *(Anonymous)*

Jesus became a leper for us. And He has washed us clean!

So, is there hope? Hope of being rescued from the enemy of our souls? Hope of an eternal cure from that disease? Hope of our debt being cancelled, not because God simply waves His hand and says the debt doesn't matter, but because Scripture says, "it was not with perishable things such as silver or gold that you were redeemed from the empty way of life . . . but with the precious blood of Christ, a lamb without blemish or defect" (1 Pet. 1:18-19)? Is there hope of our defilement being cleansed? Yes, oh, yes! But there is still a battle at hand.

✓ Practical Action Points

1. We must call sin what it is. Weak, defensive, watered-down terms for sin do not help us to combat it.

2. We must choose to believe the Bible about our alienation from God because of sin. If we do not submit to Scripture's assessment of our spiritual condition before God, we will fail to appreciate God's mercy in Christ.

3. We are not alone in our struggle against temptation and sin. We must return to the biblical doctrine of the church as the place where we can confess to each other and find help.

4. We must claim by faith what the Scriptures say about our new life in Jesus Christ. The debt has been paid; the defilement has been removed. We are no longer condemned!

2

Chapter Two

Getting Our Terms Straight

Why shouldn't we quarrel about a word? What is the good of words if they aren't important enough to quarrel over?
(G.K. Chesterton)

Everyone who sins breaks the law; in fact, sin is lawlessness.
(1 John 3:4)

We mentioned in Chapter 1 that our tendency is to try to edit God, to replace His words with our own. Or we euphemize sin, calling it something less offensive (at least to us and our culture) for various reasons. But exactly what terms does God use in His Word to describe what He declares several times that He "hates"?

God's Holy Hatred

Before we examine several of those biblical terms, let's look at a truth that has escaped many believers, the concept that God *hates*. In a culture whose mantra is "God is love (if there is a God)," it seems very foreign to hear the Lord con-

demn the Canaanites by saying to His people in Deuteronomy 12:31, "You must not worship the LORD your God
in their way, because in worshiping their gods, they do all
kinds of detestable things the LORD *hates*. They even burn
their sons and daughters in the fire as sacrifices to their gods."
The God of the Bible doesn't have much respect for religious pluralism, does He?

Notice how God is described in Psalm 5:5: "The arrogant cannot stand in your presence; you *hate* all who do
wrong." It seems a bit difficult to reconcile this with the
common Christian saying that God "hates the sin but loves
the sinner." Similarly we read in Psalm 11:5, "The LORD
examines the righteous, but the wicked and those who love
violence his soul *hates*." In fact, one passage even tells us that
the Lord turns from loving to hating those who commit sin:
"Because of all their wickedness in Gilgal, I *hated* them there.
Because of their sinful deeds, I will drive them out of my
house. I will no longer love them; all their leaders are rebellious" (Hos. 9:15).

We learn from Scripture that God despises empty religion, rituals that have lost their meaning. "Your New Moon
festivals and your appointed feasts my soul *hates*. They have
become a burden to me; I am weary of bearing them" (Isa.
1:14). The prophet Amos records the Lord's words: "I *hate*,
I despise your religious feasts; I cannot stand your assem-
blies" (Amos 5:21). When we just go through the religious
motions, leaving our hearts at home, I wonder what the Lord
feels about *our* meetings?

God has a hate list and it includes such sins as robbery,
iniquity (Isa. 61:8), plotting evil against one's neighbor, loving to swear falsely (Zech. 8:17), divorce, addiction to vio-

lence and breaking faith (Mal. 2:16). The Lord speaks of certain practices as "detestable things" that He "hates," such as not turning from wickedness or not ceasing to worship other gods (Jer. 44:4–5). Proverbs 6:16-19 tells us that "There are six things the LORD *hates*, seven that are detestable to him . . ." The list includes "haughty eyes, a lying tongue, hands that shed innocent blood, a heart that devises wicked schemes, feet that are quick to rush into evil, a false witness who pours out lies and . . ." (I'll leave the seventh for you to look up. The wording indicates that this is something God especially despises.)

Not only does God hate wickedness (Ps. 45:7), but the Psalmist says that God's followers are to do the same: "Let those who love the LORD *hate* evil, for he guards the lives of his faithful ones and delivers them from the hand of the wicked" (97:10). The Psalmist even follows his own advice: "I *hate* and abhor falsehood but I love your law" (119:163). In fact, the very definition of fearing the Lord, says Proverbs 8:13, is "to *hate* evil."

> A Mormon used-car salesman was asked, "How can you be a used-car salesman when your Mormonism prohibits lying?" "I don't lie," he answered, "I'm just vague. When people ask me, 'What's the gas mileage on this car?' I answer, 'Hmmm. Gas mileage. That's pretty important.'"

There is "a time to love and a time to *hate*," Solomon reminds us (Eccl. 3:8). Amos 5:15 tells the believer to "*Hate* evil, love good; maintain justice in the courts. Perhaps the LORD God Almighty will have mercy on the remnant of Joseph."

And it is not just the Old Testament that contains such hate speech. Paul tells us that "Love must be sincere. *Hate* what is evil; cling to what is good." (Rom. 12:9). John compliments the church in Ephesus by saying, "But you have this in your favor: You *hate* the practices of the Nicolaitans, which I also hate" (Rev. 2:6). And Paul sets an example to believers to even hate their own actions if they are are inconsistent with God's Word: "I do not understand what I do. For what I want to do I do not do, but what I *hate* I do" (Rom. 7:15).

New York Mayor Michael Bloomberg once said, "I never liked anyone who didn't have a temper. If you don't have any temper, you don't have any passion." While there are differences between anger and hatred, we must realize that there is a holy hatred that we must have. Hating what God hates shows a passion for Him and His truth. It may sound crazy in a culture that expects Christians to show only love, but could it be that one of our biggest problems is we have not learned how to *hate*?

Some people view the God of the Old Testament as a God of anger, fury and wrath, but the God of the New Testament as a God of mercy, love and forgiveness. This old liberal saw does not survive serious examination, especially in light of Jesus' declarations about hell in the Gospels and the book of Revelation's descriptions of the Lake of Fire.[1] We learn in Daniel 12:2 that "Multitudes who sleep in the dust of the earth will awake: some to everlasting life, others to shame and everlasting contempt." Those who die outside of the saving work of Christ will be in the end not eternal objects of God's love, but of His wrath and holy hatred.

What response to sin would we *want* God to have? Some think He is actively torturing His creation—a cosmic sadist who entertains Himself with human misery. Others believe

He contains both good and bad in Himself, the *yin* and the *yang*, that there is a dark side to God. Still others suggest that God is impassive, that He doesn't care one way or the other what happens in His universe, that He is really "beyond all that." But as Sam Mikolaski says, "Unless God is angry with sin, let us put a bullet in our collective brain, for the universe is mad."[2]

An Inquiry into Iniquity

One of the primary words for sin is "iniquity," and is defined by the Random House Dictionary as "gross injustice or wickedness; a violation of right or duty; wicked act; sin." The term comes from two words which mean "uneven." Of course, these definitions pertain to the English word. The Hebrew and Greek terms translated "iniquity" carry with them several word pictures which we must grasp.

> *I've never really thought about what my adult entertainment does to men. I don't stay awake at night wondering if I'm doing the right thing.*
>
> *I can't talk any longer. Gotta get back to work."*
> *(Manager of a local strip club)*

We learn from Psalm 73:7 that the source of iniquity is our callous hearts. In fact, the psalmist here says about the wicked, "the evil conceits of their minds know no limits." An insensitivity to God's truth plus the over-esteeming of one's own thinking lead to iniquity.

Micah pronounces judgment on the conspirators of iniquity: "Woe to those who plan iniquity, to those who plot evil on their beds! At morning's light they carry it out because it is in their power to do it" (Mic. 2:1). Plotting iniquity is condemnable before God. And before man, believe it or not. I once served on a jury that found several men guilty of conspiring to rob the bank where my wife and I had our $23.17! They never even made it into the building. They were arrested for suspicious behavior outside in the parking lot (one was caught with a sawed-off shotgun, by the way), and found guilty of conspiracy to commit armed bank robbery. I must admit that at the trial I felt like standing up and shouting Isaiah 61:8 to the defendants: "God hates robbery and iniquity"!

How wonderful to learn, from texts like Psalm 25:11, that iniquity, even though it is great, can be forgiven. But it must be acknowledged and not covered up (Ps. 32:5). This involves one's being troubled by his iniquity, by his sin (Ps. 38:18).

David's sin with Bathsheba (which we will look at in more detail in Chapter 6) is the background for his confession of sin in Psalms 32 and 51. David felt filthy after succumbing to temptation and willfully turning from God. The images of washing and cleansing are used by David to speak of his iniquity being dealt with by God (Ps. 51:2). In that same Psalm he pleads with God, "Hide your face from my sins and blot out all my iniquity" (51:9).

In another context the sons of Korah speak of iniquity as being forgiven as God covers all their sins (Ps. 85:2). The writers of the Psalms do not sugarcoat evil. We learn in Psalm 89:32 that iniquity deserves punishment with the rod and flogging! The psalmist even prays an imprecatory prayer against his enemy, imagining the worst fate for him that he can: "May the iniquity of his fathers be remembered before the LORD; may the sin of his mother never be blotted out" (109:14).

We learn much about our iniquity by looking at what the promised Messiah would do for us. Isaiah tells us that "We all, like sheep, have gone astray, each of us has turned to his own way; and the LORD has laid on him the iniquity of us all." (Isa. 53:6). When we minimize our iniquity we need to take another look at the cross. Try to minimize that.

> *"Iniquity" has the meaning of unevenness. "Transgression" has the meaning of stepping across.*

A Treatise on Transgression

The Random House Dictionary defines "transgression" as "an act of transgressing [don't you love it when a dictionary does that?], violation of a law, command, etc.; sin." It suggests the root meaning is a "stepping across."

When I was a young boy, part of growing up was learning how to appropriately threaten other boys in the neighborhood. I don't mean in a seriously harmful way, but marking out one's territory, arranging the pecking order. I must have seen someone in an old Western in a standoff with a rival, and the one fellow drew a line in the sand with the toe of his boot and said, "I dare you to step over this line!" If he stepped over the line, there would be a fight. If he didn't, then a point (not sure what point) would have been made.

I tried that once with a neighborhood bully who had stolen my marbles. I drew a line and challenged him to step over it. When he did with hardly a thought, I drew another line and dared him to step over that one too! He just laughed and walked away. I was glad. It meant I lived to threaten other boys, smaller boys, another day.

God doesn't re-draw His lines. He doesn't step back and change the rules. And His lines are not nearly as squiggly as we sometimes like to think.

What do we learn about transgression from the Scriptures? The psalmist prays in Psalm 19 to be kept from willful sins. He says that he would then be blameless, "innocent of great transgression." (v. 13). There are *categories* of sins in the Scriptures; some are more willful than others. Some will receive greater judgment.

David says in Psalm 32 that the man is blessed whose transgressions are forgiven, whose sins are covered (v. 1). Transgressions are to be confessed, says David. When he confessed, God "forgave the guilt of my sin" (v. 5). The psalmist prays, "Save me from all my transgressions; do not make me the scorn of fools" (39:8). If we looked at sin as the enemy of our souls, we would cry out more fervently for rescue from our transgressions.

The psalmist asks the Lord to "blot out my transgressions" in Psalm 51:1, and Isaiah gives the wonderful answer to that prayer: "I, even I, am he who blots out your transgressions, for my own sake, and remembers your sins no more" (Isa. 43:25). There are two kinds of blotters. The first is a piece of thick paper used to absorb excess ink and protect a desk top. Spiritually speaking, all the ink which could be used to describe my sins in excruciating detail has been absorbed by the Lord Jesus Christ. He has blotted up my sins. The second kind of blotter is a police blotter—a book in which incidents or arrests are recorded as they occur. God has put away the police blotter of my sins, and no longer records my transgressions against me. This is a reflection of His love, which "keeps no record of wrongs" (1 Cor. 13:5).

After all, the psalmist observes, "If you, O LORD, kept a record of sins, O Lord, who could stand?" (Ps. 130:3).

Someone has said that before we can get sinners saved, we have to get them lost. That is, people must recognize their sinfulness, their need of a Savior. The Holy Spirit brings conviction of sin, and we pray for His divine work in our friends and loved ones. David speaks of a constant awareness of his sin in Psalm 51:3, "For I know my transgressions, and my sin is always before me." Such knowledge of our sins must be overwhelming, apart from God's grace. In Psalm 65:3 we read, "When we were overwhelmed by sins, you forgave our transgressions." A culture unconcerned about its transgressions is a culture cut off from God.

But the Lord does not want us wallowing in our guilt. With geographical language meant to encourage our hearts, the psalmist says, "as far as the east is from the west, so far has he removed our transgressions from us" (103:12).

God is under no obligation to do this, is He? Micah says, "Who is a God like you, who pardons sin and forgives the transgression of the remnant of his inheritance? You do not stay angry forever but delight to show mercy" (7:18). Judgment is described elsewhere as God's "strange work" (Isa. 28:21).

Concerning the Messiah, we read in Isaiah 53 the words: "But he was pierced for our transgressions, he was crushed for our iniquities; the punishment that brought us peace was upon him, and by his wounds we are healed. . . . By oppression and judgment he was taken away. And who can speak of his descendants? For he was cut off from the land of the living; for the transgression of my people he was stricken."

The prophet Daniel speaks of the glorious end of sin:

"Seventy 'sevens' are decreed for your people and your holy city to finish transgression, to put an end to sin, to atone for wickedness, to bring in everlasting righteousness, to seal up vision and prophecy and to anoint the most holy" (9:24).

Micah 6:7 reminds us that what the Lord wants from us is *us*: "Will the LORD be pleased with thousands of rams, with ten thousand rivers of oil? Shall I offer my firstborn for my transgression, the fruit of my body for the sin of my soul?" We cannot self-pay for our sins. We need a substitute.

This is literally a matter of life and death. Thank God, He has "made us *alive* with Christ even when we were *dead* in transgressions—it is by grace you have been saved." (Eph. 2:5). The lethal nature of sin is illustrated in the following Old Testament story of sin as both iniquity and transgression.

Saul: A Case Study of Transgression

In First Samuel 15 we are given the story of the collapse of the first of Israel's kings, Saul. The story begins with God's clear instructions to Saul concerning the hated Amalekites:

> Samuel said to Saul, "I am the one the LORD sent to anoint you king over his people Israel; so listen now to the message from the LORD. This is what the LORD Almighty says: 'I will punish the Amalekites for what they did to Israel when they waylaid them as they came up from Egypt. Now go, attack the Amalekites and totally destroy everything that belongs to them. Do not spare them; put to death men and women, children and infants, cattle and sheep, camels and donkeys.'" (15:1–3)

How much clearer could the instructions be? Saul is reminded by the prophet Samuel that it was the Lord who anointed Saul king. His was a divinely-given power. The Lord lays out specific directions concerning the Amalekites. He wants them utterly wiped out for what they did to Israel back in Exodus 17. The expression "totally destroy" occurs seven times in this chapter. In no uncertain terms Saul is commanded by God to attack and "totally destroy everything that belongs to them." (1 Sam. 15:3). Saul is being used by God as a dispenser of divine judgment. This is not a normal case of conquering another people group. God even gives Saul a list of what is included in the prescribed total destruction: "Do not spare them; put to death men and women, children and infants, cattle and sheep, camels and donkeys." (v. 3). We might not like God's command to annihilate the Amalekites (one is reminded of the pogroms in the book of Joshua), but we must admit that God's instructions here do not lack clarity. There is no room for "interpretation."

Does Saul carry out God's specific order? No, we read in the next several verses:

> So Saul summoned the men and mustered them at Telaim—two hundred thousand foot soldiers and ten thousand men from Judah. Saul went to the city of Amalek and set an ambush in the ravine. Then he said to the Kenites, "Go away, leave the Amalekites so that I do not destroy you along with them; for you showed kindness to all the Israelites when they came up out of Egypt." So the Kenites moved away from the Amalekites.
>
> Then Saul attacked the Amalekites all the way from Havilah to Shur, to the east of Egypt. He took Agag king of the Amalekites alive, and all his people he totally destroyed with the sword. But Saul and the army spared Agag and the best of the sheep and cattle, the fat calves and lambs—everything that

was good. These they were unwilling to destroy completely, but everything that was despised and weak they totally destroyed. (15:4–9)

With 210,000 soldiers Saul set an ambush. He allowed the Kenites to escape the attack because they had showed kindness to Israel. Saul attacked the Amalekites, but he took Agag the Amalekite king alive. Saul and his army sorted out the livestock, keeping the good sheep and cattle, but totally destroying the "despised and weak" animals. They used their powers of discernment to separate out the good from the bad. The Bible says, "they were unwilling to destroy completely" what God had told them to destroy.

Let's briefly review Saul's case. Saul was to be on God's mission, a mission of utter judgment against the wicked Amalekites. God's evaluation of the Amalekites was that there was nothing worth preserving of their culture. Saul is specifically told not to spare them. He is even given a list of what God wants destroyed. Saul attacks the Amalekites, takes their king alive, and spares carefully-selected livestock. We next read,

> Then the word of the LORD came to Samuel: "I am grieved that I have made Saul king, because he has turned away from me and has not carried out my instructions." Samuel was troubled, and he cried out to the LORD all that night.
>
> Early in the morning Samuel got up and went to meet Saul, but he was told, "Saul has gone to Carmel. There he has set up a monument in his own honor and has turned and gone on down to Gilgal." (15:10–12)

God tells the prophet Samuel what Saul did. Saul's disobedience grieved the Lord. God describes the choices that

Saul made as a turning away from the Lord, a failure to carry out His instructions. Samuel was himself so moved by Saul's sin that he didn't sleep, crying out to the Lord all that night. Samuel has to track down Saul who has set up a monument in his own honor.

We then read,

> When Samuel reached him, Saul said, "The LORD bless you! I have carried out the LORD's instructions."
>
> But Samuel said, "What then is this bleating of sheep in my ears? What is this lowing of cattle that I hear?"
>
> Saul answered, "The soldiers brought them from the Amalekites; they spared the best of the sheep and cattle to sacrifice to the LORD your God, but we totally destroyed the rest." (15:13–15)

Saul claimed he had carried out the Lord's instructions, but if he had, there should have been silence in the land. Samuel essentially replies, "Hark! Animal noises. Why are there signs of life where God had decreed death?" Saul's response is to blame others: "The soldiers brought them from the Amalekites; they spared the best of the sheep and cattle to sacrifice to the LORD your God, but we totally destroyed the rest." Saul is not accepting responsibility for what his soldiers did. Human discrimination was employed in sorting out the best of the animals from the rest. The excuse is used that those animals would be sacrificed to the Lord. (Interesting that Saul says to Samuel they would be sacrificed to "the LORD *your* God.")

We then read in the text,

> "Stop!" Samuel said to Saul. "Let me tell you what the LORD said to me last night."

"Tell me," Saul replied.

Samuel said, "Although you were once small in your own eyes, did you not become the head of the tribes of Israel? The LORD anointed you king over Israel. And he sent you on a mission, saying, 'Go and completely destroy those wicked people, the Amalekites; make war on them until you have wiped them out.' Why did you not obey the LORD? Why did you pounce on the plunder and do evil in the eyes of the LORD?" (15:16–19)

Samuel can't bear to hear Saul's lies. He reminds Saul that God exalted him to become Israel's leader. He reminds Saul of his mission—to completely destroy the Amalekites. Finally, he confronts him directly with his sin: "Why did you not obey the LORD? Why did you pounce on the plunder and do evil in the eyes of the LORD?"

Notice the charges that Samuel makes: 1) You forgot your own smallness before God; 2) You forgot it was the Lord who elevated and anointed you; 3) You forgot your mission, a mission that was clear; 4) You did not obey the Lord; 5) You pounced on the plunder (greed); 6) You did evil in the eyes of the Lord.

We then read,

"But I did obey the LORD," Saul said. "I went on the mission the LORD assigned me. I completely destroyed the Amalekites and brought back Agag their king. The soldiers took sheep and cattle from the plunder, the best of what was devoted to God, in order to sacrifice them to the LORD your God at Gilgal." (15:20–21)

For a second time, Saul claims to have carried out the Lord's instructions (see v. 13), when he obviously didn't. What is going on here? Does Saul really think he was obedient to the Lord? Is he trying to deceive Samuel? It appears that he honestly believes he has done what God required him to do. Sin perverts our reason and brings self-deceit.

It's interesting to compare Saul's two claims of obeying the Lord. In verses 13–15 Saul did not hide from Samuel; he greeted him enthusiastically, proud of his "obedience." In his mind he had carried out the Lord's instructions. He blamed his soldiers for sparing the animals, then defended their action with a religious excuse. He quickly adds, "But we totally destroyed the rest."

˙In verses 20–21, when he is accused of not obeying the Lord, with "pouncing on the plunder," with "doing evil in the eyes of the Lord," Saul contradicts God's prophet: "But I did obey the Lord." (v. 20). Note Saul's claims: He says "I obeyed the Lord," "I went on the mission," "I completely destroyed . . ." He defends the soldiers in taking the best of the animals to sacrifice to the Lord.

Sin has terrible effects on us. The lies we tell others can begin to look like the truth to us. We can convince ourselves that we are living in obedience to God when we aren't. We can blame others, even others under our authority, for not doing God's will. We can excuse disobedience for religious reasons. We can turn a deaf ear to God's appointed spokesman who is speaking God's truth. We can emulate the practices of others around us (capturing the Philistine leader rather than executing him reflected the practice of pagan warriors).

We next read,

> But Samuel replied:
>
> "Does the LORD delight in burnt offerings and sacrifices
> as much as in obeying the voice of the LORD?

To obey is better than sacrifice,
  and to heed is better than the fat of rams." (15:22)

Our God has not left us in the dark about what pleases Him. Samuel confronts Saul's idea that he can do what he jolly well pleases, as long as there is a religious dimension to it. "NO!" says Samuel. "You chose something other than OBEDIENCE!" Samuel asks the poignant question: "Does the Lord delight in burnt offerings and sacrifices as much as in obeying the voice of the Lord?" This question certainly reminds us of Micah 6:6–8:

With what shall I come before the LORD
  and bow down before the exalted God?
Shall I come before him with burnt offerings,
  with calves a year old?
Will the LORD be pleased with thousands of rams,
  with ten thousand rivers of oil?
Shall I offer my firstborn for my transgression,
  the fruit of my body for the sin of my soul?
He has showed you, O man, what is good.
  And what does the LORD require of you?
To act justly and to love mercy
  and to walk humbly with your God.

God was looking for *obedience* from Saul and He got meaningless religious rituals instead. We next read Samuel saying,

"For rebellion is like the sin of divination,
  and arrogance like the evil of idolatry.
Because you have rejected the word of the LORD
  he has rejected you as king." (15:23)

Samuel delivers a scorching simile: "Rebellion is like the sin of divination!" (Interesting that Saul resorts to divination when he has Samuel conjured up from the dead thirteen chapters later in First Samuel 28.) Samuel's second scorching simile concerns arrogance: "Arrogance [is] like the evil of idolatry." Samuel accuses Saul of both divination and idolatry in one fell swoop.

There is a reciprocity with the Lord: Saul rejected God's Word; the Lord rejected Saul as king. How serious was Saul's sin? It lost him the kingdom of Israel. We next read,

> Then Saul said to Samuel, "I have sinned. I violated the LORD's command and your instructions. I was afraid of the people and so I gave in to them. Now I beg you, forgive my sin and come back with me, so that I may worship the LORD."
>
> But Samuel said to him, "I will not go back with you. You have rejected the word of the LORD, and the LORD has rejected you as king over Israel!" (15:24–26)

Saul "confesses." He acknowledges that he has sinned and admits it was because he was afraid of the people. (Proverbs 29:25 tells us that "Fear of man will prove to be a snare, but whoever trusts in the LORD is kept safe.") But there is more to Saul's "confession" than repentance. He wants something more than forgiveness. He wants to keep the kingdom. When he pleads with Samuel to come back with him, "so that I may worship the Lord," he is asking Samuel to make it appear to the people that Saul is right with God!

There is no room for negotiation with the Lord's prophet; Samuel refuses to go back with Saul, insisting that he has been rejected by the Lord as Israel's king.

We next read,

As Samuel turned to leave, Saul caught hold of the hem of his robe, and it tore. Samuel said to him, "The LORD has torn the kingdom of Israel from you today and has given it to one of your neighbors—to one better than you. He who is the Glory of Israel does not lie or change his mind; for he is not a man, that he should change his mind." (15:27–29)

In trying to force Samuel to go back with him, Saul tears his robe, so the prophet uses the event as an object lesson: "The Lord has torn the kingdom of Israel from you today and has given it to one of your neighbors." Saul has not only lost his throne but also the line of succession: The kingdom will not go to a family member (such as Jonathan), but to one of his neighbors. Finally, Samuel teaches some important theology: In contrast to sinful Saul, Israel's God never lies or changes His mind. Deceit and double-mindedness is a mark of fallen, fallible humanity.

We then read,

> Saul replied, "I have sinned. But please honor me before the elders of my people and before Israel; come back with me, so that I may worship the LORD your God." So Samuel went back with Saul, and Saul worshiped the LORD. (15:30–31)

A second time Saul admits, "I have sinned," but he begs Samuel to honor him before the elders and go back with him, which Samuel agrees to do. But the relationship between them is irretrievably broken. We read that "until the day Samuel died, he did not go to see Saul again, though Samuel mourned for him" (15:35). Sin destroys relationships. Sin also wounds the heart of God. The text tells us: "And the Lord was grieved that he had made Saul king over Israel" (15:35).

Some momentous events take place in the succeeding chapters, most of which involve David: He is anointed as rightful king, he kills Goliath, he becomes a great warrior, he becomes a fugitive. Saul remains somewhat of a background figure until chapter 28, when we read,

> Now Samuel was dead, and all Israel had mourned for him and buried him in his own town of Ramah. Saul had expelled the mediums and spiritists from the land.
>
> The Philistines assembled and came and set up camp at Shunem, while Saul gathered all the Israelites and set up camp at Gilboa. When Saul saw the Philistine army, he was afraid; terror filled his heart. He inquired of the LORD, but the LORD did not answer him by dreams or Urim or prophets. Saul then said to his attendants, "Find me a woman who is a medium, so I may go and inquire of her."
>
> "There is one in Endor," they said. (28:3–7)

People do strange things out of fear. Saul was terrified of the Philistines, so he tried to get wisdom from the Lord, but the Lord "did not answer him by dreams or Urim or prophets." He then made a foolish choice: He sent for a medium to inquire of her. Consulting mediums was strictly forbidden in Jewish law—in fact, *Saul himself* had outlawed mediums (v. 3)! It is no surprise then, to see in verse 8 that "Saul disguised himself" when he went to see the medium. Sin causes us to disguise ourselves. The further into sin we go, the more our life becomes one of hypocrisy and compromise.

We next read,

> But the woman said to him, "Surely you know what Saul has done. He has cut off the mediums and spiritists from the

land. Why have you set a trap for my life to bring about my death?"

Saul swore to her by the LORD, "As surely as the LORD lives, you will not be punished for this."

Then the woman asked, "Whom shall I bring up for you?"

"Bring up Samuel," he said. (28:9–11)

You see the two ironies in all this? The medium hesitated to help because she was afraid of King Saul, who had cut off the mediums and spiritists from the land. Yet Saul, in disguise, was the one asking for her help! And the second irony is that Saul is so desperate for a word from the Lord that he is resorting to the black arts to get it.

Not only does sin cause us to disguise ourselves, but it causes us to pervert what is most holy—the very name of the Lord. Saul swore to her "by the LORD" that she would not be punished for helping him. How twisted! Saul used the Lord's name to assure a condemned spiritist that she would not be judged for engaging in the hated practice of conjuring up a dead person. Saul put the final nail in the coffin of his perversion by saying ".Bring up Samuel"—the one man in Israel who would be most appalled by this practice.

What happens next is truly amazing. We do not know if this woman was a charlatan who only pretended to contact the dead, or if she had connections with demons who impersonated dead people. All we know is that the biblical text makes it clear that the woman saw Samuel—the real one—and it was a dreadful surprise! "When the woman saw Samuel, she cried out at the top of her voice and said to Saul, 'Why have you deceived me? You are Saul!'" (28:12).

Although some Christians work hard at arguing that this

could not really have been Samuel, the obvious shock on the part of the woman, coupled with the fact that the biblical text calls him "Samuel," leads us to no other conclusion. At any rate, this text shows Saul's great fear and his need of a word from God. In the remaining verses of the chapter, he admits his panic to Samuel, describes the threat from the Philistine army, and speaks of God's silence toward him. In his mind Saul is out of options. God refused to answer him by prophets or by dreams. So he used his own reasoning powers (remember the trouble he got into in First Samuel 15 when he did that?) and decided to consult Samuel, come death or high water. The text continues:

> Samuel said, "Why do you consult me, now that the LORD has turned away from you and become your enemy? The LORD has done what he predicted through me. The LORD has torn the kingdom out of your hands and given it to one of your neighbors—to David. Because you did not obey the LORD or carry out his fierce wrath against the Amalekites, the LORD has done this to you today. The LORD will hand over both Israel and you to the Philistines, and tomorrow you and your sons will be with me. The LORD will also hand over the army of Israel to the Philistines." (28:16–19)

The final evidence that this is truly Samuel is that the message sounds like him. Samuel minces no words in rebuking Saul for what he has done, and makes it clear that the Lord has turned away from him and has "become your enemy." That kind of indisputable truth does not come from a demon. And Samuel's post-mortem lecture is only getting started. He goes on to say that "the LORD has done what he predicted through me"—torn the kingdom out of Saul's hands and given it to a neighbor, David.

What Saul hoped would be some military strategy actually becomes a post-mortem rendition of "I-told-you-so." And if these words were not hard-hitting enough, Samuel dredges up the past: "Because you did not obey the LORD or carry out his fierce wrath against the Amalekites, the LORD has done this to you today."

Saul failed to obey because he didn't see himself as the one God had chosen to carry out His mission. We read in Exodus 17:14 that the Lord said to Moses, "Write this on a scroll as something to be remembered and make sure that Joshua hears it, because I will completely blot out the memory of Amalek from under heaven." In Exodus 17:16 the Lord says that He "will be at war against the Amalekites from generation to generation." Saul's military campaign against the Amalekites was not just another battle with another nation. Saul was to have served as the instrument of God's "fierce wrath" against that perverted people group.

Samuel then brings the most startling information to Saul. Saul had wanted military strategy from Samuel. Instead, he gets a funeral announcement—his own. Reminded of his disobedience, Saul is told, "tomorrow you and your sons will be with me." (v. 19). I'm sure that was not the type of military advice that Saul had been hoping for from Samuel.

The effect on Saul of this meeting with Samuel was devastating, as is evident in verses 20–25. He was filled with fear, his strength was gone and he was greatly shaken. And he had reason for his fear, because everything Samuel predicted comes true in chapter 31:

> Now the Philistines fought against Israel; the Israelites fled before them, and many fell slain on Mount Gilboa. The Phi-

listines pressed hard after Saul and his sons, and they killed his sons Jonathan, Abinadab and Malki-Shua. The fighting grew fierce around Saul, and when the archers overtook him, they wounded him critically.

Saul said to his armor-bearer, "Draw your sword and run me through, or these uncircumcised fellows will come and run me through and abuse me."

But his armor-bearer was terrified and would not do it; so Saul took his own sword and fell on it. When the armor-bearer saw that Saul was dead, he too fell on his sword and died with him. So Saul and his three sons and his armor-bearer and all his men died together that same day. (31:1–6)

We are told in Romans 15:4 that "Everything that was written in the past was written to teach us, so that through endurance and the encouragement of the Scriptures we might have hope." What lessons can we learn from the disobedience of King Saul? Even though Saul's situation was unique, his disobedience illustrates many truths about sin that can benefit us.

✓ Practical Action Points

1. We notice that lack of clarity concerning God's will is usually not the issue. We disobey because we want to. In Saul's case God's command to him was crystal clear. Ambiguity was not the problem. Perhaps ambition or autonomy was the underlying cause of Saul's rebellion. God does not want us in doubt about His will.

2. Sin affects us. It is not a victimless crime. In Saul's case sin perverted his understanding, deceiving him into thinking he had done God's will. There are consequences to sin.

3.   Sin brings on God's silence. Saul's relationship with
      God was so broken that he no longer received any an-
      swers from the Lord. His prayers to God did not make
      it past the ceiling. When we sin, how dare we think
      that God will hear our prayers, that He will come to
      our aid?

4.   Sin can escalate in our lives. When Saul did not receive
      a word from the Lord in the face of the Philistine threat,
      he resorted to necromancy. That which God despised,
      the consulting of the dead, became Saul's last resort.
      Sin distorts our reason, plunging us into deeper and
      deeper offense against God. (We'll see how this works
      out in David's sin with Bathsheba in Second Samuel
      11, which we will consider in Chapter 6.)

5.   Sin leads to death. In Saul's case it was literal death.
      Saul is gravely wounded by a Philistine archer. To keep
      his enemies from torturing him, Saul asks his armor-
      bearer to run him through, but he would not. Saul has
      to take his own life by falling on his sword. Sin is like a
      sword which we fall on when we choose to do our will
      instead of the Lord's. In many ways Saul was his own
      worst enemy. He dies by his own hand. Sin is spiritual
      suicide.

3

Chapter Three

Our Enemy's M.O.

The devil is only a convenient myth invented by
the real malefactors of our world. (Robert Anton Wilson)

I often laugh at Satan, and there is nothing that makes
him so angry as when I attack him to his face, and tell him that
through God I am more than a match for him. (Martin Luther)

In order that Satan might not outwit us.
For we are not unaware of his schemes.. (2 Cor. 2:11)

On October 2, 2006, Charles Roberts, a thirty-two-year-old local milk truck driver, walked into a one-room Amish schoolhouse in Pennsylvania, ordered the fifteen boys in the room along with several adults (including a pregnant woman and three women with infants) to leave, barred the doors with desks and wood and secured them with nails, and systematically executed five little girls, wounding seven others before killing himself.

Roberts had prepared himself for a long siege. He had a 9-mm semiautomatic pistol, two shotguns, a stun gun, two knives, two cans of gunpowder and 600 rounds of ammunition. He confessed to his wife on the phone minutes before the slaughter that he had assaulted two female relatives, ages three and four, twenty years ago. Police said Roberts was also haunted by the death of his first-born daughter, who lived only twenty minutes after a premature birth in 1997. He was "angry with himself and angry toward God," they said.

On March 7, 2007, Eric Johnson did the unthinkable. Divorced from his wife Beth about a year previously, he had a restraining order issued against him. Their eight-year-old daughter Emily had spent the weekend with her father, but failed to show up for school Monday morning. "I've got her, and you're not going to get her," were the last words Johnson spoke to his wife before he crashed a rented, single-engine Cessna into the side of his estranged mother-in-law's home Monday morning, killing himself and his daughter.

On April 16, 2007, Seung-Hui Cho killed thirty-two people at Virginia Tech. After fatally shooting a student and the resident assistant on her dormitory floor, Cho took the time to mail videos of his crazed tirades to NBC News. Two hours later, he entered four classrooms, fired more than 170 rounds (one shot every three seconds), killing thirty Norris Hall students and faculty—the worst shooting in American history. Cho had chained the building's doors to keep police from entering.

As you survey the world around you, do you ever suspect that there must be more to this world's evil than just the poor choices of finite human beings?

Don't get me wrong. We humans are capable of absolutely horrendous sins against one another, against ourselves and against the Lord. In the cartoon strip *Calvin and Hobbes*, Calvin asks his stuffed tiger Hobbes, "Do you believe in the devil? You know, a supreme evil being dedicated to the temptation, corruption, and destruction of man?" Hobbes responds, "I'm not sure that man needs the help."

And yet, as we look at the world, it appears that something beyond human nature is stirring up the evil tendencies in our society. And it is not only mass killings that reveal this supernatural influence. In our own experience we can see a connection between *our* sin and the purposes and work of the Evil One.

In League with the Devil?

The Bible is very clear about the connection between our sin and Satan: "He who does what is sinful is of the devil, because the devil has been sinning from the beginning. The reason the Son of God appeared was to destroy the devil's work" (1 John 3:8). We learn from this passage that the one who "does" sin (the Greek implies making a regular *practice* of sin) is "of" the devil.

"In Bangladesh Satan seemed to be more bold. The attacks were more brazen and obvious and also easier to deal with. We had a fakir freak out at one of our meetings and begin spinning around in a way that seemed physically impossible to me. . . . The brothers confronted the demon, cast it out in the name of Jesus and the man was delivered and converted. He is still a faithful member of the fellowship as far as I know." (Dr. David Cashin, missiologist)

This does not mean that the person who sins is demon-possessed, but there is an identity, an affinity, with the Evil One when a person practices sin. John further explains, "because the devil has been sinning from the beginning," alluding to Satan's unholy history of prideful rebellion against God and his expulsion from heaven (see Isa. 14 and Ezek. 28). John concludes by declaring that Jesus Christ came to "destroy the devil's work"—a mission of destruction!

Before we too easily exempt ourselves from the implications of this verse, we need to realize that believers are quite capable of doing the devil's work. Job's wife provides an example of that. Satan had bragged to the Lord twice that he could provoke Job to the point that he would "curse you to your face." (Job 1:11, 2:5). Just after this second taunt, Mrs. Job challenges her husband to "curse God and die" (2:9). Chrysosthom, a teacher in the early church, made this comment about Job's wife:

> Often under the appearance of friendship he [Satan] insinuates the venom of his cruel malice. In this way it was that he suborned Job's wife, by putting on the mask of natural affectionateness, to give that wretchless advice. . . . When he had gone through all, and had thoroughly tried his mettle, because he made no way, he ran to his old weapon, the woman, and assumes a mask of concern, and makes a tragical picture of his calamities in most pitiable tone, and feigns that for removal of his evil he is introducing that deadly counsel.[1]

The devil shows no gender favoritism, for in the New Testament he entices Simon Peter to do his dirty work. Jesus had begun to explain to His disciples that He must suffer at the hands of Israel's religious leaders, be killed, and on the third day be raised to life (Matt. 16:21). Peter takes the Lord aside and rebukes Him with the strongest Greek expression: "Never, Lord! This shall never happen to you!" (v. 22). Jesus responds to Peter by saying, "Get behind me, Satan! You are a stumbling block to me; you do not have in mind the things of God, but the things of men." (v. 23). What is particularly fascinating is that the Lord Jesus had earlier used almost these exact same words in resisting Satan's third temptation in the wilderness (4:10).

We do not want to see ourselves as in league with the devil. We relegate his actions to the massive and the malevolent, to the Charles Roberts, the Eric Johnsons, and the Seung-Hui Chos of this world. But when we sin, we are aligning ourselves with the Accuser. "He who does what is sinful is of the devil." When *I* sin, I am of the devil! There is a connectedness, a co-conspiracy, between the devil and the one who sins. It may well be unconscious, but it is nonetheless real. It is to his advantage when we sin against the Lord.

Jesus' Demolition Business

What is the answer to this union? John gives us the answer when he writes, "The reason the Son of God appeared was to destroy the devil's work."

If we asked the question, "Why did the Son of God come to earth?" several answers could be given, such as: "to serve and to give His life as a ransom for many" (Mark 10:45); "to lay down his life for the sheep" (John 10:11, 17); "that they may have life, and have it to the full" (John 10:10). But First John 3:8 gives a very different answer: Jesus came "to destroy the devil's work." Jesus came to *destroy*! The Carpenter from Nazareth is in the demolition business.[2]

What are the "*works* of the devil" that Jesus has come to destroy? (This expression is unique to First John 3:8; it is found nowhere else in the New Testament.) Perhaps the expression refers to all that Satan does in rebellion against God. *De*struction is sometimes as important as *con*struction. The One who came to "destroy the devil's works" has also come to *disarm* his forces: "And having disarmed the powers and authorities, he made a public spectacle of them, triumphing over them by the cross" (Col. 2:15).

Christians are also to struggle in opposition to the devil's forces: "For our struggle is not against flesh and blood, but against the rulers, against the authorities, against the powers of this dark world and against the spiritual forces of evil in the heavenly realms" (Eph. 6:12). In First John 3:8 the devil is mentioned three times in this one verse. He is a real enemy who wants us to follow his pattern. We must resist and war against him if we are to follow Christ's pattern.

The Devil's "Devices"

A second basic text we want to think about in relation to sin and Satan is Second Corinthians 2:11, where Paul warns the Corinthians—and us—to turn away from an unforgiving spirit "in order that Satan might not outwit us. For we are not unaware of his schemes."

We are in a battle against a supernatural schemer. When Paul challenges us here not to be *outwitted* by Satan, he uses a verb that can be translated "get an advantage over" and comes from a word meaning *exploit* or *cheat*. I can't help but think of unscrupulous used-car salesmen or time-share representatives.

Recently my wife and I went on a "45-minute tour" of a time-share resort's facilities. Located near one of our nation's top vacation spots, it was absolutely gorgeous. Golf course, indoor and outdoor swimming pools, arts and crafts building, gift shop—this place seemed to have it all. We agreed to a "tour" because we were promised a gift certificate to a local restaurant for listening to the sales pitch. A "45-minute" sales pitch.

Two hours later we had toured the facilities, talked about trading our time-share week for vacations all over the world, and had several financial "packages" meticulously explained to us by the salesman and his supervisor. The $29,000 price tag for one week of vacation time a year was, to say the least, not in our budget. But these salesmen would not let us go. They "reworked" the numbers, rehashed the resort's amenities and made us feel that any answer other than "Yes! Oh, YES!" would have been the height of stupidity.

After we said repeatedly "I think we'll pass," the supervisor—who had become our "best friend" during the salespitch —abruptly shook our hands and walked away. The regular salesman grudgingly slinked away to get our gift certificate. We sat there feeling drained, used, exploited, taken advantage of—and we hadn't even bought anything! He came back with the $25 dinner certificate. I'd lost my appetite.

I'm not making the case that these time-share salesmen were tools of the devil (that would be too easy!). I'm just saying that no one wants to feel exploited, outwitted, cheated or talked into something he or she would reject in a saner moment. The next time you're tempted, ask yourself what Satan is trying to talk you into.

The word translated "devices" refers to the results of directing one's mind to a subject. It can mean what is in the mind (Phil. 4:7), one's capacity for thinking or reasoning (2

Cor. 3:14, 4:4), or the purposes conceived by thinking. Satan wants to spring his clever mental mousetraps on us. How do we keep from being "outwitted"? We mentally prepare ourselves for battle.

Wouldn't you feel foolish if you bought a lemon of a used car because you were overwhelmed by the "new car" smell or the smoothness of the salesman, and were too lazy to do your homework? When you buy a used car you need to prepare for battle by pouring over Kelley Blue Book® or hiring a mechanic friend to examine the vehicle. We have to do the same when we go out into the marketplace of ideas.

We underestimate the power of our thoughts, of our minds. We don't connect a daily time of meditating on God's Word with our mental preparation to do battle. The Evil One is engaged in a 24/7 propaganda campaign. He is the "father of lies." He speaks fluent falsehood. Jesus tells us in John 8:44, "You belong to your father, the devil, and you want to carry out your father's desire. He was a murderer from the beginning, not holding to the truth, for there is no truth in him. When he lies, he speaks his native language, for he is a liar and the father of lies."

Satan plays mind-games with us. One could almost say that our battle is not psycho-somatic, but psycho-*satanic*. I don't believe he can read our minds, but he has studied the human creature for thousands of years and knows how to bring us down.

One Reason for the Incarnation

We read in Hebrews 2, "Since the children have flesh and blood, he too shared in their humanity so that by his death he might destroy him who holds the power of death—that is, the devil—and free those who all their lives were held in slavery by their fear of death" (2:14–15). First John 3:8 says that the Son of God came to destroy the devil's work. Here in Hebrews 2 we learn that God the Son became incarnate to destroy the devil himself! We have a different word for "destroy" here in Hebrews 2:14, translated in other Scriptures to mean such things as "use up" (Luke 13:7), "nullify" (Rom. 3:3, 31; 1 Cor. 1:28) or make "worthless" (Rom. 4:14). But the writer of Hebrews is clearly declaring that Jesus came to directly challenge the Evil One. He came on a mission of setting the captives free!

How ironic that by the death of the Son of God He might destroy the master of death. Nullifying the devil was not merely one of the many effects of His Incarnation, according to this text. It was the <u>reason</u> for the Incarnation. God the Son chose to share in our humanity "so that by his death he might destroy him who holds the power of death—that is, the devil."

> *"The devil's already defeated. Accept it! Live in light of his defeat! We're fighting from victory rather than FOR victory!" (Seminary student)*

Our Enemy's M.O.

What is Satan's *modus operandi*, his method of operating? What are his habits or manner of working? A study of Adam and Eve's temptation in Genesis 3 and Jesus' temptation in Matthew 4 will help us understand how we can resist the devil on a practical, daily level.

Now the serpent was more crafty than any of the wild animals the LORD God had made. He said to the woman, "Did God really say, 'You must not eat from any tree in the garden'?"

The woman said to the serpent, "We may eat fruit from the trees in the garden, but God did say, 'You must not eat fruit from the tree that is in the middle of the garden, and you must not touch it, or you will die.'"

"You will not surely die," the serpent said to the woman. "For God knows that when you eat of it your eyes will be opened, and you will be like God, knowing good and evil."

When the woman saw that the fruit of the tree was good for food and pleasing to the eye, and also desirable for gaining wisdom, she took some and ate it. She also gave some to her husband, who was with her, and he ate it. Then the eyes of both of them were opened, and they realized that they were naked; so they sewed fig leaves together and made coverings for themselves. (Gen. 3:1–7)

The first truth we notice from this text is that Satan is crafty. Revelation 12:9 calls him "that ancient serpent called the devil, or Satan, who leads the whole world astray." This may call to your mind Paul's warning in Second Corinthians 2:11 that Satan will try to "outwit" us with his "schemes." He is a shrewd, conniving old snake.

Second, we see that Satan's approach violated God's ordained order. He spoke "to the woman" (Gen. 3:1). If it is true that God intended the man to be the leader from creation (in other words, that such leadership is not a result of the fall), then Satan violated that order by appealing first to Eve.

Notice, third, that Satan majored in questions. He asked Eve, "Did God really say . . . ?" If he can cause God's children to doubt God's Word, he has won a major victory. In his efforts to instill doubt, Satan focused on God's *restriction*. He asked, "You must not eat from any tree in the garden?" (v. 1). *God's* focus had been on Adam and Eve's *freedom*: "You are free to eat from any tree in the garden; but you must not eat from the tree of the knowledge of good and evil . . ." (Gen. 2:16). The devil wanted Eve to doubt God's goodness, to think that God was holding out on them.

Eve seemed to feel an obligation to respond to Satan's challenge. She should have done what Michael did: "But even the archangel Michael, when he was disputing with the devil about the body of Moses, did not himself dare to condemn him for slander but said, 'The Lord rebuke you!'" (Jude 9). Instead, Satan's emphasis on God's restriction apparently influenced her to add to God's word in her response to the serpent: "You must not eat fruit from the tree . . . and *you must not touch it*, or you will die" (Gen. 3:3). Was she ready to believe Satan's lie that God was holding out on them?

It also appears that Eve subtracted from God's word by leaving out the word "surely" from God's warning that "when you eat of it you will *surely* die." (2:17). Minimizing God's word is as serious—and perhaps less noticeable—than outright denial of His word.

At this point Satan moved from sowing doubts and questions and shifted to outright contradiction of God's word. He said, "you will not surely die." (3:4). If deceit will not work, he will move to denial.

Satan called into question God's goodness. He said, "You will not surely die. For God knows that when you eat of it your eyes will be opened, and you will be like God, knowing good and evil" (vv. 4–5). The Evil One majors in half-truths, for Adam and Even were already like God—at least, in the way that God wanted them to be like God!

Eve used her reasoning to justify taking the fruit. Immediately after Satan had implied that God was holding out on them, we read, "When the woman saw that the fruit of the tree was *good for food* and *pleasing to the eye*, and also *desirable for gaining wisdom*, she took some and ate it" (v. 6). The threefold reason that Eve ate the fruit is often compared to the threefold description that John gives of the world:

> Do not love the world or anything in the world. If anyone loves the world, the love of the Father is not in him. For everything in the world—the *cravings* of sinful man, the *lust of his eyes* and *boasting* of what he has and does—comes not from the Father but from the world. The world and its desires pass away, but the man who does the will of God lives forever.(1 John 2:15–17)[3]

Satan takes advantage of good things —taste, aesthetic beauty, desire for knowledge—and entices us to follow them rather than the Lord. This does not make these things wrong, just our disobedience. There is nothing evil in enjoy-

> *"I think the greatest test of the western missionary is in the area of trusting God's sovereignty. We expect to win. After all, we're the good guys! What happens when Satan uses other Christians to seemingly destroy the work you've spent years building up? Does the work then seem 'impossible for God'? Satan triumphs with the lie, 'God cannot accomplish what He sent you to do!' God is sovereign and it is a great lie if we think that everything ultimately depends on us." (Missionary)*

ing good food, those things that are pleasing to the eye, or that which is desirable for gaining wisdom. They only become wrong when they, rather than the Lord, control our lives. Satan is not really into the repulsive, the ugly, or the foolish, unless they can serve his purposes.

We then learn that after Eve ate, "she also gave some to her husband, who was with her, and he ate it" (Gen. 3:6). Adam was not off somewhere attending to business in the Garden of Eden; he was with his wife. Why didn't he stop her? One of my theology students said, "Adam should have stood up for Eve! He should have pulled her away from the conversation, told the serpent to take a hike, and reminded Eve of the Creator's goodness. That's what he should have done!" Another student spoke up and said, "No, there was a better way. Rather than eating the prohibited fruit, Adam and Eve should have feasted on roast snake in the grass!"

The Fall affected each of the individuals in Genesis 3. There was a loss of innocence (v. 8) as Adam and Eve recognized their nakedness and covered themselves. They attempted to hide from God (v. 8), for they feared Him (v. 10). When God began questioning Adam and Eve, Adam is marked by blame-shifting and unthankfulness (v. 12). On the surface it sounds like he blames Eve, but his statement is deeper than that; he says to the Lord, "the woman *you* put here with me . . ." Adam blamed the Creator.

God pronounced a curse upon the serpent (vv. 14–15), the woman (v. 16) and Adam (vv. 17–19). Adam and Eve were then banished from the Garden (vv. 22–24). Some theologians suggest that such banishment was for their own good, lest they should partake of the tree of life and live in a fallen state forever.

The God-Man Is Tempted

Satan's successful temptation of Adam and Eve gives us many lessons concerning his way of operating. As foundational to the issue of temptation and sin as Genesis 3 is, God has provided another key text that shows how Satan tempts us. In Matthew 4 we read of the temptation of the God-Man Himself—Jesus.

The Son of God became fully human and, as we learn in the book of Hebrews, "We do not have a high priest who is unable to sympathize with our weaknesses, but we have one who has been tempted in every way, just as we are—yet was without sin. Let us then approach the throne of grace with confidence, so that we may receive mercy and find grace to help us in our time of need" (Heb. 4:15–16). We can be confident of having victory over temptation, because our Great High Priest showed us how:

> Then Jesus was led by the Spirit into the desert to be tempted by the devil. After fasting forty days and forty nights, he was hungry. The tempter came to him and said, "If you are the Son of God, tell these stones to become bread."
>
> Jesus answered, "It is written: 'Man does not live on bread alone, but on every word that comes from the mouth of God.'"
>
> Then the devil took him to the holy city and had him stand on the highest point of the temple. "If you are the Son of God," he said, "throw yourself down. For it is written:
>
> > "'He will command his angels concerning you, and they will lift you up in their hands, so that you will not strike your foot against a stone.'"
>
> Jesus answered him, "It is also written: 'Do not put the Lord your God to the test.'"

Again, the devil took him to a very high mountain and showed him all the kingdoms of the world and their splendor. "All this I will give you," he said, "if you will bow down and worship me."

Jesus said to him, "Away from me, Satan! For it is written: 'Worship the Lord your God, and serve him only.'"

Then the devil left him, and angels came and attended him. (Matt. 4:1–11)

Even though the book of James says, "God cannot be tempted by evil" (James 1:13), here we have the incarnate Son of God being tempted. Christ's humanity was the avenue of His temptations. Matthew 4 makes it clear that Jesus was in a weakened condition, having fasted forty days and nights. So the devil issued three tests with which to tempt Jesus (notice the threefold pattern—just like with Eve):

Test #1

Satan's first temptation of Jesus is aimed at a very basic need: hunger. "Change these stones into bread." (Some commentators have suggested that the rough terrain of the wilderness was covered by smooth rocks which looked like little loaves of bread or sections of matzo.)

What was Satan's motive in this first temptation? Jesus' response helps us understand what the Evil One was trying to accomplish: "It is written: 'People do not live on bread alone, but on every word that comes from the mouth of God'" (v. 4). This first temptation was to entice Jesus to act independently of the Father. One is reminded of John 5 where the Lord Jesus says, "I tell you the truth, the Son can do nothing by himself; he can do only what he sees his Father doing, because whatever the Father does the Son also does" (v. 19).

There is so much more to life than "Have a need? Meet your need!" What is more important than satisfying one's physical hunger? Living on the word of God! We are much more than our appetites. We are creatures made in the image of the "God [who will] supply all [our] need according to his riches in glory by Christ Jesus" (Phil. 4:19, KJV).

In past generations tuberculosis was called *consumption*, because its symptoms (a bloody cough, fever, pallor and a long relentless wasting away) seemed to consume people from within. A case could be made that many today are wasting away, being consumed from within by a spiritual malignancy. Our deepest need is for "every word that comes from the mouth of God."

Test #2

In the second temptation[4] we read that "the devil took him to the holy city and had him stand on the highest point of the temple" (v. 5). I believe we should take this text literally. The devil actually transported Jesus from the wilderness to Jerusalem and somehow placed Him on the highest point of the temple. Then Satan said, "If you are the Son of God, throw yourself down" (v. 6).

What is the temptation here? The devil apparently wanted Jesus to prove His Sonship by putting Himself in a dangerous position in which the Father would be forced to act. Satan goes beyond merely suggesting Jesus' action. He tries to support his enticement by quoting from the Word of God—Psalm 91, a Psalm which guarantees security and protection to the one who trusts the Lord.[5] It is as if Satan is saying, "What? You don't trust God?!"

Satan will do *anything*—even quote Scripture!—to get us to tempt God, to put God to the test. The irony here is that Satan is tempting God (the Son) to test God (the Father). Much like the first temptation (of turning the stones into bread), Satan is seeking to drive a wedge between the Father and the Son. The Lord Jesus' response to him is simply, "It is also written: 'Do not put the Lord your God to the test'" (v. 7). Here the Lord Jesus is quoting Deuteronomy 6:16 where Israel is told, "Do not test the LORD your God as you did at Massah."[6]

Test #3

The third temptation of the Lord Jesus, like the second, involved transportation. The devil took Jesus to a "very high mountain" in order that Satan might entice Him, to give Him a better view of what He could have if He would only worship Satan. Satan does that, doesn't he? He offers us a better view—or so it appears. He offered Eve and Adam a "better" understanding in Genesis 3 ("For God knows that when you eat of it your eyes will be opened, and you will be like God, knowing good and evil," v. 5). Satan's "new and improved" is really only "old and inferior." Adam and Eve were like God in the way He intended them to be like Him. And here in Matthew 4, the fact is that Jesus already owned all the kingdoms of the world as the Second Person of the Trinity. They ultimately were not Satan's to give.

Was Satan on a mission to get Jesus to avoid the cross? We do not know with certainty if Satan understood Jesus' mission to come to the earth to go to the cross. Was his purpose to get Jesus to take a short-cut to glory? This seems clear, for he offers the kingdoms of this world now. In a moment of His greatest physical weakness, Jesus has to look at the very best that this world has to offer—"all the kingdoms of the world and their splendor."

Jesus' response was succinct: "Away from me, Satan! For it is written: 'Worship the Lord your God, and serve him only'" (v. 10). Jesus tells Satan to take a hike.

Again Jesus says, "It is written." In response to each of the three temptations, He quotes Scripture.[7] To this third challenge Jesus makes it clear that Satan does not deserve and will not receive Jesus' worship. In fact, Jesus commands him to do that which he failed to do and, as a result, got him booted out of heaven: "to worship the Lord your God and serve Him only."

The proper response to Satan's temptations is to tell him to *flee*. We read in James 4:7, "Submit yourselves, then, to God. Resist the devil, and he will flee from you."

Were Jesus' victories over these three temptations easy? Not according to Scripture: "Because he himself suffered when he was tempted, he is able to help those who are being tempted. . . . Although he was a son, he learned obedience from what he suffered and, once made perfect, he became the source of eternal salvation for all who obey him" (Heb. 2:18, 5:8–9). Peter reminds us, "For even hereunto were ye called: because Christ also suffered for us, leaving us an example, that ye should follow his steps" (1 Peter 2:21, KJV).

A Garden Versus a Wilderness

What lessons do we learn about Satan's *modus operandi* from Genesis 3 and Matthew 4? Although there are numerous contrasts between Adam and Eve's failure in the Garden and Jesus' victory in the wilderness,[8] our question concerns the similarities, which reveal how Satan operates in the process of temptation:

1. Satan speaks in both passages. He uses language to sow doubt, to question, to challenge the already-revealed will of God. He is a master of the "if/then" proposition: "If you eat, then . . ."; "If you are the Son of God, then . . ."

2. Satan appeals to a point of need. To both Eve and the Lord Jesus, he appealed to hunger, to the need to eat. In both situations it was a real need. It must at least be said that Satan is a quick study and an excellent student of man and his needs. Our appetites and our needs are clearly apparent to the Evil One.

3. Satan wants real needs satisfied in an inappropriate way. Eve is enticed to disobey a clear command from God; Jesus is tempted to act independently of His Father.

When we know these steps in the process, we can be on the lookout for them. Remember, if we are aware of his "devices," Satan will not "outwit" us (2 Cor. 2:11).

There is, incidentally, also a fourth similarity between Genesis 3 and Matthew 4: Both are direct, personal confrontations. Both events were so critical that Satan acted immediately and directly on his "subjects." Adam and Eve, the first human beings and vice-regents with the Creator, merited his direct assault. From Satan's perspective they needed to be "brought down." And of course, the Son of God, the Lord Jesus, entering into His public ministry in Matthew 4, was such a threat that He was bound to become a personal target of Satan.

Should we expect Satan himself to speak to us, to directly tempt us to turn away from the Lord? Not really; we're not that important for him to personally concern himself with each of us. We must not forget, however, Satan's minions, his army of fallen angels who wish to do us harm. Some scholars suggest that the devil took one-third of the angels in heaven with him in his mutiny. Although we have little evidence of how many fallen angels there are, the simplest truth is that there are *enough*—enough to do his bidding and enough to plague believers.

Satan is a powerful enemy. By bringing down Adam and Eve, he brought down the whole human race. One could make the point that his action of tempting them to sin and turn away from God led to the crucifixion of God the Son. Satan holds the power of death, according to Hebrews 2:14 which says, "Since the children have flesh and blood, he too shared in their humanity so that by his death he might destroy him who holds the power of death—that is, the devil."

How wrong Mark Twain was when he said about the devil, "All religions issue bibles against him, and say the most injurious things about him, but we never hear his side." We hear his side from the moment we are born into this fallen world. We are saturated in his lies throughout our lives. He hates God; he hates us, and he actively pursues us to get back at God.

As we will see in our next chapter, the believer has *three* enemies. We dare not live our lives ignoring two-thirds of the forces that oppose us.

✓ Practical Action Points

1. We must acknowledge the reality and power of our supernatural foe, the devil. C.S. Lewis said we commit two errors about Satan: We either think about him too little, or we think about him too much. Many believers fail to make any connection between their own sins and the works of the Evil One.

2. We are not to be outwitted by Satan, but must learn how he seeks to trip us up and exploit us. When we meditate on Scripture, we prepare ourselves for spiritual battle. If you have not already done so, read *The Screwtape Letters* by C.S. Lewis for some understanding of Satan's tricks.

3. The devil loves to get God's people to doubt God's Word. He spreads the propaganda that God is not good and that He is holding out on us. He will not hesitate to contradict or even mis-quote the Word of God to accomplish his purposes.

4. The Lord Jesus Christ is our model for defeating Satan and his minions. Study His actions and reactions in the four Gospels.

4

The Other Two-Thirds of Our Enemies

I read the book How to Be Your Own Best Friend *last week,
went out and gained 20 pounds, and haven't trusted myself since!*
(Erma Bombeck)

*If we were brought to trial for the crimes we have committed
against ourselves, few would escape the gallows. (Anonymous)*

*Do not love the world or anything in the world. If anyone loves the
world, the love of the Father is not in him. For everything in the
world —the cravings of sinful man, the lust of his eyes and the
boasting of what he has and does—comes not from the Father but
from the world. The world and its desires pass away, but the man
who does the will of God lives forever. (1 John 2:15–17)*

As we saw in our last chapter, the believer in Christ has a
supernatural Enemy who seeks to kill and destroy. We
must never underestimate, minimize or overlook his tricks.
He is cunning and crafty. His reality and opposition to us
must drive us to the Lord for protection and wisdom. James
4 says, "Submit yourselves, then, to God. Resist the devil,

and he will flee from you. Come near to God and he will come near to you." (vv. 7–8).

But there are two other enemies which are equally opposed to God and the things of God. And opposed to *us*. They are "the world" and "the flesh." As we examine each of these enemies, we will see that they have their M.O.s as well; each follows certain methods of operating on us.

Let's begin with a consideration of "the world." What does Scripture mean by "the world," how is it the enemy of the believer, and what steps can we take in standing against its enticements to sin?

A Definition of "The World"

The term *cosmos*, or "the world," occurs 186 times in the New Testament. Over forty percent of those occurances are in the Gospel of John. The term seems to have three possible meanings:

1) the physical planet where we live (Jesus came into the "world," John 1:10–14);

2) the people on the planet ("God so loved the *world*," John 3:16);

3) the pagan system opposed to God and the things of God ("Do not love the *world* or the things in the *world*," 1 John 2:15).

Notice that the same biblical writer, John, uses the term with all three different meanings. One text (John 3:16) tells us that God loves the world; another text (1 John 2:15–17), using the same term "world" six times, tells us that we had better not love the world!

> Do not love the *world* or anything in the *world*. If anyone loves the *world*, the love of the Father is not in him. For everything in the *world*—the cravings of sinful man, the lust of his eyes and the boasting of what he has and does—comes not from the Father but from the *world*. The *world* and its desires pass away, but the man who does the will of God lives forever. (1 John 2:15–17)

Unless one is willing to acknowledge a genuine contradiction in the Scriptures, John is obviously using the term "the world" in different senses. I'm to love the world of people that God loved in giving His Son, but I'm not to love the worldly system which opposes God and the things of God.

What in the World Is Real Worldliness?

What do we notice in First John 2:15–17 about this worldly system?

First we notice that John gives us a *command*—not to love the world or anything in the world. The proper response to a command is, of course, obedience. Am I loving the world and the things in the world? We need to realize, however, that this text is not teaching asceticism, the view that we are not to enjoy the physical pleasures of life. God "richly provides us with eveything for our enjoyment" (1 Tim. 6:17). I am not wrongly loving the world when I enjoy God's good gifts.

Next we see that this command is followed by a conditional statement. "If you love the world, love for the Father is not in you." Wow! Could the cost for loving the world be any greater than that? Some might even say it sounds like a threat. Is that an acceptable way to motivate us to faith?

A close friend from a few years ago, with whom I served in a Christian ministry, recently informed me that he has turned his back on the gospel. John (and that *is* his first name; please pray for him) says he no longer believes the Bible is trustworthy or that Jesus is the Savior. He is convinced that Christians have been deluded. Through phone conversations and emails, I set forth my best case for the truth of Biblical Christianity, and none of it mattered. I challenged him about the impact of his apostasy upon his wife and two sons; I pled with him to talk with other Christians. None of my persuasive powers had any success.

At one point in our discussions, I felt it important to warn him of the danger of departing from the Christian faith, so I quoted texts such as Matthew 16:26 which asks, "What good will it be for a man if he gains the whole world, yet forfeits his soul?" He has read my book, *The Other Side of the Good News*, a defense of the doctrine of hell. How did he react?

He said indignantly, "I will not respond to a threat!" He angrily told me that Christians, when they can't answer honest questions, resort to threatening people with hell and damnation. I told him that I loved him and that I was trying to be faithful to the Scriptures in warning him of God's judgment.

I must agree with my friend John, however—none of us like threats. None of us like being bullied into belief. We particularly resent it when a threat is wielded instead of a good argument, when a person who has power but does not deserve it tries to force an action or a belief, or when the threat is out of proportion with the seriousness of the matter at hand. But when God threatens us, He does so to shock us into belief, to tell us the truth about present and future reality. He has the power to carry out the judgment. A true threat is not offensive to those who appreciate being warned of imminent—or eternal—danger.

Here in First John 2, this conditional statement includes the threat, "If you love the world, love for the Father is not in you." We cannot love the world which God says not to love and love the Father at the same time. Paul sadly says this of a co-worker in the gospel: "For Demas, because he loved this world, has deserted me and has gone to Thessalonica" (2 Tim. 4:10).

This conditional statement in First John 2:15 is then followed by an explanation: "For everything in the world—the cravings of sinful man, the lust of his eyes and the boasting of what he has and does—comes not from the Father but from the world. The world and its desires pass away, but the man who does the will of God lives forever." John breaks down what he means by the world into three expressions of worldliness: "the cravings of sinful people"; "the lust of their eyes"; and "their boasting about what they have and do."

Before we look at these three expressions carefully, let's notice how the text begins: "Do not love the world." The expression carries with it the idea of "stop loving the world." These believers were already loving the world that God did not want them to love. John goes on to say, "If you love the world . . ." Again the idea is that of continually loving the world: "If you continually love the world [that God says not to love] . . ."

Love is discriminating. Love is not simply an automatic

response to everything we encounter. (In fact, as we discussed in Chapter 2, there are some things we are supposed to hate.) The Beatles, great theologians that they were, were wrong when they sang, "All You Need Is Love." Sometimes we need godly hate. And sometimes we need to be told to "stop loving."

We must be blunt with ourselves. Our natural tendency is to love that which agrees with our sinful natures. We come into this world in rebellion against God and find ourselves in an environment that encourages us to actively participate in and even advance that revolt. We are not to love anything in that system which rejects God.

In order to stop a behavior or an attitude, we must recognize that it is operating in our lives. How do we recognize that we are loving this world that God says don't love? The answer is found in the three expressions John uses to describe the love of the world: "the cravings of sinful people, the lust of their eyes and their boasting about what they have and do."

"The Cravings of Sinful People"

C.S. Lewis once said, "It would seem that our Lord finds our desires, not too strong, but too weak. We are half-hearted creatures, fooling about with drink and sex and ambition when infinite joy is offered us, like an ignorant child who wants to go on making mud pies in a slum because he cannot imagine what is meant by the offer of a holiday at the sea. We are far too easily pleased."[1] The term "cravings" (also translated "desires") is a common word, used eighty-four times in the Septuagint and thirty-four times in the New Testament.

Used in a positive sense, Jesus says in Luke 22:15, "I have eagerly *desired* to eat this Passover with you before I suffer." Paul considers what awaits him in heaven and writes, "I *desire* to depart and be with Christ, which is better by far" (Phil. 1:23). This term sometimes simply means great longing, as in Paul's comment to the Thessalonican believers: "Out of our intense longing [desire, KJV] we made every effort to see you" (1 Thess. 2:17).

The great majority of New Testament occurrences of this term, however, are negative. For example, Jesus said that some people hear the truth but "the worries of this life, the deceitfulness of wealth and the *desire* for other things come in and choke the word, making it unfruitful" (Mark 4:19). This desire, this passion, for other things can keep a person from responding to the gospel! In John 8:44 Jesus has some hard words for the Jewish leaders: "You belong to your father, the devil, and you want to carry out your father's *desire*." Jesus teaches that the devil has desires—and even the best religious leaders can adopt his agenda!

This term is translated "lusts" in Romans 1:24: "Therefore God gave them over in the sinful desires [*lusts*, KJV] of their hearts to sexual impurity for the degrading of their bodies with one another." We pollute ourselves when we follow our evil desires. It is translated "passions" in Romans 6:12: "Therefore do not let sin reign in your mortal body so that you obey its evil desires [*passions*, KJV]." Sin seeks to control us through bodily passions. (Not surprisingly, a current TV soap opera is named "Passions"!)

Paul uses the verb form of this word to speak about "coveting": "For I would not have known what *coveting* really was if the law had not said, 'Do not *covet*.' But sin, seizing the opportunity afforded by the commandment, produced in me every kind of *covetous* desire" (Rom. 7:7–8). We are commanded in Romans 13:14 to "Clothe yourselves with the Lord Jesus Christ, and do not think about how to gratify the desires of the sinful nature." When I think of the term "provision," the image of a camping trip comes to mind. If you forget your provisions, you'll starve. We are to starve to death the desires of the flesh.

Paul reminds us of our before-Christ life in Ephesians 2:3 when he says, "All of us also lived among them at one time, gratifying the the cravings of our sinful nature and following its desires and thoughts." Paul is equating living "in the cravings of our sinful nature" with "following its desires and thoughts." We are often critical of those who pursue the passions of their body. But what about those who chase the instincts of the intellect? Intellectual desires which conflict with God's revealed truth are temptations and sins which must also be resisted.[2]

We learn in James 1:14 that "each one is tempted when, by his own evil *desire,* he is dragged away and enticed." In the next verse we are told "Then, after *desire* has conceived, it gives birth to sin; and sin, when it is full-grown, gives birth to death." We cannot always blame outside forces when we are tempted. We carry our temptations inside us![3]

That is why Paul challenges the Ephesian believers "with regard to your former way of life, to put off your old self, which is being corrupted by its deceitful *desires*; to be made new in the attitude of your minds" (Eph. 4:22–23). Our former self, our "old man," can corrupt us by its deceitful *desires*—the same term that John uses for "*cravings* of sinful people." Paul issues an order for the old man's execution:

"Put to death therefore what is earthly in you: fornication, impurity, passion, evil *desire* and covetousness, which is idolatry." This kind of spiritual suicide involves coming out from under the control of unrestrained, wicked thoughts and actions, which in reality are the worship of a false god! We are to put to death anything in us which leads us away from the true God.

Our earthly desires are not innocent, but "foolish and harmful" (1 Tim. 6:9)—self-destructive. Paul warns us that living by our passions is spiritual slavery (Titus 3:3). Peter reminds us that they "war against your soul" (1 Pet. 2:11). Our passions are in a battle for our souls! The Christian life provides spiritual emancipation. We can become freed from those passions and pleasures which waste our lives and harm our neighbors.

God does not merely tell us to kill our desires, however; He calls us to replace them with that which is good: "Flee the evil desires of youth, and pursue righteousness, faith, love and peace, along with those who call on the Lord out of a pure heart" (2 Tim. 2:22). God does not take something away without replacing it with something far better.

"The Lust of Their Eyes"

The next expression John uses to describe the world is "the lust of their eyes." The phrase contains the same word as in the previous expression, the "cravings" of sinful people.

Dr. Ronald Thiemann, for thirteen years the Dean of Harvard Divinity School, put in a request in 1999 for a larger hard drive for one of his university-owned computers. When the transfer of those files was taking the better part of a full day, technicians discovered that thousands of pornographic images had filled the hard drive to capacity. Harvard University President Neil L. Rudenstine asked Thiemann to resign for "conduct unbecoming a dean" after he was alerted about the matter.

Statistics abound concerning this one example of "the lust of the eyes." As of 2003 there were 1.3 million pornographic websites totaling over 260 million pages. Adult DVD/video rentals in 2005 amounted to almost 1 billion. More than 70% of men ages18–34 visit a pornographic site in a typical month. Child pornography is a $3 billion annual industry, with over 100,000 websites offering illegal child pornography.

According to Divorcewizards.com,

> At a 2003 meeting of the American Academy of Matrimonial Lawyers, two-thirds of the 350 divorce lawyers who attended said the Internet played a significant role in the divorces in the past year, with excessive interest in online porn contributing to more than half such cases. Pornography had an almost non-existent role in divorce just seven or eight years ago.

More than one out of every three pastors say that pornography is a current struggle. Almost half of all families say pornography is a problem in their home. The largest consumer of internet pornography is the 12–17 year-old age group. The U.S. Department of Justice said in 1996: "Never before in the history of telecommunications media in the United States has so much indecent (and obscene) material been so easily accessible by so many minors in so many American homes with so few restrictions."[4]

According to research published in 2006 by *Christianity Today* and ChristiaNet:

- 50 percent of all Christian men are addicted to pornography.
- 20 percent of all Christian women are addicted to pornography.
- 33 percent of pastors admit to visiting a sexually explicit website.
- 36 percent of laity admit to visiting a sexually explicit website.[5]

Pornography may be the most blatant form of eye-lust, but it is not the only example we could cite. Advertisers spend millions of dollars making their products visually appealing. Years ago a friend in television commercial production explained to me the hours it took to make a beer commercial. "The beer has to be poured just right for maximum appeal to the viewer's thirst," she said.

Arthur W. Hunt III's book, *The Vanishing Word: The Veneration of Visual Imagery in the Postmodern World*,[6] sets forth the thesis that Western civilization has devolved from a word-based culture to an image-based culture, now resembling many aspects of ancient pagan idolatry. Are believers to be primarily people of the ear—or of the eye? When the verbal medium gives way to the visual medium, respect for the Word of God and its authoritative proclamation may suffer. The God who gave both the ear and the eye requires us to "walk by faith, not by sight" (2 Cor. 5:7, KJV).

We need to be careful lest we deny God's gift of vision. The evidence of worldliness in First John 2 is not what can be seen, but rather the lust for what can be seen. In fact, the text indicates that this "lust of the eyes" which is "in the world" (which God says not to love) does not come from the Father, and passes away. The expression is not a condemnation of the visual arts, but of visual lusts.

Let's think some more about the expression "the lust of

the eyes." Is it used anywhere else in Scripture? We do have our famous text about Eve's falling into temptation in Genesis 3: "When the woman saw that the fruit of the tree was good for food and pleasing to the eye, and also desireable for gaining wisdom, she took some and ate it. She also gave some to her husband, who was with her, and he ate it" (v.6). The Greek translation (the Septuagint) of that verse indicates that the fruit was "eye-pleasing." The fruit was attractive. She saw that it was good for food and pleasing to the eyes. The Evil One is not into ugliness, is he? He appeals to our aesthetics, our sense of beauty.[7]

The beauty of the fruit in Genesis was not the problem. Just as its usefulness for food was not the problem. God did not say that the fruit of the tree of the knowledge of good and evil was not good for food or was not pleasing to the eyes.

John is warning us against the "lust" of the eyes. Is it possible that he had Genesis 3:6 in mind as he wrote these words? Did not Adam and Eve fall into worldliness when they disobeyed God? Both Eve and Adam were dominated by the fruit and themselves. They did not even stop to think about God and His clear prohibition.

The triplet nature of the two texts is fascinating:

Genesis 3:6	First John 2:16
When the woman saw that the fruit of the tree was good for food	For everything in the world—the cravings of sinful man,
and pleasing to the eye,	the lust of his eyes
and also desireable for gaining wisdom	and the boasting of what he has and does

The bottom line? The three-pronged temptation to worldliness that we struggle with is the very thing that tripped up Eve. The devil may be shrewd, but he doesn't seem to be very imaginative. He keeps using the same old bag of tricks. And sadly, he's successful far too often.

"Boasting about What They Have and Do"

If our task is to define worldliness, then this third expression says a great deal. Loving the world means boasting in what one "has" and what one "does"—both *possessions* and *profession* can get our eyes off the things of the Lord.

First, we must notice from the Scriptures that not all boasting is sin. Like anger, jealousy and hatred (which can be righteous emotions), there is both evil boasting and godly (biblical) boasting.

Good or godly boasting includes: boasting in our weaknesses (2 Cor. 11:30); boasting in God's character and in the fact that we know Him (1 Sam. 2:1, Jer. 9:23–24); and boasting in God's work in others (2 Cor. 1:14). Galatians 6:4 says, "Each one should test his own actions. Then he can take pride in himself, without comparing himself to somebody else." The Old Testament even commands us to boast: "Let him who boasts boast . . . in the Lord" (Jer. 9:24). And Jeremiah's challenge is repeated twice in the New Testament (1 Cor. 1:31, 2 Cor. 10:17).

Paul engages in sarcastic boasting for various purposes in Second Corinthians 11. He gives a virtual treatise on boasting in Chapter 12, after describing his experience of being "caught up to paradise."

Boasting only becomes evil when we focus on our own

strength, wisdom or riches (Jer. 9:23–24, Judg. 7:2), or when we ignorantly or presumptuously speak about the future (Prov. 27:1, James 4:13–16). Evil boasting is a particular characteristic of false teachers (Rom. 1:30, Jude 16, Rev. 18:7). Real love does not boast in these ways (1 Cor. 13:4).

John says that boasting about what we "have and do" gets our eyes off the Lord and entices us to worship the worldly system which God says not to love. Boasting about one's *possessions* (what we have) causes us to forget the One who owns it all. Boasting about one's *profession* (what we do) causes us to forget that God enables us to earn our living, to be productive, to accomplish our goals.

How silly to boast about what we have when it can all be taken from us in a matter of moments. One summer night a few years ago, my wife was asleep in the main bedroom. Around midnight she heard a sound like children playing with little cars on the floor of our attic. She pulled down the trap door in the ceiling to find the entire attic engulfed in flames! She and the rest of the family—I was out of town at the time—barely got out of the house alive. We lost everything.

We found out later that a ventilation fan had shorted out and caught fire. The sound that woke my wife, by the way, was the springs on a plastic cot which were zipping across the attic floor as the cot was melting.

On the rare occasion when we ask each other if something survived the fire, our usual response is, "No, that's now in heaven with Jesus." How ridiculous to boast about what we have when our possessions can vanish in a moment! Our possessions can possess us.

Boasting about what we do can also be short-lived. Our positions can delude us into thinking that we have made ourselves important. A popular radio personality introduces his show by talking about himself and how his great talent is "on loan from God." He pronounces the word "God" in a way that gives the impression that God should be happy He has someone who is worthy of such talent. Oh, how quickly our talents, gifts and abilities can be taken away from us, or simply fade away.

In considering the other two-thirds of our enemies, we need to be on guard against the "world"—not the physical planet or the people of the planet, but the *world system* opposed to God and the things of God. Worldliness is loving what God tells us not to love. It is evidenced by following sinful cravings, pursuing the lust of our eyes, and boasting about our possessions and professions.

Worldliness is far more than a culturally-defined, temporary list of do's and don't's legalistically followed by Christians. Garrison Keillor talks about his conservative Christian upbringing and how legalism was the dominant way of being "spiritual." Most card games were outlawed, he says, with one exception. Keillor writes (quoting Clarence Bunsen),

> Most Brethren I knew were death on card-playing, beer-drinking, and frowned on hand-holding, and of course they wouldn't go near a dance. They thought it brought out carnal desires. Well, maybe theirs lay closer to the surface. I don't know. Some were not only opposed to dancing but also felt that marching in formation was wrong, so we called them the Left-Footed Brethren. Some others were more liberal. Mr. Bell for example, he thought cards were okay so long as you didn't play with a full deck. The Bijou used to show good movies

but the Brethren and some Lutherans ganged up on Art and made him stop, so now you have to drive to St. Cloud if you want to see unmarried people together in one room with the door closed. It's a shame. I think if the church put in half the time on covetousness that it does on lust, this would be a better world for all of us.[8]

Worldliness is a spirit, an attitude of choosing one's own way of sin instead of following hard after the Savior. As Screwtape says in *The Screwtape Letters*, "Prosperity knits a man to the world. He feels that he is 'finding his place in it,' while really it is finding its place in him."[9]

A Focus on the Flesh

"Self is a stealth enemy! We need to choose our mirror carefully. If our mirror is the Word of God (James 1:23), then we don't look nearly as good as we think we do!"
(Businessman)

Finally, in addition to the devil and the world, we have a great enemy in "the flesh." This term occurs 228 times in the Greek Old Testament and 153 times in the New Testament—a total of 381 occurrences! Obviously we can't look at all 381 uses of the term throughout the Bible, so let's give our attention to two primary sources: (1) the Gospel of John, and (2) the Apostle Paul's use of the term in the Epistle to the Romans.

John's Use of "the Flesh"

We learn in John 1:13 that salvation is not a matter "of the *flesh*" but of God. In John's third chapter we learn that "flesh" and "spirit" are mutually exclusive categories: "Flesh gives birth to flesh, but the Spirit gives birth to Spirit" (3:6).

Contrasting the spirit and the flesh, Jesus teaches that "The Spirit gives life, the *flesh* counts for nothing; The words I have spoken to you are spirit and they are life" (6:63). He criticizes the religious leaders of the Jews by saying, "You judge by human standards" (8:15). It appears from these verses that God sees the flesh in a negative way.

And yet other verses are more positive. We learn that the Word "became *flesh* and made his dwelling among us" (1:14). Jesus speaks of Himself as the living bread which came down from heaven in John 6. There He teaches that one must "eat of this bread" in order to live forever and that the bread which He gives for the life of the world "is my *flesh*." (v. 51). When the Jews react to this cannibalistic-sounding language by asking, "How can this man give us his *flesh* to eat?" (6:52), Jesus intensifies His point: "I tell you the truth, unless you eat the *flesh* of the Son of Man and drink his blood, you have no life in you. Whoever eats my *flesh* and drinks my blood has eternal life, and I will raise him up at the last day" (6:53–54). It is the one who "eats my *flesh* and drinks my blood who remains in me," Jesus says (6:56).[10]

How do we resolve this apparent contradiction between positive and negative uses of "the flesh" by John? A clue to the answer is found in the very last use of "flesh" in John's Gospel and how it is translated in different Bible versions. This last use of the term is in Jesus' high priestly prayer, in which He speaks of Himself in the third person. He prays to the Father, "Thou hast given him power over all *flesh*, that he should give eternal life to as many as thou hast given him" (John 17:2, KJV). The NIV reads, "For you granted him authority over all *people* that he might give eternal life to all those you have given him."

It appears, then, that "flesh" refers to the world of people—humans. That is why the term "the flesh" can refer to that which opposes the Spirit who saves us (our salvation is from God, not by human effort), *or* to the truth of Christ's incarnation (His becoming "flesh"—human—for us). Receiving eternal life is a matter of "eating" His flesh, which obviously refers to a lifelong faith relationship with Him. And when Jesus criticized the Jewish leaders for judging according to "the flesh," He meant that they were using human standards.

The Use of "Flesh" in the Apostle Paul

Paul uses the term "the flesh" over ninety times in his writings, twenty-six times in the epistle we will now examine, the book of Romans.[8] Like John, Paul sometimes uses the term in Romans to refer to the Incarnation (as in 8:3, where he says that Christ was sent in the "likeness of sinful *flesh*" [KJV]). Sometimes the term simply refers to being human (as in 3:20). Paul speaks of our pre-conversion days as "living in the *flesh*" [KJV] (7:5). The flesh is contrasted with the Spirit in Romans 8:4 (we are to walk not "according to the sinful nature but according to the spirit"). In fact, setting one's mind "on the *flesh*" is death; setting one's mind on the Spirit is life and peace (Rom. 8:6).

We learn further that those who are "in the *flesh*" cannot please God (8:8). What does this mean? It cannot mean that those who are human cannot please God, for we will always be human—though in the resurrection we will receive new bodies like Christ's (1 Cor. 15, 1 John 3). In fact, Paul says that we are not "in the *flesh*," but "in the Spirit" (Rom. 8:9). So what does being "in the *flesh*" mean?

It must mean the same as living *according to the flesh*, because Paul says, "For if you live according to the sinful nature [*flesh*], you will die; but if by the Spirit you put to death the misdeeds of the body, you will live" (Rom. 8:13). We are to actively execute the "misdeeds of the body." In this text "the flesh" and "the body" seem synonymous.

Sometimes the word simply means race (9:3, "those of my own race"). Both the humanity and the deity of the Lord Jesus are affirmed by Paul in Romans 9:5 which reads in the NIV: "Theirs are the patriarchs, and from them is traced the *human ancestry* of Christ, who is God over all, forever praised! Amen." The children of "the *flesh*" are contrasted with the children of "the promise" in Romans 9:8. Paul commands us to "clothe yourselves with the Lord Jesus Christ, and do not think about how to gratify the desires of the sinful nature" in Romans 13:14.

In summary, the Apostle Paul uses the term "flesh" in a variety of ways. Positively, it may refer to the Incarnation or to one's race or to simply being a human being.

Negatively, the word can refer to one's pre-conversion days and is contrasted with the Spirit. To speak of someone "living according to the flesh" means nothing short of death! When the mind is set on the flesh, one is showing hostility to God and cannot please Him. The "children of the flesh" are contrasted with the "children of the promise."

The believer is in a *war* with the flesh, but this does not suggest self-abuse. We are not to torture ourselves physically, thinking that flagellation or asceticism will somehow enhance our souls or spirits. Abusing our bodies is not a Christian concept. God gave us our bodies to be used for Him. We are to "offer [our] bodies as living sacrifices, holy and pleasing to God—this is [our] spiritual act of worship" (Rom. 12:1).

The Bible recognizes that humans are both immaterial (soul or spirit) and material. We will forever be human; we will receive resurrection bodies like Christ's (1 Cor. 15). Although it is easy to identify the "flesh" with the physical body, that is hardly a full biblical understanding. We are to honor God with our bodies, but also turn away from, cleanse ourselves from, and execute the "flesh." According to Galatians 2:20, "I have been crucified with Christ and I no longer live, but Christ lives in me. The life I live in the body, I live by faith in the Son of God, who loved me and gave himself for me." The expression "in the body" is literally "in the *flesh*."

✓ Practical Action Points

1. We dare not forget the other two-thirds of our enemies. Without minimizing the devil's schemes to drag down the believer, the follower of Christ must also be aware of the worldly system opposed to God and the things of God. The "world" is a much more nuanced and subtle enemy than any list of culturally-confined taboos we Christians may seek to avoid. We also have the enemy of the "flesh." We carry with us our own sinful nature (one meaning of the term the "flesh"), and must be biblically and brutally honest with ourselves that truly we are often our own worst enemies.

2. On the other hand, it is not honoring to the Creator when we make the physical the enemy of the spiritual. C.S. Lewis says, "There is no good trying to be more spiritual than God. God never meant man to be

a purely spiritual creature. That is why He uses material things like bread and wine to put the new life into us. We may think this rather crude and unspiritual. God does not: He invented eating. He likes matter. He invented it."[12]

3. Finally, we must recognize that the Lord wants us to give ourselves to Him, body and all. This is "holy and pleasing" and is our "spiritual act of worship" (Rom. 12:1).

5

Chapter Five

Seven Deadly Mistakes We Make about the Seven Deadly Sins

Life is a movie, and you're the star. Give it a happy ending.
(Joan Rivers)

Wanted—Man or woman for part-time cleaning. Must be able to recognize dirt. (From the Holland, Michigan, *Evening Sentinel*)

A little sleep, a little slumber, a little folding of the hands to rest —and poverty will come on you like a bandit and scarcity like an armed man. (Prov. 6:10–11)

My, how easy it is for us to take sin seriously—in our *culture*! Whether it's the perfume "My Sin" or the Hershey candy bar "Temptation" (sold only in Canada, I think), we Christians have 20/20 vision in pointing out the transgressions of our times. The Broadway play *Wicked: The Untold Story of the Witches of Oz* played to sold-out audiences. The dark movie *Sin City* or the daytime drama *Passions* illustrate the fact that the sins of our society are in our face—much like a new installment of Jerry Springer's "Too Hot for TV" DVD.

But it's too simple to pick on society's sins. What about *our* sins? What about pride, anger, spiritual laziness, lust?

We need to consider a subject developed mostly by Roman Catholic scholars, the subject of the so-called "Seven Deadly Sins." Now, don't misunderstand me. I do not affirm the Catholic method of dealing with sin through confession to an anonymous priest who prescribes acts of penitence to make up for one's failures. And it must immediately be pointed out that *all* sin separates us from God—apart from the finished work of the Lord Jesus. James 2:10 says, "For whoever keeps the whole law and yet stumbles at just one point is guilty of breaking all of it."

I heard a youth speaker say, "Imagine that you painted a circle on a pane of glass. You then divided the circle into ten pie-like sections, naming each after one of the Ten Commandments. If you took a hammer and struck one section of the glass, what would happen? You would have broken all of the law."

When we examine the subject of the Seven Deadly Sins, we discover right at the start that there is no list of such sins in the Word of God, the Bible. (I googled for a list of the Seven Deadly Sins and got an advertisement which said, "Looking for the seven deadly sins? Find exactly what you want today—on *eBay.com*!")

Lists of Sins

There are, however, several biblical passages which list sins. For example, as we noticed in Chapter 2, Proverbs 6:16–19 says, "There are six things the Lord hates, seven that are detestable to him: haughty eyes, a lying tongue, hands that shed innocent blood, a heart that devises wicked schemes, feet that are quick to rush into evil, a false witness who pours out lies and a man who stirs up dissension among brothers." Scholars tell us that the writer of Proverbs is *not* saying, "There are six sins God hates—no, wait, I miscounted—there's *seven*!" It is actually a Hebrew literary device which means, "There are six sins God hates—but there is a seventh that He *really* despises!" (Note what that seventh sin is.)

We get a list of sins in First Corinthians 5:11 where we read, "But now I am writing you that you must not associate with anyone who calls himself a brother but is sexually immoral or greedy, an idolater or a slanderer, a drunkard or a swindler. With such a man do not even eat."[1] Paul is quite clear that an unrepentant Christian is a contradiction in terms and should, as a last resort, be tearfully excluded from God's people.

In the very next chapter Paul writes,

> Do you not know that the wicked will not inherit the kingdom of God? Do not be deceived: Neither the sexually immoral nor idolaters nor adulterers nor male prostitutes nor homosexual offenders nor thieves nor the greedy nor drunkards nor slanderers nor swindlers will inherit the kingdom of God. And that is what some of you were. But you were washed, you were sanctified, you were justified in the name of the Lord Jesus Christ and by the Spirit of our God. (6:9–11)

These are all serious offenses and each disqualifies a person for heaven. Only the atoning work of the Lord Jesus can wash, sanctify and justify sinners so that they can "inherit the kingdom of God."

We get another list of sins in Galatians 5:19–21:

> The acts of the sinful nature are obvious: sexual immorality, impurity and debauchery; idolatry and witchcraft; hatred, discord, jealousy, fits of rage, selfish ambition, dissensions, factions and envy; drunkenness, orgies, and the like. I warn you, as I did before, that those who live like this will not inherit the kingdom of God.

Significantly, the phrase "and the like" confirms that this list is *not* exhaustive.

A similar list is found in Ephesians 5:

> But among you there must not be even a hint of sexual immorality, or of any kind of impurity, or of greed, because these are improper for God's holy people. Nor should there be obscenity, foolish talk or coarse joking, which are out of place, but rather thanksgiving. For of this you can be sure: No immoral, impure or greedy person—such a man is an idolater—has any inheritance in the kingdom of Christ and of God. (5:3–5)

Our last list of sins we want to point out is found in Revelation 21:8: "But the cowardly, the unbelieving, the vile, the murderers, the sexually immoral, those who practice magic arts, the idolaters and all liars—their place will be in the fiery lake of burning sulfur. This is the second death."

What do we learn from these six lists of sins? First, we see that the lists differ from each other. There is no single list of sins which, if avoided, will guarantee a person eternity in heaven with God. Second, it is quite obvious that God hates sin, that sin disrupts Christian fellowship, and that sin will keep people from inheriting the kingdom of God.

We do read in First John 5 of the "sin unto death": "If

anyone sees his brother commit a sin that does not lead to death, he should pray and God will give him life. I refer to those whose sin does not lead to death. There is a sin that leads to death. I am not saying that he should pray about that. All wrongdoing is sin, and there is sin that does not lead to death" (5:16–17). Interpretations vary, but this text may refer to an unbeliever's adamant and persistent refusal of the gospel, or perhaps to a believer who commits a sin which leads to physical death. At any rate, as we have seen, there is no list of "Seven Deadly Sins" in the Bible.

So Why Deal with the "Seven Deadly Sins"?

I believe, however, that the so-called Seven Deadly Sins —lust, gluttony, greed, sloth, wrath, envy and pride—merit our serious study and our concerted avoidance. We want to briefly define each of these sins, suggest a biblical character who was marked by that sin, and provide some steps to avoid that particular sin. We then lastly want to ask, "What are the Seven Deadly Mistakes we make about the Seven Deadly Sins?"

A Little Bit on Lust

Traditionally, *lust* involves obsessive or excessive thoughts or desires of a sexual nature. Biblically, lust refers to desires contrary to the will of God. The term for "desires," "lusts" and "cravings" is the same Greek word and is used 118 times in the Old and New Testaments.[2] Most of the uses of the term "lust" or "desire" are in a negative context, such as the desire for other things choking out the gospel (Mark 4:19). Paul challenges believers not to live in the passions of the flesh, but rather to execute those worldly passions which keep us enslaved (Rom. 8:13). We can have freedom from our self-destructive pleasures (Rom. 7:23).

A number of years ago filmmaker Woody Allen claimed to have fallen in love with Soon-Yi, the daughter of his former girlfriend, Mia Farrow. He outraged much of society when he defended himself with the words, "The heart wants what the heart wants." Our culture communicates the message that lust is a must, that whatever one desires one should pursue, regardless of the consequences. The Apostle Paul tells us just the opposite: "Put to death, therefore, whatever belongs to your earthly nature: sexual immorality, impurity, lust, evil desires and greed, which is idolatry" (Col. 3:5).

When I think of the sin of lust, the biblical character who immediately comes to mind is Samson. His story is told us in Judges 13–16. Although Samson was greatly used to deliver Israel from the Philistines (we read that "the Spirit of the Lord began to stir him" while he was young), he demanded a young Philistine wife for himself (14:1). Later he spent the night with a prostitute (ch. 16) and thereafter bound himself with Delilah, who would prove to be his downfall. King David, whose sin we consider in our next chapter, also followed his lust to his own shame.

What steps may be taken to avoid lust? First, if lusts are desires contrary to the will of God, then we must know His will by knowing His Word. One passage that pertains directly to this is Psalm 37:4: "Delight yourself in the Lord and he will give you the desires of your heart." This sounds very much like Augustine and Luther's advice to "Love God and do as you please." Our desires are not naturally God-honoring, but when we delight ourselves in the Lord and grow in His Word, our desires get re-ordered.

Second, we must acknowledge our sexual needs and satisfy them in a biblical way (see 1 Cor. 7:1–5; Eph. 5:3, 22–33; Prov. 5; etc.).

Third, we must recognize the propaganda of our culture which uses all of its resources to encourage us to indulge our lusts. Someone has said, "Love is essentially the effort to sacrifice yourself to another person. Passion [or lust] is essentially the effort to sacrifice another person to yourself."

Some Guidance on Gluttony

Traditionally, *gluttony*, the second of the Seven Deadly Sins, is overindulgence or over-consumption of anything, but it is usually seen as an excessive desire for food, or withholding food from the needy. Thomas Aquinas said that it can involve eating too soon, too expensively, too much, too eagerly or too daintily!

Biblically, gluttony refers to craving the food of the rich. We read in Proverbs, "When you sit to dine with a ruler, note well what is before you, and put a knife to your throat if you are given to *gluttony*. Do not crave his delicacies, for that food is deceptive" (23:1–3). The Apostle Paul is tough on the inhabitants of Crete when he writes, "Even one of their own prophets has said, 'Cretans are always liars, evil brutes, lazy gluttons.' This testimony is true. Therefore, rebuke them sharply, so that they will be sound in the faith" (Titus1:12–13).

The prime biblical example of gluttony which comes to mind is that of Eli the priest in First Samuel 1–4. Eli raised the young boy Samuel (ch. 1), but failed miserably in disciplining his own sons, Hophni and Phineas. We learn in First Samuel 2 that Eli's sons were wicked men with no regard for the Lord. They brutalized those who came to bring sacrifices to the Lord by stealing food from them, thereby "treating the Lord's offering with contempt" (1 Sam. 2:17).

Eli tried to rebuke his sons (who were even sleeping with the women who served at the Tent of Meeting), but to no avail. One wonders if they didn't listen to Eli because of his own hypocrisy—he ate the meat his sons stole from the worshipers at the temple. A man of God was sent to rebuke Eli with this question: "Why do you honor your sons more than me by fattening yourselves on the choice parts of every offering made by my people Israel?" (2:29).

In First Samuel 4 we learn of the deaths of Eli's sons Hophni and Phineas and of the capture of the ark of the covenant. We then read that the aged Eli "fell backward off his chair by the side of the gate. His neck was broken and he died, for he was an old man and heavy." (v. 18). Eli's weight problem appears to have been the result of gluttony—eating the meat stolen by his sons Hophni and Phineas.

What steps may be taken to avoid gluttony? First, we need to acknowledge God's good gift of appetite and food. Paul tells us that the Lord "richly provides us with everything for our enjoyment." (1 Tim. 6:17). Second, we should resist our culture's insistence that we over-indulge in the good gifts that God has given.[3] Paul wrote to the Philippians, "Let your moderation be known unto all men. The Lord is at hand" (Phil. 4:5, KJV). Third, we must look for opportunities to share our abundance with others (Acts 4:34, 10:2; Eph. 4:28).

Got Greed?

The third of the Seven Deadly Sins is *greed*, traditionally understood to be the sin of excess. It also includes hoarding, theft and robbery. The believer is not to "associate with anyone who calls himself a brother but is sexually immoral or *greedy*, an idolater or a slanderer, a drunkard or a swindler. With such a man do not even eat" (1 Cor. 5:11).

The Old Testament provides the example of Gehazi, Elisha's servant, as one overtaken by greed. In Second Kings 5 we read of Naaman, the commander of the king of Aram, who came to Elisha to be cured of leprosy. He brought with him silver, gold and clothing to compensate Elisha, but after Naaman was cured, the prophet refused any payment.

Gehazi, Elisha's servant, said to himself, "My master was too easy on Naaman, this Aramean, by not accepting from him what he brought. As surely as the LORD lives, I will run after him and get something from him" (v. 20). Gehazi met up with Naaman, fabricated a story about two young prophets who had come to visit, and asked for gifts of silver and clothing. Naaman generously gave Gehazi more than he asked for, and he hid the treasures from Elisha. When Elisha asked Gehazi where he had been, Gehazi lied again and said, "Your servant didn't go anywhere" (v. 25). God's judgment then fell on this greedy conniver:

> But Elisha said to him, "Was not my spirit with you when the man got down from his chariot to meet you? Is this the time to take money, or to accept clothes, olive groves, vineyards, flocks, herds, or menservants and maidservants? Naaman's leprosy will cling to you and to your descendants forever." Then Gehazi went from Elisha's presence and he was leprous, as white as snow. (5:26–27)

It is not too much to say that greed is spiritual leprosy.

Luke 12 records the story of a man who has the opportunity to ask Jesus a question. If you had the opportunity to ask Jesus a question, what would it be? "Lord, how do you want me to serve You?" Or, "Lord, why did such and such a tragedy happen to me?" Or, "Lord, when will you return for Your children?"

Not this man—he asked a question about money! "Teacher, tell my brother to divide the inheritance with me" (v. 13). In fact, it's a demand and not really a question, isn't it?

Jesus' response seems abrupt and dismissive: "Man, who appointed me a judge or an arbiter between you?" (v. 14). Our Lord may have been alluding to Moses' experience, where we read, "The next day [Moses] went out and saw two Hebrews fighting. He asked the one in the wrong, 'Why are you hitting your fellow Hebrew?' The man said, 'Who made you ruler and judge over us?'" (Exod. 2:13–14). The Greek translation of Exodus 2:14 is very similar to Luke 12:14. Perhaps Jesus' point is that His mission on earth was not to impose Himself on human situations or to settle mere matters of material possession. He did not come as a trusts and estates attorney!

Jesus said to this man, "Watch out! Be on your guard against all kinds of greed; a man's life does not consist in the abundance of his possessions" (v. 15). The man came to ask for guidance; Jesus warned him of greed. Uppermost in this man's mind was getting his share, obtaining what he thought was rightfully his. And perhaps he was being cheated out of his inheritance. The text does not tell us. It only tells us what he asked of Jesus and how Jesus responded.

The text says that Jesus said "to them." It seems reasonable to believe that this man's brother, whom he implied was cheating him out of his fair share of the inheritance, was standing right there. So Jesus' warning against greed was issued to this man—and probably his brother as well.

It's one thing to be told, in front of a crowd, that you've come to the wrong person to straighten out an inheritance. It's quite another to be scolded publicly for the sin of greed. And then the man is told a story by Jesus to illustrate the condition of his heart.

Before we look at the parable which Jesus gave, let's notice two points that Jesus makes about greed. First, He refers to "all kinds of greed"—there is more than one kind. There is the greed for power, for respect, for independence, for material prosperity. But Jesus' main point is that "a man's life does not consist in the abundance of his possessions." One of the primary effects of greed is that it causes us to think of one another in terms of possessions. But what we own is not what we are.

As the master storyteller, Jesus illustrates His point about the danger of greed by talking about a rich man. (We all love to hear stories about rich people, and especially about rich people who mess up!) Jesus says,

> The ground of a certain rich man produced a good crop. He thought to himself, "What shall I do? I have no place to store my crops." Then he said, "This is what I'll do. I will tear down my barns and build bigger ones, and there I will store all my grain and my goods. And I'll say to myself, 'You have plenty of good things laid up for many years. Take life easy; eat, drink and be merry.'" But God said to him, "You fool! This very night your life will be demanded from you. Then who will get what you have prepared for yourself?" (Luke 12:16–20)

In Jewish culture, this farmer was obviously considered to have been blessed by God, for he had a problem every farmer would love to have: too many crops! To solve his problem, he crafted a business plan which was simple and straightforward, but woefully short-sighted. His strategy of replacing his smaller barns with larger ones was sound. But he got into trouble when he started talking to himself. (We always get into trouble when the primary voice we hear is our own.) He imagines what it will be like when he surveys his new storage barns, bursting with an abundance of grain, and predicts his own conversation with himself: "I'll say to myself, 'You have plenty of good things laid up for many years. Take life easy; eat, drink and be merry'" (v. 19).

There are many problems with what he says to himself. How is "plenty" to be defined? How can one be sure that the "good things" are really "good"? Who can know how "many years" he has on earth?

Perhaps James was thinking of this parable when he wrote,

> Now listen, you who say, "Today or tomorrow we will go to this or that city, spend a year there, carry on business and make money." Why, you do not even know what will happen tomorrow. What is your life? You are a mist that appears for a little while and then vanishes. Instead, you ought to say, "If it is the Lord's will, we will live and do this or that." (James 4:13–15)

Biblical self-talk recognizes the brevity of life and the sovereignty of God in the affairs of men.

My friend and colleague Dr. Terry Hulbert suggests that there is much more to this parable of Jesus than we first notice. The man asking Jesus to help him with his inheritance may well have only recently buried his father (after all, that's how one receives an inheritance). Perhaps Jesus' parable is not an out-of-thin-air story made up on the spot to teach a lesson. Perhaps Jesus is speaking directly about *this* man's father, whom they had just buried! Perhaps the man's father had been greatly blessed of God, had made provisions for storing his abundant crops, but had made no provision for meeting God.

The question, "Then who will get what you prepared for yourself?" is the critical issue for the one who had asked for Jesus' involvement in his inheritance. Could it be that one point Jesus is making with him is "Don't be like your father, unprepared for eternity because you are focusing all your energy on material possessions"?

Jesus concludes His lecture with the words, "This is how it will be with anyone who stores up things for himself but is not rich toward God" (v. 21). Greed causes us to build the wrong barns, to pour over the wrong ledger, to give our attention to the wrong bottom line.

We all know how we store up things for ourselves. But how is one "rich toward God"? Two passages help us here. The Lord Jesus teaches us in Matthew 6: "Do not store up for yourselves treasures on earth, where moth and rust destroy, and where thieves break in and steal. But store up for yourselves treasures in heaven, where moth and rust do not destroy, and where thieves do not break in and steal. For where your treasure is, there your heart will be also" (vv. 19–21).

To the rich young ruler who claimed to have kept all the commandments of God, Jesus said, "You still lack one thing. Sell everything you have and give to the poor, and you will have treasure in heaven. Then come, follow me." We read in the next verse: "When he heard this, he became very sad, because he was a man of great wealth." Jesus then said to His disciples, "How hard it is for the rich to enter the kingdom of God! Indeed, it is easier for a camel to go through the eye of a needle than for a rich man to enter the kingdom of God" (Luke 18:22–25). Greed makes it hard to have two bank accounts (one on earth and one in heaven) at the same time.

> *"Financial prosperity is the divine right of every Christian. In fact, it's more than a divine right. It's a divine obligation!"*
> *(Leroy Thompson, Sr.* [4]*)*

What steps may be taken to avoid greed? First, we must acknowledge that all that we have, all that we own, is really a stewardship from God: "Do you not know that your body is a temple of the Holy Spirit, who is in you, whom you have received from God? You are not your own; you were bought at a price. Therefore honor God with your body" (1 Cor. 6:19–20); "You were bought at a price; do not become slaves of men" (1 Cor. 7:23); "What do you have that you did not receive?" (1 Cor. 4:7).

Second, we first give ourselves to the Lord, then we give our resources (2 Cor. 8:4). The solution to greed is giving! Paul commended the Macedonian Christians for their generous giving, even out of extreme poverty.

And that leads to the third point: We do not give in order to get. Prosperity theology churches frequently preach a greed message which only feeds our lust for more.

The Ease Disease

The fourth of the Seven Deadly Sins is *sloth*. Traditionally, sloth was originally called the sin of sadness (involving apathy, depression and joylessness, the last being a refusal to enjoy the goodness of God and the world He created). This sin referred to a feeling of discontent or dissatisfaction. Dante called sloth the failure to love God with all one's heart, all one's mind and all one's soul, expressed in the failure to utilize one's talents and gifts. Sloth also involves an unwillingness to act or to care. Biblically, *laziness* is a common translation (although the common understanding of "laziness" misses the implications of sadness or depression).[5]

We read in Ecclesiastes 10:18, "If a man is *lazy*, the rafters sag; if his hands are idle, the house leaks." Proverbs 6 challenges us:

> *Go to the ant, you sluggard;*
> *consider its ways and be wise!*
> *It has no commander,*
> *no overseer or ruler,*
> *yet it stores its provisions in summer*
> *and gathers its food at harvest.*
> *How long will you lie there, you sluggard?*
> *When will you get up from your sleep?*
> *A little sleep, a little slumber,*
> *a little folding of the hands to rest—*
> *and poverty will come on you like a bandit*
> *and scarcity like an armed man. (vv. 6–11)*

I have a "Calvin and Hobbes" cartoon in my files where he is in school, reluctantly sitting in his desk, face scrunched up in great frustration, saying to himself, "I don't want to

study. I don't want any tests. I don't want any homework."
Many Christians are like that—especially when it comes to
digging into the Word of God for themselves.

Slothfulness, laziness, is a disease. I call it "the ease disease." Many believers act as if they are entitled to be idle.
What is the opposite of idleness? Being proactive, curious,
energetic about learning, looking for opportunities to serve,
to grow, to engage. We sometimes speak of those who watch
a lot of television as "couch potatoes." I believe many Christians are "pew potatoes," sitting back listening to the study
of others, watching the church service take place in front of
them. When we choose to be spectators instead of partici-
pants, consumers instead of contributors, we have given in
to the sin of sloth.

I would not have immediately connected sloth or laziness
with sadness, but there is much to be said for the fact that
depression paralyzes. Joylessness immobilizes one into pas-
sivity.

My choice for the biblical character who comes to mind
illustrating the sin of sloth might surprise you: Elijah in First
Kings 19. There we read,

> So Jezebel sent a messenger to Elijah to say, "May the gods
> deal with me, be it ever so severely, if by this time tomorrow I
> do not make your life like that of one of them."
> Elijah was afraid and ran for his life. When he came to
> Beersheba in Judah, he left his servant there, while he himself
> went a day's journey into the desert. He came to a broom
> tree, sat down under it and prayed that he might die. "I have
> had enough, LORD," he said. "Take my life; I am no better
> than my ancestors." Then he lay down under the tree and fell
> asleep. (vv. 2–5)

Now I don't wish to criticize Elijah. I'm not saying I would have responded any differently than he did. There is a genuine threat to his life (wicked Jezebel). He feels that he is the only prophet left (see v. 10). And so he separates himself from others, sits under a broom tree, and prays that he might die, even asking the Lord to take his life.

The Lord responds to Elijah's depression and thoughts of suicide by sending an angel to feed him (vv. 5–8), commanding him to appoint his successor (v. 16), and reminding him that there were 7,000 other servants who had not bowed down to Baal (v. 18). Fear and depression immobilize Elijah. Sloth seems to be a result of depression and sadness rather than their cause.

What steps may be taken to avoid sloth? I believe the Scriptures make several challenges very clear:

First, what we do and how we live matters greatly to God. We must continually remind ourselves that He cares about the choices we make and the way we invest our lives.

Second, all believers have been entrusted with various gifts for the building up of the local body of Christ. Looking at texts like First Corinthians 12, Romans 12, Ephesians 4 and First Peter 4 exposes the Christian to the concept that God has given every believer certain talents and abilities which are to be used for encouraging the rest of the church.

Third, we were never created to become content and satisfied in this world alone. A story called "Disillusionment" by Thomas Mann, written when he was only twenty, begins with the narrator sitting in St. Mark's Square in Venice when he falls into a conversation with a fellow countryman.

The man asks, "Do you know what disillusionment is? Not a miscarriage in small unimportant matters, but the great and general disappointment which everything, all of life, has in store?" He tells how, as a small boy, the house caught fire; yet as they watched it burn down he was thinking, "So this is a house on fire? Is that all?" And ever since then, life has been a series of disappointments; all the great experiences have left him with the feeling, "Is that all?"

Only when he saw the sea for the first time, he says, did he feel a sudden tremendous craving for freedom, for a sea without a horizon. And one day, death will come, and he expects it to be the last great disappointment. "Is this all?"

A song based on the story, sung by Peggy Lee, leaves out the part about the sea, but ends, just as Mann's story does, with the idea that death will be just one more disappointment. The verse to this song is actually spoken rather than sung. The refrain, the only part which is sung, goes,

> *Is that all there is?*
> *Is that all there is?*
> *If that's all there is, my friend,*
> *Then let's keep dancing,*
> *If that's all there is.*

One writer says that this little piece of existentialism could have made it onto the pop music charts of the late 1950s. And it's especially amazing that it was written by songwriters who were known for such lighthearted rock classics as "Yakety Yak," "Poison Ivy," "Hound Dog" and "Charlie Brown."[6]

Living one's life solely for this world brings dissatisfaction and soul sadness. C.S. Lewis said, "If I find in myself a desire which no experience in this world can satisfy, the most probable explanation is that I was made for another world."[7]

Although there are forms of depression which are greatly helped by medication and therapy, soul sadness which manifests itself in sloth is best remedied by the truth of God. My life matters. I have been gifted to serve others. I am not to seek my deepest contentment in this world. Rather than dwelling on my feelings of sadness and depression, perhaps the best solution is to go out and serve someone!

It must also be pointed out that, as Eugene Peterson says, "Busyness—which is essentially laziness—is the enemy of spirituality. A busy person is a lazy person because they are not doing what they are supposed to do."[8] Most of us think of the busy person as the very opposite of the lazy person. The key is not filling our lives with activities, appointments and stuff, but investing our lives in what counts.

Righteous Wrath?

The fifth of the Seven Deadly Sins is *wrath*. Traditionally, wrath is defined as inordinate and uncontrolled feelings of hatred and anger. Wrath may be shown by a vehement denial of the truth, an impatience with the procedure of law, or a desire to seek revenge outside the workings of the justice system (vigilantism). Wrath can also simply involve a general wishing to do evil or harm to others. Biblically, wrath can be godly or ungodly.

I grew up on the King James Bible, and sometimes its language is unique: "Wherefore, my beloved brethren, let every man be swift to hear, slow to speak, slow to wrath: For the wrath of man worketh not the righteousness of God. Wherefore lay apart all filthiness and superfluity of naughtiness, and receive with meekness the engrafted word, which is able to save your souls" (James 1:19–21). It's that "super-fluity of naughtiness" that gets me every time.

The phrase, "the wrath of man worketh not the righteous-ness of God," translated in the NIV as "man's anger does not bring about the righteous life that God desires," is certainly referring to ungodly wrath. However, the Scriptures are clear that God is a God of wrath (as we'll see in a moment) and that wrath is His righteous expression of anger against sin. We read in Romans 12:19, "Do not take revenge, my friends, but leave room for God's wrath, for it is written: 'It is mine to avenge; I will repay,' says the Lord." Some understand-ings of God today ("theologies") leave precious little room for God's wrath. One writer even says that "God's mercy has His hands of holy wrath tied behind His back."

Earlier generations, however, had no qualms about em-phasizing God's wrath. Jonathan Edwards' famous sermon "Sinners in the Hands of an Angry God" had such phrases as "The bow of God's wrath is bent and the arrow made ready on the string, and justice bends the arrow at your heart, and strains the bow, and it is nothing but the mere pleasure of God, and that of an angry God, without any promise or obligation at all, that keeps the arrow one moment from being made drunk with your blood."[9] Edwards' sermon con-cludes with the invitation: "Therefore, let every one that is out of Christ, now awake and fly from the wrath to come."

Briefly surveying the Scriptures on the topic of God's wrath,[10] we learn that one of the blessings of the gospel is being rescued from God's wrath. Although we are told three times in the book of Ezekiel that "God takes no delight in the death of the wicked" (Ezek. 18:23, 32; 33:11), that same book warns again and again of the wrath of God: "Wrath is upon the whole crowd" (7:12); God's wrath is something to be "spent" (13:15), "poured out" (21:31), and "blown" upon sinners (22:21). God says, "I will pour out my wrath on them and consume them with my fiery anger, bringing down on their own heads all they have done" (22:31). God speaks of His "zeal and fiery wrath" (38:19).

Other Scriptures teach us that the Lord is One who is "provoked to anger" (Deut. 9:7), that the wicked sometimes "stir up more of His wrath" (Neh. 13:18), and that "the desire of the righteous ends only in good, but the hope of the wicked only in wrath" (Prov. 11:23). Isaiah warns that "the day of the Lord is coming—a cruel day, with wrath and fierce anger—to make the land desolate and destroy the sinners within it" (Isa. 13:9). The prophet Nahum declares that "the Lord is a jealous and avenging God; the Lord takes vengeance and is filled with wrath. The Lord takes vengeance on his foes and maintains his wrath against his enemies" (Nah. 1:2).

John the Baptist's message was to "flee from the coming wrath" (Matt. 3:7). The Apostle Paul argues that the wicked are "storing up wrath against [themselves] for the day of God's wrath" (Rom. 2:5). The concept of God's avenging wrath is not an embarrassment to Paul, for he admonishes the Roman believers with the words: "Do not take revenge, my friends, but leave room for God's wrath, for it is written: 'It is mine to avenge; I will repay,' says the Lord" (Rom. 12:19). Believers in Christ should see themselves as those who once "were by nature objects of wrath" (Eph. 2:3), but are not objects of God's mercy: "God did not appoint us to suffer wrath but to receive salvation" (1 Thess. 5:9). Still, we shouldn't take God's wrath lightly. Paul argues this point when he writes, "Since, then, we know what it is to fear the Lord, we try to persuade men" (2 Cor. 5:11). Similarly, the writer to the Hebrews asserts that "It is a fearful thing to fall into the hands of the living God" (Heb. 10:31, KJV).

In his classic work *Knowing God*, J.I. Packer writes, "God's wrath in the Bible is never the capricious, self-indulgent, imitable, morally ignorable thing that human anger so often is. It is, instead, a right and necessary reaction to objective moral evil. God is only angry where anger is called for."[11] Packer further says,

> No doubt it is true that the subject of divine wrath has in the past been handled speculatively, irreverently, even malevolently. No doubt there have been some who have preached of wrath and damnation with tearless eyes and not pain in their hearts. No doubt the sign of small sects cheerfully consigning the whole world, apart from themselves, to hell has disgusted many. Yet if we would know God, it is vital that we face the truth concerning his wrath, however unfashionable it may be, and however strong our initial prejudices against it. Otherwise we shall not understand the gospel of salvation from wrath, nor the propitiatory achievement of the cross, nor the wonder of the redeeming love of God.[12]

> *"Unless God is angry with sin, let us put a bullet in our collective brain, for the universe is mad."*
> *(Sam Mikolaski)*

What biblical examples do we see of wrath? Negatively, we have the illustration of Moses' striking the rock in Numbers 20. Moses had already struck the rock at God's command back in Exodus 17. In Numbers 20 the people complained again: "This place has no grain or figs, grapevines or pomegranates. And there is no water to drink!" (v. 5).

Moses and Aaron met with the Lord at the Tent of Meeting; the Lord told Moses to take the staff, gather the assembly together, and *speak* to the rock before the people. By following God's instructions, the Lord says, "You will bring water out of the rock for the community so they and their livestock can drink" (v. 8).

Moses took the staff from the Lord's presence and gathered the assembly together in front of the rock, but then he goes beyond the Lord's command. He lectures God's people saying, "Listen, you rebels, must we bring you water out of this rock?" (v. 10). We then read, "Moses raised his arm and struck the rock twice with his staff. Water gushed out, and the community and their livestock drank" (v. 11). He went beyond God's command with an expression of anger at the Lord's people.

What are the consequences of Moses' outburst? We read, "But the Lord said to Moses and Aaron, 'Because you did not trust in me enough to honor me as holy in the sight of the Israelites, you will not bring this community into the land I give them'" (v. 12). Moses reflects on this judgment when he says to God's people, "Because of you the LORD became angry with me also and said, 'You shall not enter it, either'" (Deut. 1:37). In fact, when Moses pleaded with God to permit him to cross the Jordan and enter the Promised Land with his people, God responded by saying, "That is enough . . . do not speak to me anymore about this matter" (Deut. 3:26).[13]

Positively, we have a clear example of righteous wrath in Mark 3 when Jesus encountered what appeared to be a set-up. A man with a shriveled hand was sitting in the front row of the synagogue, probably at the invitation of the synagogue leaders, who wanted to trap Jesus into healing the man on the Sabbath: Not about to shrink back from a critical challenge, Jesus had the man stand up in front of everyone. Before healing the man, Jesus asked, "Which is lawful on the Sabbath: to do good or to do evil, to save life or to kill?" (v. 4). Mark adds this pointed observation: "But they remained silent."

The biblical text then tells us, "He looked around at them in anger and, deeply distressed at their stubborn hearts, said to the man, 'Stretch out your hand.' He stretched it out, and his hand was completely restored. Then the Pharisees went out and began to plot with the Herodians how they might kill Jesus" (vv. 5–6).

We learn from this passage that one form of righteous anger or wrath is to be deeply distressed at stubborn hearts. The combination of wrath and grief at spiritual stubbornness is the key.

One might ask, what was the difference between Moses' striking the rock in anger and Jesus' anger in Mark 3? Moses (and Aaron) clearly go beyond God's Word in striking the rock (twice), rather than merely speaking to it. What may appear as merely getting caught up in the moment God characterizes as Moses and Aaron not trusting "in me enough to honor me as holy in the sight of the Israelites" (Num. 20:12). On the other hand, the Lord Jesus in Mark 3 is not inconvenienced by the religious leaders of Israel, but rather deeply distressed. He "looked around at them in anger and, deeply distressed at their stubborn hearts," healed the man with the withered hand.

What steps may be taken to avoid wrath? First, we would suggest that we familiarize ourselves with what makes *God* angry and we follow His example.[14] Second, we need to be brutally honest with ourselves when ungodly anger rears its ugly head.

For me, I struggle sometimes with road rage. I get frustrated with slow drivers or with drivers who talk on their cell phone, apply make-up and eat a Whopper—all at the same time! When I am on an entrance ramp onto the highway, I get angry when people won't let me merge in. When I am on the highway, I get angry with people on the entrance ramp who want to merge in!

I suppose anger may be a reasonable response to poor and dangerous drivers, but my road rage is usually because I am inconvenienced or delayed in getting where I want to go. Sometimes I start flashing my high beams at other drivers and my wife says, "Sweetheart" (I know I'm in trouble when she calls me that), "some of these people carry deer rifles in their trucks." She has a point!

I've needed to be honest with the Lord and acknowledge my road rage. One step that is helping me is to mentally prepare myself before I get on the highway to look for opportunities to show kindness to other drivers as I commute to work. Kindness can be contagious. On those days I am being spiritual, other drivers are shocked that I am putting them before myself. Another thing that helps me is—are you sitting down?—*prayer!* I find that if I pray for those who make me angry, it's hard to intercede for them and be mad at them at the same time. Trust me—I've tried it, and it works![15] XXXXXXXXXXXX

Envy: The Green-Eyed Monster

The sixth of the Seven Deadly Sins is *envy*. Traditionally, envy involves an insatiable desire for that which someone else has. Dante called envy "love of one's own good perverted to a desire to deprive other men of theirs."

Biblically, envy is a cancer that consumes the sinner himself. We read in Proverbs, "A heart at peace gives life to the body, but *envy* rots the bones" (14:30). Peter tells us, "Therefore, rid yourselves of all malice and all deceit, hypocrisy, *envy*, and slander of every kind" (1 Peter 2:1).

One of my favorite Sunday afternoon activities is to go through the flyers in the Sunday paper, especially those for stores like BestBuy and Circuit City. Circuit City had an advertisement for a new cell phone. The ad reads, "Get the fully-loaded 'enV.' In bold letters the ad continues, "Now available in *green*." And they say there's no imagination left in marketing!

Envy, the green-eyed monster, must be recognized and resisted in our lives. Titus 3:3 says, "At one time we too were foolish, disobedient, deceived and enslaved by all kinds of passions and pleasures. We lived in malice and *envy*, being hated and hating one another."

Perhaps the biblical character most clearly portrayed as consumed by envy would be Cain. We read in Genesis 4,

> Now Abel kept flocks, and Cain worked the soil. In the course of time Cain brought some of the fruits of the soil as an offering to the LORD. But Abel brought fat portions from some of the firstborn of his flock. The LORD looked with favor on Abel and his offering, but on Cain and his offering he did not look with favor. So Cain was very angry, and his face was downcast.

Then the LORD said to Cain, "Why are you angry? Why is your face downcast? If you do what is right, will you not be accepted? But if you do not do what is right, sin is crouching at your door; it desires to have you, but you must master it." (4:2–7)

We then read of the result of Cain's anger:

Now Cain said to his brother Abel, "Let's go out to the field." And while they were in the field, Cain attacked his brother Abel and killed him.

Then the LORD said to Cain, "Where is your brother Abel?"

"I don't know," he replied. "Am I my brother's keeper?"

The LORD said, "What have you done? Listen! Your brother's blood cries out to me from the ground. Now you are under a curse and driven from the ground, which opened its mouth to receive your brother's blood from your hand. When you work the ground, it will no longer yield its crops for you. You will be a restless wanderer on the earth." (4:8–12)

Cain's disappointment in his offering not being acceptable to the Lord leads him to the premeditated murder of his brother. Cain is then put under a curse by the Lord and doomed to be a restless wanderer on the earth. Envy is a destructive force which can easily lead to other sins. One writer has said, that "Envy is the art of counting the other fellow's blessings instead of your own."

What steps may be taken to avoid envy? First, we need to recognize the presence of envy when it is in our lives. A lack of peace, according to Proverbs 14:30, may open the door to envy, which "rots the bones." Brutal honesty with ourselves will help us combat this sin. We must simply say to ourselves, "My problem is that I am envious of _____."

Second, we are to get rid of the sin of envy in our lives.

First Peter 2:1 clearly commands us to "rid yourselves of all . . . envy." Thanking God for His blessings upon *others* is a great place to start. Thankfulness (for God's gifts to us and to others) may well be a kind of all-purpose virtue for vices like envy, wrath, jealousy, etc.

The Peril of Pride

The Seventh Deadly Sin, *pride*, is considered the most original and most serious of the seven, the source from which the others arise. This sin involves an excessive love of self. Pride led to Lucifer's exclusion from heaven. C.S. Lewis writes,

> There is one vice of which no man in the world is free; which every one in the world loathes when he sees it in someone else; and of which hardly any people, except Christians, ever imagine they are guilty of themselves. . . . It was through Pride that the devil became the devil: Pride leads to every other vice: it is the complete anti-God state of mind.[16]

Biblically, we need to recognize that there can be *godly* pride:

> *This is what the LORD says:*
>
> *"Let not the wise man boast of his wisdom*
>   *or the strong man boast of his strength*
>   *or the rich man boast of his riches,*
> *but let him who boasts boast about this:*
>   *that he understands and knows me,*
>   *that I am the LORD, who exercises kindness,*
>   *justice and righteousness on earth,*
>   *for in these I delight,"*
>   *declares the LORD. (Jer. 9:23–24)*

However, the Bible is quite clear that there is an ungodly pride which keeps people from the Lord. We read in Psalm 10:4, "In his *pride* the wicked does not seek him; in all his thoughts there is no room for God." Proverbs 11:2 says, "When *pride* comes, then comes disgrace, but with humility comes wisdom." We further read in Proverbs 16:18, "*Pride* goes before destruction, a haughty spirit before a fall."

In our culture we are constantly bombarded with messages encouraging the sin of pride. The "great theologian" Joan Rivers writes in her book *Bouncing Back*, "Life is a movie and you're the star. Give it a happy ending."[17] Well, she's wrong on three counts: (1) Life is not a movie. Movies usually deal with fiction—and life is neither fantasy nor fiction; (2) You and I are not the stars of our lives. Left to ourselves and our sin natures, we may think we are the stars, but the truth is quite the opposite. For the believer, Jesus Christ is to be the star of our lives; (3) It may be that God does not want all of our lives to have a "happy ending." Hebrews 11 indicates that many of God's servants lost their lives for the sake of the gospel and counted eternity far more important than mere earthly happiness.

I am constantly amazed how even the most anti-Christian writers occasionally stumble over a biblical concept. George Bernard Shaw, no friend of Christianity, could not have written a more direct challenge to sinful pride than when he wrote, "This is the true joy of life: the being used up for a purpose recognized by yourself to be a mighty one; being a force of nature instead of a feverish, selfish little clot of ailments and grievances, complaining that the world will not devote itself to making you happy."[18]

The biblical character that immediately comes to my mind

when thinking of the deadly sin of pride is none other than Simon Peter:

> Then Jesus told them, "This very night you will all fall away on account of me, for it is written:
>
>> 'I will strike the shepherd,
>> and the sheep of the flock will be scattered.'
>
> But after I have risen, I will go ahead of you into Galilee."
>
> Peter replied, "Even if all fall away on account of you, I never will."
>
> "I tell you the truth," Jesus answered, "this very night, before the rooster crows, you will disown me three times."
>
> But Peter declared, "Even if I have to die with you, I will never disown you." And all the other disciples said the same. (Matt. 26:31–35)

What do we notice about this text? We notice that Jesus made a clear prediction that *all* of His disciples would fall away on account of Him. Such a falling away, Jesus says, is actually a fulfillment of Scripture, as Jesus quotes Zechariah 13:7. Peter's response was essentially, "You're right, Lord. I've had my doubts about these other guys for a long time. But, you can count on me! I will never fall away on account of you."

Now, it's bad enough when one directly contradicts the clear statement of Jesus about all falling away. It's even worse when one essentially says that an Old Testament prophecy is somehow incorrect. But it's absolutely terrible when one has the opportunity to back down from one's prideful opinion— and chooses not to do so!

How much clearer could Jesus' words have been? We read, "Then Jesus told them, 'This very night you will all fall away on account of me'" (v. 31). Peter's response? "Even if all fall away on account of you, I never will." Perhaps Peter is not aware of how prideful his words are. He challenges the words of God Incarnate, essentially saying, "I'm sure your 'all' does not include me, Jesus. It was really an exaggeration for effect, right?" To use the words "I never will" is the height of arrogance.

Jesus does not sugarcoat His response to Peter. He says, "I tell you the truth . . . this very night, before the rooster crows, you will disown me three times." He reiterates not only that His "all" includes Peter, but that Peter would surpass the other disciples' disowning of Christ: Peter would deny Christ "three times."

What *should* Peter have said? When Jesus said, "'This very night you will all fall away on account of me,'" Peter's response should have been, "Lord, please tell me what to do. I do not want to deny You. But I believe You and Your words above my own opinion of myself. What am I to do? Can I somehow avoid denying You? How will I be able to quickly come back into fellowship with You?"

According to Luke's Gospel, Jesus clearly warns Peter that Satan has desired to sift all the disciples. We read, "Simon, Simon, Satan has asked to sift you as wheat. But I have prayed for you, Simon, that your faith may not fail. And when you have turned back, strengthen your brothers" (Luke 22:31–32). In verse 31 the "you" is plural (Satan wanted to sift *all* the disciples as wheat). But Jesus says that He has prayed for Peter specifically: "I have prayed for you [singular], Simon, that your [singular] faith may not fail. And when you [singular] have turned back, strengthen your [singular] brothers" (v. 32). The sifting text occurs just before Jesus' predicts

Peter denial in Luke 22.

Peter's pride caused him not to believe the words of God Incarnate, caused him to deny the truth of Old Testament prophecy, and contributed to his refusal to acknowledge Christ.

I understand that G. Gordon Liddy, Watergate conspirator, said, "I have found within myself all I need and all I ever shall need. I am a man of great faith, but my faith is in George Gordon Liddy. I have never failed me."[19] Ungodly pride causes us to fail the Lord, for our eyes are on ourselves instead of on Him.

What steps may be taken to avoid pride? First, recognize that we are to boast in the Lord and in His goodness to us: "In God we make our boast all day long, and we will praise your name forever. Selah" (Ps. 44:8). When we seek to magnify Him, we will find ourselves much less committed to magnifying ourselves.

Second, confess ungodly pride wherever it manifests itself. We read in Proverbs 21:4, "Haughty eyes and a proud heart, the lamp of the wicked, are sin!" James 4:6 tells us that "God opposes the proud but gives grace to the humble." First Corinthians 13:4 reminds us that "love . . . does not boast, it is not proud."

Third, express godly pride in the accomplishments of others. Communicate to others your thankfulness for them and for their commitment to the things of the Lord. Paul expressed godly pride in the Thessalonians: "Therefore, among God's churches we boast about your perseverance and faith in all the persecutions and trials you are enduring" (2 Thess. 1:4). He also told the Philippians,

Do everything without complaining or arguing, so that you may become blameless and pure, children of God without fault in a crooked and depraved generation, in which you shine like stars in the universe as you hold out the word of life—in order that I may boast on the day of Christ that I did not run or labor for nothing. (Phil. 2:14–16)

Seven Deadly Mistakes We Make about the Seven Deadly Sins

We've examined the Seven Deadly Sins—lust, gluttony, greed, sloth, wrath, envy and pride—suggesting several biblical characters that had been taken captive by them. But as we mentioned at the beginning of this chapter, it is so easy to see someone else's sin or the sins of our society. What about us as individuals? Where do we struggle with these sins?

The Illusion of Immunity

The first mistake many of us make about these sins I would call *the illusion of immunity*. This is the believer who either outwardly or inwardly says, "I'm no longer tempted by any of these sins!" He or she might even be insulted or have their pride (!) bruised if we suggested that they might struggle with lust, gluttony, greed, sloth, wrath, envy or pride just like the rest of us.

James, however, reminds us that we are all in the same boat: "*Each one* is tempted when, by his own evil desire, he is dragged away and enticed. Then, after desire has conceived, it gives birth to sin; and sin, when it is full-grown, gives birth to death" (1:14–15). Of course, James is *not* saying that we must *inevitably* fall into sin! He is simply describing the cycle of temptation, sin and death that all human beings are prone to. If we resist temptation, with the Lord's help we can break that cycle.

James is, however, clearly teaching us that *every* believer is tempted—enticed by "his own evil desire." We should never arrogantly imagine that we have reached a plane where we are "above" the enticements of sin. Perhaps the place to begin in discussing these Seven Deadly Sins is not with lust, gluttony or greed, but with the last—*pride!*

Former heavyweight boxer James (Quick) Tillis is a cowboy from Oklahoma who fought out of Chicago in the early 1980s. He still remembers his first day in the Windy City after his arrival from Tulsa. "I got off the bus with two cardboard suitcases under my arms in downtown Chicago and stopped in front of the Sears Tower. I put my suitcases down, and I looked up at the Tower and I said to myself, 'I'm going to conquer Chicago.' When I looked down, the suitcases were gone."[20]

The Dilemma of Definition

Some followers of Christ may fall into the error I call *the dilemma of definition*. This is the person who (inwardly or outwardly) says, "I'm not sure these are really sins anymore." Here the issue is what constitutes one's personal dictionary. If we consult our culture, sins like lust, gluttony, greed, sloth, wrath, envy and pride fade away—or become redefined as virtues. Lust is seen as the normal sexual need of humans. Greed becomes healthy, entrepreneurial motivation. Pride is set forth as justifiable under almost all circumstances.

I found a cartoon on the Internet of two guys with a book

on the ground between them. One says to the other, "Yeah, I spent two years typing up all the words that exist. And then I made it into a book. I call it 'the dictionary.'" For followers of Jesus Christ, we don't create our own dictionaries. The Bible is our dictionary. The Word of God defines these Seven Deadly Sins (as well as many others) clearly and concisely.

The Conceit of Comparison

A third deadly mistake we all make I call *the conceit of comparison*. This is the person who says or thinks, "At least I'm not as bad as _____" —and they fill in the name of a friend, co-worker, neighbor, fellow church-goer or relative. But the test is not "Where am I compared to others?" but "Where am I compared to where *I* should be?" Galatians 6:4 says, "Each one should test his own actions. Then he can take pride in himself, without comparing himself to somebody else."

An old preacher's story fits here. A hundred years ago there was a young pastor who was trying to build a church out West. In that town were two of the most hateful, nastiest, no-good brothers in American history. Their names were Billy and Tex. Both were mean as snakes. Both were guilty of multiple crimes. It came to pass that Tex died. Billy came up to the pastor and said, "Reverend, I know you're trying to build a church, and I've got the money to help you do it. If you will do my brother's funeral and just once refer to him as a saint, I'll give you the money!" The pastor thought about it and then agreed to do the funeral.

At the funeral the pastor said, "The man we're burying

today was a murderer, a thief, a cattle rustler. Tex was a mean, nasty skunk, and deserved to die! But," the pastor paused, "compared to his brother Billy over there, he was a *saint!*"

The Excuse of Externalism

A fourth deadly mistake we make about the Seven Deadly Sins could be called *the excuse of externalism*. This is the person who says, "At least I don't do any of these sins in public!" The problem with this excuse is that sins begin as matters of the heart. Jesus said, "What comes out of a man is what makes him 'unclean.' For from within, out of men's hearts, come evil thoughts, sexual immorality, theft, murder, adultery, greed, malice, deceit, lewdness, envy, slander, arrogance and folly. All these evils come from inside and make a man 'unclean'" (Mark 7:20–23).

If one basic definition of sin is saying "No!" to God, then, as so often has been said, the heart of the problem is the problem of the heart. We say "No!" to God through Lust when we desire what we should not have, through Gluttony when we take more than we need, through Greed when we covet what someone else has, through Sloth when we refuse to exercise our gifts for the building up of the body of Christ, through Wrath when our anger is anything but godly, through Envy when we allow jealousy to invade our minds, through Pride when we think we're fine and have no sins to repent of.

The Presumption of the Past

A fifth deadly mistake we make concerning these sins I call *the presumption of the past*. This believer says (or thinks), "I used to struggle with these sins, but no longer!" We should all be grateful when God gives us victory over certain un-holy habits, but we dare not presume these temptations will never again crouch at our doors!

The last words of Josè Cubero, one of Spain's most bril-liant matadors, were "Pali, this bull has killed me." Then he lost consciousness and died. Only 21 years old, he had been enjoying a spectacular career until the conclusion of a fateful 1958 bullfight. After thrusting his sword a final time into a bleeding, delirious bull, which then collapsed, Josè made a tragic mistake. Considering the struggle finished, he turned to the crowd to acknowledge the applause.

The bull, however, was not dead. It rose and lunged at the unsuspecting matador, its horn piercing his back and puncturing his heart. Just when we think we've finished off sin, just when we turn to accept the congratulations of the crowd, sin stabs us in the back. We should never consider sin dead before we are.

I find great encouragement from the Apostle Paul's cry of exasperation: "What a wretched man I am! Who will rescue me from this body of death? Thanks be to God—through Jesus Christ our Lord!" (Rom. 7:24–25). Notice that Paul says, "What a wretched man I *am*," not "I *was*." We, like Paul, will have to fight temptation and sin until we die or the Lord returns. Only the fool thinks he can glide to glory on the successes of the past.

The Hold of Helplessness

A sixth mistake we make about these Seven Deadly Sins could be called *the hold of helplessness*. This mistake is of a different kind than the ones we've looked at so far. The believer who makes this mistake is not seeking to excuse his or her sin, but is crying out in despair, "I will never be free from this secret sin!"

The answer to this helpless condition is obvious, though difficult: "If we confess our sins, he is faithful and just and will forgive us our sins and purify us from all unrighteousness" (1 John 1:9). *Confession* is the antidote to helplessness. The Apostle John assures us that the confessor can count on God's character of faithfulness and justice. The first step to victory, ironically, is to admit defeat!

Occasionally I get to teach first-year Greek in our seminary and First John 1:9 is one of my favorite verses to inflict on (I mean, *to share with*) my students. After we have translated the verse in our Greek New Testaments, I ask, "Why did John use these two adjectives about God: 'faithful' and 'just'?" Various answers will be given, some good, some creative. But eventually one student will say, "Because God is faithful to His character and His promises! He has *promised* to forgive those who confess their sins! And," the student continues, "He is just and righteous because He forgives us on a righteous basis—the substitutionary death of His Son for our sins!" At such times I just look at the class and reply, "Amen!"

The Error of Isolation

Confession to the Lord, while a necessary step, may not in itself immediately rescue us from the sin with which we struggle. This leads us to the seventh deadly mistake we make about the Seven Deadly Sins: what I call *the error of isolation*. This believer says, "I am alone in my struggle—no one is able to help me!" This mistake effectively separates the believer from the body of Christ, the church, and produces only feelings of powerlessness and hopelessness. But the truth of the matter is that one purpose of the church is to help us find victory over sin: "Brothers, if someone is caught in a sin, you who are spiritual should restore him gently. But watch yourself, or you also may be tempted. Carry each other's burdens, and in this way you will fulfill the law of Christ" (Gal. 6:1–2).

Notice that Paul is not writing about those who have pursued sin and refuse to turn away from it. To be "caught in a sin" indicates a desire to get uncaught. So the text is speaking of a "caught" Christian. Notice also that Paul's challenge is for a gentle restoration. He is not to be whipped back into line or humiliated into conformity, but gently restored. Note that the effort to restore such a Christian is described as carrying each other's burdens and thus fulfilling the law of Christ. This kind of restoration is a burden-bearing work.

Two statements are made about those seeking to do the restoration. First, the challenge is given to "you who are spiritual." "Ah," I can hear someone say, "I would not classify myself as spiritual! Therefore, I'm not 'called' to this 'ministry.'" The problem with this excuse, of course, is that every believer is called to be spiritual. The one who says, "I'm not spiritual" should be challenged to get spiritual—so he or she can help other believers.

Second, those seeking to do the restoration are challenged to watch themselves, "or you also may be tempted." The spirituality of those seeking to restore does not make them immune from temptation.

We need to be accountable to each other. Galatians 6:1–

2 assumes that we are aware when another believer is "caught in a sin." The normal Christian life includes a desire to restore fellow believers gently. We are not alone—nor should we carry our burdens alone. God comforts His people by His people. And He restores His people by His people.

In a sense we should be grateful to our Catholic friends who have worked so hard on understanding these Seven Deadly Sins. Although we do not affirm their practices of confession or penitence, they have at the very least raised our awareness of these lethal practices.

The real question is, do we want escape, do we long for deliverance from the sins with which we struggle—or ought to be struggling? I'm reminded of the poem by A.J. Langguth entitled "Not Ready":

A brazen girl possessed of seven devils
Was brought before Jesus to be cured.
"I am going to cast out those seven devils from you," He said.
"May I ask you a favor?"
"What is it, child?"
"Cast out six." [21]

✓ Practical Action Points

1. With which of the Seven Deadly Sins do you most struggle? What specific steps will you take to begin gaining victory over that sin?

2. Pray about and work toward developing a close relationship with another believer to whom you can confess your struggle with these sins.

3. After watching a movie, discuss which of these Seven Deadly Sins were portrayed in the story. Were they defended as normal human behavior or challenged as being self-destructive, dishonoring to God, etc.?

6

Chapter Six

Coming Clean

It is the deliberate choosing to remain in illusion and to see God and the universe as hostile to one's ego that is of the very essence of Hell. The dreadful moods when we hug our hatred and misery and are too proud to let them go are foretastes in time of what Hell eternally is. (Dorothy Sayers)

If we confess our sins, he is faithful and just and will forgive us our sins and purify us from all unrighteousness. (1 John 1:9)

If we claim that we're free of sin, we're only fooling ourselves. A claim like that is errant nonsense. On the other hand, if we admit our sins—make a clean breast of them— he won't let us down; he'll be true to himself. He'll forgive our sins and purge us of all wrongdoing. (1 John 1:8-9, The Message)

One of the key events in the Old Testament is David's sin with Bathsheba (2 Sam. 11). From this passage we can glean several valuable principles about temptation and the consequences of giving in to it. We will also look at how God uses the prophet Nathan to confront David's sin (2

Samuel 12), and two of David's penitential psalms which show his confession of his sin (Ps. 32 and 51).

David's fall into sin is recorded briefly, with no excuses. We read:

> In the spring, at the time when kings go off to war, David sent Joab out with the king's men and the whole Israelite army. They destroyed the Ammonites and besieged Rabbah. But David remained in Jerusalem.
>
> One evening David got up from his bed and walked around on the roof of the palace. From the roof he saw a woman bathing. The woman was very beautiful, and David sent someone to find out about her. The man said, "Isn't this Bathsheba, the daughter of Eliam and the wife of Uriah the Hittite?" Then David sent messengers to get her. She came to him, and he slept with her. (She had purified herself from her uncleanness.) Then she went back home. The woman conceived and sent word to David, saying, "I am pregnant." (2 Sam. 11:1–5)

"When faced by temptation, the first response should be to flee. If you can't flee, then fight that temptation. Finally, forsake the sin if you give in to the temptation." (Young mother of two).

We notice several steps leading up to and resulting in David's sin. First, David was not where he should have been (v. 1). It was a time of war; David should have been at the battlefront. Instead, he sent Joab out with Israel's army. Although they had victory over the Ammonites, Scripture clearly implies that it was wrong for David to remain in Jerusalem.

The second step in David's sin is that he did not guard his eyes (v. 2). He should have taken his cue from the testimony of Job. Job defended himself against his friends' accusations by saying, "I made a covenant with my eyes not to look lustfully at a girl" (Job 31:1). David apparently never made any such personal commitment! There is no indication in Second Samuel 11 that David was planning to commit adultery. It simply tells us that he took an evening stroll on the roof of the palace (perhaps he could not sleep because he knew he should be off at war?) and saw a woman bathing. I spoke on this passage at a church and wanted to show a picture of what that evening scene might have looked like. I could not find an artist's portrayal that did not include a topless Bathsheba. I might be wrong, but I believe the scene was much more modest than artists have portrayed it. Although it was obvious to David that Bathsheba was taking a bath, perhaps most of the battle was in David's mind. At any rate, the text tells us that she "was very beautiful."

The third step in David's sin is that he misused his power (vv. 3–4). The text tells us that "David sent someone to find out about her." A *male* servant comes back and says, "Isn't this Bathsheba, the daughter of Eliam and the wife of Uriah the Hittite?"[1] It may be that this servant knew what King David was thinking and attempted to bring David to his senses. "She's someone else's wife, King David," he essentially says. His words fell on deaf ears. (One wonders why David asked for information about her at all. His next step, taking her, could have happened without the inquiry, right?)

We read that David "sent messengers to get her" (v. 4). It sounds like she had no choice. I know of no place in the Bible where any blame is laid on Bathsheba. Would it be too much to say that she was, for all intents and purposes, raped? This seems to be David abusing his power and simply *tak-*

ing. It began with a *look*, and then David *took*.

The text makes it clear that Bathsheba had only recently completed her menstrual cycle, so she was not pregnant when she slept with David. David took her, used her and sent her back home. But then, perhaps weeks later, Bathsheba delivered to David the three most feared words an unprepared man can hear: "I am pregnant" (v. 5).

The fourth step in David's sin is that he sought to cover it up (vv. 6–25). Rather than confessing his sin and seeking forgiveness, David attempted to hide his paternity. He sent for Uriah, involving Joab in his cover-up. After engaging Uriah in some military small talk, presumably to disarm him and to identify with him, David commanded Uriah to "Go down to your house and wash your feet" (v. 8). This was a euphemism for "Go have some R&R with your wife before you go back on the battlefield."

> *"Sin will take you farther than you want to go, cost more than you want to pay, and keep you longer than you want to stay." (Local African-American pastor)*

But Uriah did not accommodate David's plan. He did not go home, but instead slept at the entrance to the palace. (v. 9). Perhaps Uriah thought to himself, "Maybe the king needs some protection. That's why he's brought me back from the battlefront."

The next day, David asked Uriah why he disobeyed a direct order from the king and did not spend the night with his wife. (v. 10). Uriah's answer was that of a good soldier: "The ark and Israel and Judah are staying in tents, and my master Joab and my lord's men are camped in the open fields. How could I go to my house to eat and drink and lie with my wife? As surely as you live, I will not do such a thing!" (v. 11). Has a more loyal and honorable statement ever been made by a soldier?

Then David detained Uriah for two more days and resorted to getting Uriah drunk, figuring he'd lose his moral inhibitions while "under the influence" and go home. But it didn't work; Uriah again slept with David's servants and did not go home to his wife (vv. 12–13).

Moving to Plan "B"

Plan "A" to cover up his sin (having Uriah sleep with his wife) didn't work, so David quickly moved to Plan "B"— Uriah had to die. And the sooner the better. A dead Uriah would allow David to take Bathsheba as his wife.

There are various ways to do someone in, but David picked a method that was the very soul of treachery. He sent Uriah's order of execution to Joab—using *Uriah* as the letter carrier! The most wicked part of the plan was that it depended on Uriah's godliness and integrity; David trusted Uriah not to read the letter, or (if he could not read) have someone read it to him. The letter read, "Put Uriah in the front line where the fighting is fiercest. Then withdraw from him so he will be struck down and die" (v. 15). Have words of greater deceit and cowardice ever been written?

Joab obeyed his commander-in-chief and set up the bogus plan of attack so that Uriah was killed—along with some of David's other soldiers (vv. 16–17). I wonder how many "some" were? How outraged the broken-hearted mothers, wives and children would have been if they knew that their men died just to cover up David's sin!

When the messenger from the front lines tells David that Uriah died in battle, he responds with a sappy aphorism: "Say this to Joab: 'Don't let this upset you; the sword devours one as well as another'" (v. 25). How heartless and demeaning to the memory of a brave soldier! The reality is that the whole situation is a ruse, an effort to cover over David's sin and clear the way for him to have what he wants—Bathsheba.

And that is exactly what takes place. After a time of mourning for her dead husband, Bathsheba becomes David's wife and bears him a son (vv. 26–27). It looks as if David has "gotten away with it." There is one witness, however, who cannot be bribed, deceived, bumped off or hushed up: "But the thing David had done displeased the LORD" (v. 27).

David was not where he should have been (v. 1), he did not guard his eyes (v. 2), he misused his power (vv. 3–5) and he sought to cover-up his sin (vv. 6–27). One sin led to another, involving others, even to the extent of others dying for David's transgressions. But above all else, David displeased God.

A Call to Confront

The Lord does not want his people to languish in sin. In David's case the Lord raises up the prophet Nathan to confront him, employing a very creative strategy. He tells King David a story which appeals to David's sense of justice and moral outrage:

> There were two men in a certain town, one rich and the other poor. The rich man had a very large number of sheep and cattle, but the poor man had nothing except one little ewe lamb he had bought. He raised it, and it grew up with

him and his children. It shared his food, drank from his cup and even slept in his arms. It was like a daughter to him.

Now a traveler came to the rich man, but the rich man refrained from taking one of his own sheep or cattle to prepare a meal for the traveler who had come to him. Instead, he took the ewe lamb that belonged to the poor man and prepared it for the one who had come to him. (2 Sam. 12:1–4)

What a dastardly thing to do—the rich man needs to provide a meal for his guest, but instead of taking one of his sheep or cattle, he steals the poor man's solitary ewe lamb and *barbecues* it! Such a selfish act would be soundly condemned in any culture. But Nathan's story does not begin with, "Once upon a time in a land far, far away . . ." No, he implies that this selfish act had actually happened, in David's own kingdom. We then read,

David burned with anger against *the man* and said to Nathan, "As surely as the Lord lives, *the man* who did this deserves to die! He must pay for that lamb four times over, because he did such a thing and had no pity." (12:5–6)

The king who had burned with lust now burned with anger, ready to bring justice to the situation: "*The man* who did this deserves to die!" Wait a minute—*capital punishment* for stealing another man's lamb? David justifies the punishment because he says, "He did such a thing and had no pity." Sin causes us to forget about others, to be cruel instead of compassionate.

Nathan's next step is to confront David directly with his sin:

Then Nathan said to David, "You are *the man*! This is what the Lord, the God of Israel, says: 'I anointed you king over

Israel, and I delivered you from the hand of Saul. I gave your master's house to you, and your master's wives into your arms. I gave you the house of Israel and Judah. And if all this had been too little, I would have given you even more.'" (12:7–8)

David says, "As surely as the LORD lives, *the man* who did this deserves to die!" Nathan takes David's words (the identical phrase in the original Hebrew) and turns it around to convict the king: "You are *the man*!"

After reminding David of God's goodness in his life, the Lord said through Nathan, "And if all this had been too little, I would have given you even more." In effect, Nathan is saying that David's sin made no sense! It was not logical. Sin is just plain stupid!

The Lord (through Nathan) then reminds David that sin shows *contempt* for God: "Why did you despise the word of the Lord by doing what is evil in his eyes?" (v. 9); "You despised me and took the wife of Uriah the Hittite to be your own" (v. 10). Despising the word of the Lord is despising the Lord Himself.

Nathan then speaks of God's judgment for his sin: "This is what the LORD says: 'Out of your own household I am going to bring calamity upon you. Before your very eyes I will take your wives and give them to one who is close to you, and he will lie with your wives in broad daylight. You did it in secret, but I will do this thing in broad daylight before all Israel'" (v. 11–12). These predictions unfortunately come true in David's life.

What was David's reaction? "I have sinned against the LORD." Nathan replied, "The LORD has taken away your sin. You are not going to die" (v. 13). David may have thought he was going to be struck down right then and there—after all, his own words of judgment against the rich man in Nathan's story ("The man that has done this deserves to die!") were actually spoken against himself. When David confesses, Nathan speaks of God's mercy, but also reminds David that sin hurts God's reputation in the world: "By doing this you have made the enemies of the LORD show utter contempt" (v. 14).

Psalm 32: The Song of a Forgiven Sinner

Two psalms—32 and 51—are traditionally associated with David's sin against Bathsheba and her husband Uriah. Psalm 32 is called a *maskil*, a term one writer says refers to "someone who is sensible, wise, insightful or prudent."[2] Another writer says the term originates from the Hebrew word *maschil*, a musical term used to define or express a melody requiring great skill in its execution. Maskil was first conceived by David in the biblical Old Testament as a way of giving instruction or spoken wisdom through song.

Little is mentioned in the Bible about the maskils, but in reading their words their message is clear. They were not meant to portray some perfect world from which pain, death and sin did not exist, nor were they meant to show the goodness of mankind. They spoke of reality. A reality where murder, violence, hatred and suffering were the constant, inescapable burden of the author. A reality where only the unfailing love and unending forgiveness of a perfect God could give wings like a dove to fly away and be at rest.[3]

Psalm 32 first begins with a blessing:

> Blessed is he
>> whose transgressions are forgiven,
>> whose sins are covered.
> Blessed is the man
>> whose sin the LORD does not count against him
>> and in whose spirit is no deceit. (vv.1–2)

How wonderful to find forgiveness with the Lord! David uses several words to describe both his own wrong actions ("transgressions," "sins" and "sin") and God's action in his life ("forgiven," "covered" and "does not count against him").[4] He then reflects on where he was before he confessed his sin to the Lord:

> *When I kept silent,*
>> *my bones wasted away*
>> *through my groaning all day long.*
> *For day and night*
>> *your hand was heavy upon me;*
> *my strength was sapped*
>> *as in the heat of summer.*
>>>>> *Selah. (vv. 3–4)*

David teaches us here that unconfessed sin can bring physical consequences in the life of the one who needs to repent. This is a revolutionary thought for many believers—the idea that God can bring physical punishment in order to convince us to confess.

Part of our difficulty, I believe, is that we think God is *safe*. Mark Buchanan has a book with the great title: *Your God Is Too Safe*.[5] I'm reminded of C.S. Lewis' *Chronicles of Narnia* where the children are to meet Aslan (who is the

Christ-figure in the stories). We read of their apprehension as they discuss Aslan with Mr. and Mrs Beaver:

> "Is—is he a man?" asked Lucy.
>
> "Aslan a man!" said Mr. Beaver sternly. "Certainly not. I tell you he is the King of the wood and the son of the great Emperor-Beyond-the-Sea. Don't you know who is the King of Beasts? Aslan is a lion—*the* Lion, the great Lion."
>
> "Ooh!" said Susan, "I'd thought he was a man. Is he—quite safe? I shall feel rather nervous about meeting a lion."
>
> "That you will, dearie, and no mistake," said Mrs. Beaver, "if there's anyone who can appear before Aslan without their knees knocking, they're either braver than most or else just silly."
>
> "Then he isn't safe?" said Lucy.
>
> "Safe?" said Mr. Beaver. "Don't you hear what Mrs. Beaver tells you? Who said anything about safe? 'Course he isn't safe. But he's good. He's the King, I tell you."[6]

David makes some strange comments here, such as "groaning all day long." Have you ever groaned all day long for your sins? What does it mean that God's hand was "heavy upon me"? Some have suggested that David was getting a kind of spiritual spanking—and it was a 24/7 one!

> Then I acknowledged my sin to you
>   and did not cover up my iniquity.
> I said, "I will confess
>   my transgressions to the LORD"—
> and you forgave
>   the guilt of my sin.
>   Selah. (v. 5)

There comes a point at which David acknowledges his sin to the Lord. Nathan's story of the heartless rich thief who

had stolen the poor man's solitary ewe lamb blew David's
moral gaskets. He burned with anger and said to Nathan,
"As surely as the LORD lives, the man who did this deserves
to die! He must pay for that lamb four times over, because
he did such a thing and had no pity" (2 Sam. 12:5–6).
Nathan's words "You are the man!" (v. 7) were used by God
the Holy Spirit to bring conviction of sin to David's heart,
and he said, "I have sinned against the LORD" (v. 13).

> Therefore let everyone who is godly pray to you
>   while you may be found;
> surely when the mighty waters rise,
>   they will not reach him. (Ps. 32:6)

David now moves from his own confession to an invitation to all who hear his words. He seems to be addressing
both those who are "godly" and the Lord Himself. "Therefore let everyone who is godly pray to you," David says. The
very One from whom Adam and Eve hid in their sin was the
very One they should have fled to. When *we* sin, hiding
from the Lord is the last thing we should do!

It is interesting that David speaks to those who are "godly."
In a psalm whose primary message is about confessing sin,
David's invitation is to the godly. Perhaps his meaning is
that the godly, those who belong to the Lord, belong to One
who wants to hear their confession and wants to forgive their
sin. At what *time* should the godly person pray to the Lord?
David says, "while you may be found." The implication seems
to be that sometimes God cannot be found! Sometimes He
hides His face from us (Deut. 32:20, Job 34:29, Ps. 10:1,
etc.).

David then gives us a promise: "Surely when the mighty

waters rise, they will not reach him." The images of people in New Orleans on rooftops waiting to be rescued after Hurricane Katrina come to mind. When we do not pray to the Lord and confess our sins, we will drown in our unforgiveness.

> You are my hiding place;
>> you will protect me from trouble
>> and surround me with songs of deliverance.
>>> Selah. (Ps. 32:7)

David then directs his comments again to the Lord Himself as he did in verse 5. He makes three statements about the Lord—one about His identity, the other two about His actions. God is identified by David as "my hiding place." How can a Spirit be a hiding place? How can a hiding place be invisible? We must remind ourselves that reality is not limited to what we can perceive with our senses. It is the Lord's actions that show how He is our hiding place. David says that the Lord both protects him from trouble and surrounds him with "songs of deliverance." Who's doing the singing? The guardian angels that surround us? Or is it the Lord Himself? It is enough to know that we are protected and serenaded—the sinner has come home.

David then shifts to first person:

> I will instruct you and teach you in the way you should go;
>> I will counsel you and watch over you. (v. 8)

Surely David is not claiming to be the one who will instruct, teach, counsel and watch over the one reading his psalm! Obviously he has once again shifted from recounting his experience of forgiveness to the *Lord's* making a promise to all who read David's psalm. We all desperately need the

Lord to "instruct," "teach," "counsel" and "watch over" us.

The psalmist then moves to a direct challenge to those who refuse to repent:

> Do not be like the horse or the mule,
>   which have no understanding
> but must be controlled by bit and bridle
>   or they will not come to you. (v. 9)

He is reminding us that we are not mere brutes. We have the choice to surrender to the Lord. God's teaching and counsel in verse 8 should keep us from falling to the level of an ignorant beast in verse 9 who must be hurt in order to hear. But he also reminds us that the Lord is not impotent in the face of our stubbornness, but all-powerful—He will do all that is necessary to drive us to repentance and restoration. One of the weapons of His arsenal is pain—and He will not hesitate to use pain to prod us to repentance. As the prophet Hosea said,

> "Come, let us return to the LORD.
> He has torn us to pieces
>   but he will heal us;
> he has injured us
>   but he will bind up our wounds.
> After two days he will revive us;
>   on the third day he will restore us,
>   that we may live in his presence.
> Let us acknowledge the LORD;
>   let us press on to acknowledge him.
> As surely as the sun rises,
>   he will appear;
> he will come to us like the winter rains,
>   like the spring rains that water the earth." (Hos. 6:1–3)

As David concludes this Psalm, he says,

> Many are the woes of the wicked,
>   but the LORD's unfailing love
>   surrounds the man who trusts in him. (Ps. 32:10)

There is a clear contrast between the life of the "wicked" and the life of "the man who trusts in him." For the former, there are many "woes." Why? Because of unconfessed, unforgiven sins. For the latter, there is the surrounding presence of the Lord's unfailing love. David has used the verb "surrounded" twice in this psalm: The believer is surrounded by songs of deliverance (v. 7) and the Lord's unfailing love (v. 10).

Are there not many *unrealized* woes of the wicked? That longing for a right relationship with the Lord which is ignored and stifled, that wooing of the Holy Spirit which may be spurned time and time again, will result in unbelievable woes, eternal regrets for the wicked.

David concludes this Psalm by writing,

> Rejoice in the LORD and be glad, you righteous;
>   sing, all you who are upright in heart! (v. 11)

These three challenges—to rejoice, to be glad and to sing—are critical to my spiritual health. I have to rejoice in the Lord, or otherwise I would be drowned by my circumstances. I need constant reminders to "be glad," for my culture tells me to be down, depressed, discontent. And oh, how I need to sing! The One who sang songs of deliverance over me (v. 7) fills *my* heart with singing! He gives us the song, the notes and the voice.

By the way, the text indicates that this singing is from

those who are "upright in heart." Only salvation in Jesus
Christ makes one upright in heart. As much as our culture is
always on the prowl for new talent, new voices, new singing
sensations, it seems that the Lord wants to hear music from
one and only one choir: the redeemed!

Psalm 51: The Song of a Confessing Sinner

Psalm 51 begins with a historical superscription: "For the
director of music. A psalm of David. When the prophet
Nathan came to him after David had committed adultery
with Bathsheba." There is great debate among scholars
whether these titles are reliable, but they date all the way
back to the time of Ezra in the fifth century B.C.[7] It is interesting that although Psalm 32 is thought to relate to David's
sin with Bathsheba, Psalm 51 actually states it. The details
of this psalm fit that period in David's life quite well, and we
can learn a lot from a close look at this ode to confession.

David begins this psalm with a petition to the Lord:

> Have mercy on me, O God,
>   according to your unfailing love;
>   according to your great compassion
>   blot out my transgressions. (v. 1)

Forgiveness is a matter of mercy, isn't it? We do not demand it from a holy God. The basis for that forgiveness is
"mercy," "unfailing love" and His "great compassion." God
is under no obligation to forgive us. We are truly "debtors to
mercy alone."

> Wash away all my iniquity
>   and cleanse me from my sin.

> For I know my transgressions,
>   and my sin is always before me. (vv. 2–3)

Sin dirties our lives. David wants to be clean, but he immediately realizes that this is not a do-it-yourself project. When our children were small, my son could not see why we made him wash his hands even when he could not see any dirt on them. I remember needing to explain the concept of "invisible dirt" (germs). Sin is like "invisible dirt" which clings to our souls and makes us feel unclean.

Sometimes the deepest cleansing that the Lord can do in our lives is in our consciences, our thought-life. David says, "For I know my transgressions, and my sin is always before me" (v. 3). God uses our conscience to bring us to a sense of guilt and shame[8] so that we will seek forgiveness and cleansing. The Evil One Satan wants us to set up camp in our sin, to wallow in our remorse, to see nothing other than our offense before God. He uses God's good gift of conscience to torture us with a constant reminder of our transgression.[9]

> Against you, you only, have I sinned
>   and done what is evil in your sight,
> so that you are proved right when you speak
>   and justified when you judge. (v. 4)

David then says one of the most astounding things in the entire Bible. In reflecting on his adultery with Bathsheba and his murder of her godly husband Uriah, David says, "Against you, you only, have I sinned." Wait! Can't David count? Several people *died* due to David's uncontrolled lust— Uriah, a number of brave Israelite soldiers, and let's not forget about the baby born to David and Bathsheba. How can

David say, "Against you, you only, have I sinned"?

The expression "and done what is evil in your sight" might give us a clue. David is thinking of God's perfect standard of righteousness. Ultimately sin is an offense to God. David is not denying having hurt many others by his selfish acts. His focus is on how sin has hurt God.

> Surely I was sinful at birth,
>> sinful from the time my mother conceived me. (v. 5)

In this critical next verse, David reflects upon his own coming into existence. "Surely I was sinful at birth," he says. This is hardly how we greet the entrance of a new life into the world! No one would ever say to a new mother, "My, what a beautiful bundle of hell-deserving wickedness you have there!"[10] No, we rejoice with the new parents and re-mark how beautiful the new one is (whether they really are or not!).

I'm not saying that the labor/delivery room needs to be-come a place of deep theological pronouncement about origi-nal sin and the need for salvation, but we must listen to what David says. "Surely I was sinful at birth, sinful from the time my mother conceived me." He is not teaching that the sexual act which results in a pregnancy is itself sinful. No, he is saying, "I was sinful at birth, sinful from the point of conception." (Isn't it ironic, by the way, that this passage is a strong biblical argument that human life begins at con-ception and that the fetus is fully human and deserves our protection?)

> Surely you desire truth in the inner parts;
>> you teach me wisdom in the inmost place. (v. 6)

David next deals with what really matters to the Lord. He desires "truth in the inner parts." Our tendency is to focus on the externals, the ease of legalism. Outward conformity to a set of standards does not necessarily indicate heart transformation. God wants to work on our insides, teaching us "wisdom in the inmost place."

This, of course, was one of the major contentious issues between the Lord Jesus and the Pharisees. They were experts in the externals: how much one tithed, whether one ceremonially washed his hands, how one appeared. Jesus' focus was clearly on the heart when He said, "What comes out of a man is what makes him 'unclean.' For from within, out of men's hearts, come evil thoughts, sexual immorality, theft, murder, adultery, greed, malice, deceit, lewdness, envy, slander, arrogance and folly. All these evils come from inside and make a man 'unclean'" (Mark 7:20–23).

> Cleanse me with hyssop, and I will be clean;
> wash me, and I will be whiter than snow. (v. 7)

Returning to the picture of sin's impurity, David prays for cleansing. The herb hyssop was used in the ritual of passover where it was mixed with lamb's blood and the mixture was sprinkled on the door posts and lintels. It was also used in the ritual for cleansing from leprosy. In the Psalms, the use of hyssop refers allegorically to the purification of one's heart.

> Let me hear joy and gladness;
> let the bones you have crushed rejoice. (Ps. 51:8)

How can there be joy and gladness and rejoicing in a Psalm that has to do with one's sin and God's judgment? The answer, of course, is that David has been forgiven! Forgiveness and cleansing bring with them not only a sense of relief, but of joy and gladness.

What does David mean when he says, "Let me *hear* joy and gladness"? Perhaps David is thinking of being restored to God's people and their songs of praise. Unconfessed sin breaks our fellowship with the family. Maybe he is thinking of his own voice. Unconfessed sin blocks our own worship of the Lord.

When we combine the first line of verse 8 with the second ("Let the bones you have crushed rejoice"), we see that David is speaking of *himself*. It was *his* bones that the Lord had "crushed" because of his sin. David's unconfessed sin had silenced his own voice of praise. Let's not move too quickly past the second line of verse 8. God crushes bones— even the bones of His children. He will do anything consistent with His nature to compel His children to come clean with their sin.

We don't normally connect bone-crushing with the Lord. In fact, the one Bible passage I am reminded of is Daniel 6:24, where the king had those who had falsely accused Daniel thrown into the lions' den: "And before they reached the floor of the den, the lions overpowered them and crushed all their bones." Our sins threaten *us*—and the Lord is not beyond breaking our bones so that we will confess and once again find joy.

> Hide your face from my sins
>   and blot out all my iniquity. (Ps. 51:9)

David asks God to "hide His face" from his sins. Notice that this is a *request*—David knows that God is not obligated to do so. David also asks the Lord to "blot out all my iniquity," because he knows that God sees right through our feeble efforts to blot out our sins. But when He blots them out, it is because He has taken care of them.

> Create in me a pure heart, O God,
>   and renew a steadfast spirit within me. (v. 10)

David's prayer now turns to a positive note, a request for *restoration*. David compromised his purity when he lusted after and took Bathsheba. His greatest failure, it might be argued, was not sexual, but spiritual. He had failed to remain faithful to the Lord. After purification comes the request for a steadfast spirit. What is a "steadfast spirit"? That expression is used only here in Psalm 51:10. A clue to its meaning is found in another Psalm:

> For their heart was not steadfast toward Him,
> Nor were they faithful in His covenant. (78:37, NASB)

It seems that David is asking for another chance to prove himself faithful to the Lord. Sin, at its root, is unfaithfulness to God. Thankfully, God provides additional opportunities for His people to become (and to show themselves) faithful to His covenant.

> Do not cast me from your presence
>   or take your Holy Spirit from me.
> Restore to me the joy of your salvation
>   and grant me a willing spirit, to sustain me. (52:11–12)

Forgiveness brings the freedom to ask God for things. Here David seems primarily concerned not with his sins, but with his relationship to the Lord. He does not want to be cast from God's presence. David knew, however, that God is omnipresent, that he could never be completely separated from God: "Where can I go from your Spirit? Where can I flee from your presence?" (Ps. 139:7). So when David asks in our psalm, "Do not cast me from your presence," he is apparently referring to fellowship, not geography.

Some see the request not to "take your Holy Spirit from me" as suggesting that Old Testament believers could lose their salvation. Again I believe David is simply referring to his closeness to the Lord.

Notice that David prays in verse 12 not for salvation itself, but for the *joy* of God's salvation. Sin destroys our joy in knowing the Lord. David also asks for a "willing spirit" to sustain him. He is aware that sin can make us stubborn and unyielding to God.

David recognizes that "none of us lives to himself alone and none of us dies to himself alone" (Rom. 14:7), and so he has an obligation to use his experience of failure to help others. He prays,

> Then I will teach transgressors your ways,
>   and sinners will turn back to you.
> Save me from bloodguilt, O God,
>   the God who saves me,
>   and my tongue will sing of your righteousness.
> O Lord, open my lips,
>   and my mouth will declare your praise. (Ps. 51:13–15)

Our experiences, even our sinful ones, can be used by the Lord to impact others for good. David wants to teach transgressors God's ways, to encourage sinners to turn back to the Lord, to be an example of one who, because of forgiveness, can sing of God's righteousness and declare God's praise.

David concludes Psalm 51 with a reminder of what the Lord truly desires:

> You do not delight in sacrifice, or I would bring it;
>   you do not take pleasure in burnt offerings.
> The sacrifices of God are a broken spirit;
>   a broken and contrite heart,
>   O God, you will not despise.
> In your good pleasure make Zion prosper;
>   build up the walls of Jerusalem.
> Then there will be righteous sacrifices,
>   whole burnt offerings to delight you;
>   then bulls will be offered on your altar. (vv. 16–19)

God does not need the sacrifices of His people. He is not like the pagan deities who needed to be fed! God's delight is in His people who are broken and contrite.

✓ Practical Action Points

1. Confession of sin is required of God's people. Do you, like David, find a longing for God's mercy, for your transgressions to be blotted out? Have you daily experienced the joy of your iniquity being washed away, your sin cleansed? Do you stand in need of your "joy of salvation" being restored?

2. Do you desire to help others find freedom from their sin? One of the devil's biggest victories is to make us think that we are so dirty we can't help other dirty sinners find cleansing. David reminds us that God wants to replace that sense of uselessness with songs of deliverance.

3.   Do you ask God to give you a greater sense of your own sin? It is so easy for us to play what I call the "I'm-almost-perfect-what's-wrong-with-you?" game. Jonathan Edwards reminds us,

Often . . . I have had very affecting views of my own sinfulness and vileness; very frequently to such a degree as to hold me in a kind of loud weeping, sometimes for a considerable time together; so that I have often been forced to shut myself up. I have had a vastly greater sense of my own wickedness, and the badness of my heart, than ever I had before my conversion. It has often appeared to me, that if God should mark iniquity against me, I should appear the very worst of all mankind; of all that have been, since the beginning of the world to this time; and that I should have by far the lowest place in hell. . . . And yet it seems to me, that my conviction of sin is exceeding small, and faint; it is enough to amaze me, that I have no more sense of my sin. I know certainly, that I have very [poor] sense of my sinfulness.[11]

7

Chapter Seven

Breaking the Hold of Unholy Habits

*First we form habits, then they form us. Conquer
your bad habits or they will conquer you.* (Dr. Rob Gilbert)

*In the lowest moments of my life,
the only reason I didn't commit suicide was that I knew
I wouldn't be able to drink anymore if I was dead.* (Eric Clapton)

*Blessed is the man who can set aside all distraction . . .
Act with courage, for habit is broken by habit.* (Thomas à Kempis)

*Do not lie to each other, since you have
taken off your old self with its practices.* (Col. 3:9)

*Let us not give up meeting together, as some are
in the habit of doing, but let us encourage one another
—and all the more as you see the Day approaching.* (Heb. 10:25)

I've been assembling a kit for a storage shed. You know
you're in trouble when, just after purchasing the $800 kit,
the salesman tells you, "By the way, you know this doesn't
come with a floor, right?"

After buying the wood for the floor, I headed home to start the process. I built a level, square floor (exactly like the salesman explained to me), then followed the kit's directions perfectly. No mishaps. No wrong pieces nailed into place. No injuries.

Until last night. Last night I decided to temporarily nail a tarp over the as-of-yet-unshingled roof to keep the prophesied rain from turning my shed into a neighborhood ark. As I drove my last nail, I remember the process as if it were playing in super-slow-mo. I can still see the hammer coming down on my left thumb as it held the nail which was supposed to be the object of the blow.

There are few immediate pains as invigorating as hitting oneself on the thumb with a hammer. Oh, sure, there's childbirth, but that lasts for *hours!* And unlike women in labor, I didn't even have time to practice my Lamaze breathing. (I understand in the Korean War they sometimes drove bamboo shoots under the fingernails. Perhaps they didn't have hammers available.)

Anyway, I winced and said to myself, who was now incredibly awake and alert, "Self, let's attempt this one more time. And let's really try not to hit the pink thing holding the nail."

The hammer came down a second time – on *exactly the same spot* on my thumb as the first time. I can still see my thumb looking up at my hand holding the hammer with an expression of shock that said, "I thought we *talked* about this!" I said to myself, calmly and without any bad words (remember, I'm an Evangelical theologian), "I can't believe I did it *again!* Wow. That really hurts."

Unholy habits are sometimes like that. Someone has defined sin as not simply that which you shouldn't do, but as that which will hurt you—and hurt you bad. Frequently, the greatest damage ever done to us is that which we do to ourselves, over and over again. Even when we've had a rational conversation with ourselves not to deliver the same blow to the same spot.

Is it fair to say that often the sin we commit is not just a spontaneous action, thought or word we begrudgingly allow to escape us, but the result, the evidence, of a way of responding, thinking and speaking? Sometimes we are shocked at ourselves and say, "Where did *that* come from?" But in our saner moments, when we drop the mask of innocence and pretension and are truly honest with ourselves, we say, "Yes, that was *me*. I knew that's how I would respond. I am so ashamed." We might even quote the Apostle Paul: "Who will rescue me from this body of death?" (Rom. 7:24). What we think of as our normal pattern of responses, our typical way of relating to life's circumstances, are actually *habits* we have formed over the years. We become so identified with them that we think they are our true selves.

Transformation, Not Conformity

Come to think of it, I'm not at all sure that God's primary work is "sin management"—keeping us from doing individual acts which transgress His laws. Instead, it seems to me from Scripture that His number-one agenda item for each of us, at every moment of our lives, is to systematically and strategically transform us into the image of His Son (Rom. 8:29).

One of my favorite things to do at the end of each year is to buy myself a new appointment book. I transfer over phone

numbers and speaking engagements for the new year which
I had to write in the margins of the old appointment book
so I wouldn't forget them. Imagine God's appointment
book—what does He write each morning for His daily goal?
I believe that day after day, year after year, His entry is exactly the same: "Today I want to make [fill in your name
here] more like my precious Son."

If this is true, if God's highest goal for us is to become like
His Son,[1] then it makes sense that our habits will flow out of
that process. So, before we begin to talk about habits, let's
look into God's primary objective for our lives. A classic passage on this issue of transformation is Romans 12:1–2:

> Therefore, I urge you, brothers, in view of God's mercy, to
> offer your bodies as living sacrifices, holy and pleasing to God—
> this is your spiritual act of worship. Do not conform any longer
> to the pattern of this world, but be transformed by the renew-
> ing of your mind. Then you will be able to test and approve
> what God's will is—his good, pleasing and perfect will.

Cooperation, Please!

We learn several things from this key text. The first is that
this transformation involves our cooperation. The idea that
we simply "let go and let God," that we put our wills into
neutral and become Christ-like "by faith alone," that we
spiritually coast to consecration, is challenged by Paul's command to "offer your bodies as living sacrifices." The metaphor of sacrifice is a powerful one. We are to lay ourselves
down on the altar.

As we saw earlier in our consideration of King Saul's sin,
Micah 6:6–8 speaks powerfully of this truth of *self*-sacrifice
to the Lord:

With what shall I come before the LORD
    and bow down before the exalted God?
Shall I come before him with burnt offerings,
    with calves a year old?
Will the LORD be pleased with thousands of rams,
    with ten thousand rivers of oil?
Shall I offer my firstborn for my transgression,
    the fruit of my body for the sin of my soul?
He has showed you, O man, what is good.
    And what does the LORD require of you?
To act justly and to love mercy
    and to walk humbly with your God.

To the simple question, "What does the Lord want from me?", Micah's (and Paul's) answer is simple: YOU! He wants our individual lives laid down on the altar.

Notice that Paul teaches we are to offer our *bodies*. I would have expected him to say "minds," "hearts" or "spirits." But as we saw earlier in our consideration of "the flesh," sometimes the most difficult part of ourselves to surrender is our physical life with its appetites and demands.

Don't miss how *God* views the giving of our bodies as living sacrifices to the Lord. He views it as "holy and pleasing to God." In fact, our belief that our bodies are "unspiritual" is clearly refuted by Paul's statement that "this is your *spiritual* act of worship." Want to do something spiritual for the Lord? Then give your body with its appetites to Him![2]

Get Determined!

Giving our bodies as living sacrifices to the Lord not only involves our cooperation but also includes our determination: "Do not conform any longer to the pattern of this world"

(Rom. 12:2). We determine to no longer conform. It is interesting that Paul does not say "do not *be conformed*"—which sounds passive, like something that happens *to* us, and we might not think is our fault. Instead, he says, "do not *conform* any longer"—which is active, something that *we* choose to do, something for which we must take responsibility.

This determination requires at least two decisions on our part: First, we seek to understand something of the "pattern of this world." We study the spirit of the age, the many subtle (and not-so-subtle) ways in which worldliness is manifested in this present generation. We have to reject the idea that avoiding the taboos of the past assures us of being spiritual in the present. It is *this* world we are not to conform to, not the world of a past generation. The exact expression "of this world" is really "of this *age*." Legalistic nostalgia does not help today's believer resist the pull of the present.

The term "pattern," by the way, is from a verb which means to "fashion something by using a shaped container form." I know this is a serious study, but when I think of this verb meaning "to conform to" I can't help but think of a gelatin mold. J.B. Phillips' translation of the New Testament renders Romans 12:2 as, "Don't let the world around you squeeze you into its own mold, but let God re-mold your minds from within, so that you may prove in practice that the plan of God for you is good, meets all his demands and moves towards the goal of true maturity." The Message has "Don't become so well-adjusted to your culture that you fit into it without even thinking."

So, we determine to understand something of the "pattern of this world." But the second part of our determination is that we also admit to our past choices of adopting the pattern of this world. Paul says, "Do not conform *any longer* to the pattern of this world." We need to name the forms of worldliness in our present culture and acknowledge when we have taken on attitudes, perspectives and habits that identify us with this system opposed to God and the things of God.

The attitude in many churches is that an outbreak of worldliness among us would be as rare as an outbreak of leprosy! The real question is, Where have all the worldly Christians gone? And the real answer is, We're here and alive and well and just as worldly as past generations. We just won't admit it.

Guaranteed Understanding

We've seen that we are required to be determined not to conform to this world. This determination involves some understanding of the pattern of this world and an admission of our choices to conform to the habits, attitudes and perspectives of those who oppose God.

One last observation is important here as we conclude our discussion of Romans 12:1–2. The text involves not only our cooperation and our determination. It also promises our understanding. Paul says, "Do not conform any longer to the pattern of this world, but be transformed by the renewing of your mind. Then you will be able to test and approve what God's will is—his good, pleasing and perfect will."

Bruce Waltke points out in his book *Finding the Will of God: A Pagan Notion?*[3] that many Christians fall into a kind of divination or pagan practice of seeking to uncover God's secret, hidden will for their lives. Romans 12:1–2 makes it quite clear that when we, negatively, are no longer conforming to the pattern of this world and, positively, are being transformed by the renewing of our minds, then God's will becomes clear to us! We will be able to test and approve what God's will is and will be able to rest in His good, pleasing and perfect will.

Send in the Clones?

Although many other texts teach us that God is molding believers into the image of His Son (such as Rom. 8:29, 2 Cor. 3:18 and Col. 3:10), there is a world of difference between being conformed to Christ and being cloned by other Christians.

Years ago Steve Taylor sang a song entitled "I Wanna Be a Clone." The lyrics speak to this issue of conformity to Christian expectations rather than transformation into the likeness of Christ. In the song a new Christian is told that conversion is not enough, that he has to "play the part." But playing the part means he has to "kiss conviction goodnight" and lose a sense of "serving Him on my own."

He is threatened with losing his salvation unless he conforms, and unfortunately comes to the conclusion "who needs the Bible anyway?" He learns to speak fluent "Christianese" in striving to be a clone. Wanting to share his faith with others, he is told to "give it twenty years or so" before he tries to witness. He realizes that "my church is an assembly line," making every believer exactly like every other believer.

God has a much better plan! We read in First Thessalonians 4:3, "For this is the will of God, even your sanctification" (KJV). Sanctification is a fancy word meaning to be set apart, that is, to become like the Son. I believe that the Person of Christ is so wonderful and so rich that the Father can make every single redeemed person who has ever lived like His Son and yet each retains his or her individuality. C.S. Lewis said it quite well:

> The more we let God take us over, the more truly ourselves we become—because he made us. He invented all the different people that you and I were intended to be. . . . It is when I turn to Christ, when I give up myself to His personality, that I first begin to have a real personality of my own.[4]

Unholy habits involve the practice of sin by which we hurt ourselves. We must stop being surprised at our sins, which are really the evidence of our habits. God is not concerned with "sin management," but with transforming us into the image of His Son. In looking at Romans 12:1–2, we see that we are to cooperate with His program, to be determined not to be conformed to the pattern of this world, to acknowledge where we have given in, and to grow in our understanding of the will of God. The Father wants to transform each and every believer into the image of His Son, without resorting to cloning us.

Giving Up Ungodly Habits

This brings us back to the issue of habits. You might have heard the story about a man who was having lunch with his pastor. "Pastor," he said, "I've got to be honest with you. I really struggle with my temper. I fly off the handle at the smallest things." He sighed, then said, "I guess it's just my cross to bear."

"No, Tom," said the pastor strongly. "It's not your cross to bear. It's your *wife's* cross to bear. It's your *sin!*"

If God's highest goal for the believer is *transformation*—conforming the believer to the image of the Lord Jesus Christ—then this process has a direct application to the abandonment of unholy habits and the development of godly habits.

Mark Twain once said, "Habit is habit and not to be flung out of the window by any man, but coaxed downstairs a step at a time." I believe the Apostle Paul would strongly disagree with Twain and would say, "No! Some habits should be ruthlessly shoved down the stairs with malice aforethought!" The Bible has much to say about sinful practices and how they can be ended.

We are creatures of *habit*. The word "habit" in English refers to "an acquired behavior pattern regularly followed until it has become almost involuntary." The word can indicate a customary practice or use, a dominant or regular disposition or tendency, a prevailing character or quality. We might say, "She has a habit of looking at the bright side of things." "Habit" can also be used euphemistically for an addiction. Of course, a "habit" might also refer to the garb of a particular rank, profession or religious order, such as a monk's "habit." Apparently the term (which comes from Middle English or the Latin term *habitus* meaning state, style or practice) originally implied the *having* of something. Unfortunately, what we often think *we* have, has *us*.[5]

We are quick to judge others for their bad habits. In an article on rock stars who lived self-destructive lives, *USA Today* reported on Eric Clapton. The article said,

At the height of his heroin addiction, Clapton was spending about $16,000 a week on the drug. Years later, when he turned to heavy drinking, he was admitted to a hospital hours from death with five bleeding ulcers. [Clapton said:] 'In the lowest moments of my life, the only reason I didn't commit suicide was that I knew I wouldn't be able to drink anymore if I was dead.'[6]

Have you noticed how our culture seems addicted to, well, addictions? From Alcoholics Anonymous to Overeaters Anonymous to Procrastinators Anonymous (who always start their meetings late), we have self-help groups whose primary goal is to overcome "addictions." But aren't addictions really only a fancy name for *habits*?[7]

When I was going through seminary, I worked full-time in a detox hospital for alcoholics. My job as an orderly was to assist the nurses in admitting and caring for the patients. I learned much about alcoholism—and much about the individuals it afflicts.

Among the many lessons I learned was not to get too close to a wino when taking admission information. One guy kept whispering his answers as I was doing his paper work, so I repeated my questions, leaning close to him to catch his words. Then he breathed on me and said, "WELL . . ." I don't think he had brushed his teeth in years, and his breath could have removed four layers of paint!

Another lesson I learned is that alcoholism is an equal opportunity addiction. During one of my shifts at around 3 a.m., two weeping teenage girls brought their well-dressed but inebriated mother in. I learned that the woman's husband was the CEO of a large company in the Philadelphia area and was always away on some business trip. The wife

had found a new friend, alcohol, and now was being admit-
ted by her grieving daughters into our facility. They were
devastated; she was embarrassed as they all seemed to realize
at the same time that their mother had become what they
thought was a "hopeless drunk."

The Truth about Ourselves

The Bible does not describe the sinner before conversion to Christ as one who sometimes sins, or who once in
a while transgresses, but as one who practices sin, as one
who is marked by iniquity. For example, we read in Titus
3:3–5:

> At one time we too were foolish, disobedient, deceived and
> enslaved by all kinds of passions and pleasures. We lived in
> malice and envy, being hated and hating one another. But
> when the kindness and love of God our Savior appeared, he
> saved us, not because of righteous things we had done, but
> because of his mercy. He saved us through the washing of
> rebirth and renewal by the Holy Spirit.

This text is filled with awful adjectives about our pre-
conversion character: "foolish, disobedient, deceived and
enslaved" (v. 3). We are portrayed as slaves of sin, living "in
malice and envy." We were not accidental tourists but permanent residents in the land of the lost, practicing sins that
made us enemies of God.

Let's focus for a few minutes on our "B.C." condition as
described here in Titus 3. Each of these adjectives explains
something about our estrangement from God. Verse 3 tells
us that we were

1

"foolish"—living without God's wisdom,
"disobedient"—blithely violating God's commands,
"deceived"—not knowing that we didn't know, and
"enslaved"—prisoners to our own plans.

This enslavement was not to the devil or to any outside force, but to our own "passions and pleasures" (v. 3). We were victims of our own internal lusts, doing damage to ourselves.

A Despicable Description

How did we live in our "B.C." condition? In "malice and envy." The word "lived" has the idea of "passing the time." We talk about "spending time" with someone else as if time were money. This term is used only here in the entire Bible and literally means to "go through."

> *"If we were brought to trial for the crimes we have committed against ourselves, few would escape the gallows."*
> *(Anonymous)*

The word "malice" has the idea of "badness" and is used in Matthew 6:34 when Jesus says, "Each day has enough trouble of its own." (RSV). The term is translated "wickedness" in Acts 8:22 and as "malice" in Romans 1:29. Paul tells the Corinthians to avoid the "yeast of *malice* and wickedness" which is contrasted with the "[unleavened] bread of sincerity and truth" (1 Cor. 5:8). Later in the same letter he tells us "be not children in understanding: howbeit in malice be ye children, but in understanding be men." (14:20-KJV).

Paul also says in Titus 3 that we lived in "*envy*," which means "a state of ill will toward someone because of some

real or presumed advantage experienced by such a person"
and is used nine times in the New Testament. Perhaps Paul's
point is that we lived in malice (ill will toward God) and
envy (ill will toward other people).

Paul goes on to say that we were "being hated and hating
one another." The term "being hated" is used only here in
Titus 3:3 and has the connotation that the person is worthy
of being hated. We deserved to be hated by others. But we
were not only the rightful recipients of hatred, we lived a life
of "hating one another."

God's Kind Intervention

Titus 3 uses strong words to describe how we lived prior
to conversion. But, thank God, the text does not end there:

> But when the kindness and love of God our Savior ap-
> peared, he saved us, not because of righteous things we had
> done, but because of his mercy. He saved us through the wash-
> ing of rebirth and renewal by the Holy Spirit (vv. 4–5).

God did not leave us in our habitual, fallen condition.
He provided a Savior. And that Savior was not given by God
out of obligation, but out of "kindness" and "love." God did
not owe us a Savior. Paul says "He saved us"—it is an ac-
complished fact. We are, here and now, saved from our sins,
saved from God's wrath, saved from a wasted life. The apostle
is quick to add that it was "not because of righteous things
we had done." (After all, he has just listed all our works which
condemn us before a holy God.) He saved us "because of
His mercy." But what about those practices which betray
our profession?

Practical Steps in Shoving Unholy Habits Down the Steps

We've covered a fair amount of territory in this chapter. Our intention has been to say that unholy habits do damage to ourselves. God's priority is to make us like His Son. Our salvation involves recognizing our sinful condition before we encountered God's kindness in Christ. So how do we get rid of unholy habits?

One principle for breaking a bad habit is to replace it with a good one. We use the term "orthodoxy" to refer to right beliefs. Some use the term "orthopraxis" to refer to right behaviors. And we have orthodontists (which I guess means "right teeth-straighteners"!). I would like to coin a new term. Are you ready? *Ortho-habits!* What are the *right habits* we need to develop?

I'll answer that question with the use of the following acrostic:

H   holiness
A   attitude
B   Bible
I   intimacy
T   time
S   service

Just a few words on these steps. The first letter of HABITS stands for *Holiness*. How are my current practices helping me to become more like the Lord Jesus? If I don't have a longing for holiness, there is something wrong. Perhaps I need to examine the second letter of HABITS—my *Attitude*. Because the Lord works from the inside out,[8] He cares more about my heart than my habits. The Lord says in Proverbs 23, "My son, give me your heart!" (v. 26).

My family and I have a favorite seafood restaurant in Charleston, South Carolina. Although owned by several Jewish brothers from New York City, the restaurant prominently posts the following quote from Christian pastor Chuck Swindoll throughout their place:

> The longer I live, the more I realize the impact of attitude on life. Attitude, to me, is more important than facts. It is more important than the past, than education, than money, than circumstances, than failure, than successes, than what other people think or say or do. It is more important than appearance, giftedness or skill. It will make or break a company . . . a church . . . a home. The remarkable thing is we have a choice every day regarding the attitude we will embrace for that day. We cannot change our past . . . we cannot change the fact that people will act in a certain way. We cannot change the inevitable. The only thing we can do is play on the one string we have, and that is our attitude. I am convinced that life is 10% what happens to me and 90% of how I react to it. And so it is with you . . . we are in charge of our Attitudes.[9]

"When we do not immerse ourselves in the Scriptures, we are acting as if God is mute or not interested in training His child." (Middle-aged Bible teacher)

I frequently need an "attitude check." How about you?

When it comes to developing ortho-habits, we cannot overestimate the "B" in HABITS—the imperative of putting the ***Bible*** squarely in the center of our lives. We evangelicals do not—or at least, should not—worship the Bible. But we believe that feasting on God's Word will nourish our souls, revolutionize our lives and make us more like the Lord Jesus. "All Scripture is God-breathed and is useful for teaching, rebuking, correcting and training in righteousness, so that the man of God may be thoroughly equipped for every good work" (2 Tim. 3:16–17)

The believer in Jesus Christ *must* give himself or herself to the systematic, consistent study of the Word of God. We all need to be taught, rebuked, corrected and trained in right-eousness. A.W. Tozer once said,

> Whatever keeps me from my Bible is my enemy, however harmless it may appear to be. Whatever engages my attention when I should be meditating on God and things eternal does injury to my soul. Let the cares of life crowd out the Scrip-tures from my mind and I have suffered loss where I can least afford it. Let me accept anything else instead of the Scriptures and I have been cheated and robbed to my eternal confu-sion.[10]

The "I" in HABITS is another ortho-habit I want to challenge us to: *Intimacy*, with the Lord and with others. Cynthia Heald has said, "God does not have a secret society of intimate friends. We are as intimate with God as we choose to be."[11] As critical as growing in intimacy with the Lord is, we also desperately need to grow in intimacy with God's people—*and* with those who need to know Him.[12]

Cheer up—only two more letters to go!

The "T" in HABITS I would use to stand for *Time*. Am I exercising good stewardship over the seconds, minutes, hours, days, weeks, months, years, decades that God by His grace gives me? How I'm spending my minutes is how I'm spending my *life*! Rick Warren wrote in *The Purpose-Driven Life*, "You will not be in heaven two seconds before you cry out, why did I place so much importance on things that were so temporary? What was I thinking? Why did I waste so much time, energy and concern on what wasn't going to last?"[13] He also said, "Time is your most precious gift, because you only have a set amount of it."[14]

Our last letter in the words HABITS stands for *Service*. Are the practices of my life giving me more of a servant attitude toward life? Our Savior said, "For even the Son of Man did not come to be served, but to serve, and to give his life as a ransom for many" (Mark 10:45). Am I asking myself how I can serve others? In my conversations and interactions with others, is there "value added" by my participation? That perspective on life is rare these days.

The motivational speaker Stephen Covey has rightly said, "Our character is basically a composite of our habits. Because they are consistent, often unconscious patterns, they constantly, daily, express our character."[15] I want the character of Christ in my life. How about you?

✓ Practical Action Points

1. We recognize and cooperate with God's process of making us like His Son. To be like His Son we need to study Christ's character as recorded in the Gospels.

2. We lay our lives (including our bodies) on the altar to Him, giving up control of "our" bodies.

3. We stop conforming to this world, but allow God's Word to transform our minds.

4.   We cease being surprised at our own sin, but humbly ask for God's mercy and cleansing action in our lives.

5.   We stop trying to clone believers into our image, recognizing that God seeks to develop unique Christ-like character in each individual believer.

6.   We admit the truth about ourselves as outlined in Titus 3. We turn away from the myth of man's innate goodness and appreciate God's kindness in providing a Savior.

7.   We begin by God's grace and the Spirit's power to replace unholy habits with godly ones, what I call "ortho-habits."

8

What's the Church Got to Do with It?

In the end there's only me, mourning the things
not meant to be. (Group Tempest, "Early Winter")

Carved in wood over the door of a church
in Ohio are these words: "Enter at your own risk."
We are making choices to become risk-free, fail-safe ships
that spend entire tours of duty hugging harbors. (Leonard Sweet)

What business is it of mine to judge those outside the church?
Are you not to judge those inside? God will judge those outside.
"Expel the wicked man from among you." (1 Cor. 5:12–13)

Let's be honest. For many of us the local church has been of little help in the issues of temptation and sin. Far too many of us in the pew and the pulpit are afraid to talk about temptation, and we act as if we are beyond being enticed to do *anything* contrary to the Word of God. The local church is not, for most of us Protestants, a place of confession, but of pretension. We *pretend* that we do not struggle with sins great and small. We find no outlet to be honest, no ear to listen to our struggles—only criticism and judgment when these problems surface, usually against our will.

Gossip, not godly intervention, is the *modus operandi* of the local church. Many of our churches are worse than useless when it comes to real-life help concerning temptation and sin. So we keep our battles to ourselves, perhaps occasionally confiding in our spouse. But sometimes there is a crisis—a shocking arrest, an embarrassing discovery, a public blowup—and too late we learn of situations where secret sin has been festering below the surface.

Crises like these are certainly extreme cases, but many churches act as if no Christian ever struggles with lust, greed, jealousy, anger, resentment, gossip or any other sins. We speak little of our temptations and sins, and try to convince each other that all that is left for us to do is to purchase our ascension robes so we're ready to go home to Glory! In our privatized, isolated, independent, accountable-to-no-one-but-myself Western culture, we have effectively and efficiently cut ourselves off from the help provided by God Himself for our deliverance, recovery and cleansing: the local church.

Got Shame?

At the height of the recent controversy over unsafe Chinese imports, Cheung Shu-hung, co-owner of the Lee Der Industrial Company, hanged himself at a warehouse in Beijing. He headed the manufacturing of lead-tainted Sesame Street toys which were the center of a massive U.S. recall. Apparently it is common for disgraced officials to commit suicide in China.

America is not, to say the least, a shame-based culture

like China! Zephaniah 3:5 says that "the unrighteous know
no shame." If there is no shame, there is no possibility of
genuine repentance, and no possibility of authentic forgiveness and restoration. We would do well in our culture to
adopt not an Eastern, commit-suicide type of shame, but a
biblical understanding of the effects of sin on ourselves and
others. Lewis B. Smedes once wrote, "A healthy sense of
shame is perhaps the surest sign of our divine origin and our
human dignity. . . . We are the closest to health when we let
ourselves feel the pain of it and be led by the pain to do
something about it."[1]

Our authority is not another culture, nor our own, but
what the Word of God clearly teaches. And one aspect of
biblical accountability is shame over our sin, shame which
brings one to admit the truth, to repent of what one has
done, and to submit oneself to the loving discipline of the
local church. Perhaps "sorrow" is a more useful term. After
Paul rebuked the church in Corinth and they turned from
their sin, he wrote, "I am happy, not because you were made
sorry, but because your sorrow led you to repentance. For
you became sorrowful as God intended and so were not
harmed in any way by us. Godly sorrow brings repentance
that leads to salvation and leaves no regret, but worldly sorrow brings death" (2 Cor. 7:9–10).

There are three primary texts we want to examine as we
think about the local church and the issue of temptation
and sin.[2] The first, Matthew 5, speaks to the offender; the
second, Matthew 18, speaks to the offended one. And the
third, First Corinthians,[5] has to do with the double victory
the devil gets when we don't get involved in each other's
lives.

Matthew 5: When You've Been the *Offender*

Jesus says in Matthew 5, "Therefore, if you are offering your gift at the altar and there remember that your brother has something against you, leave your gift there in front of the altar. First go and be reconciled to your brother; then come and offer your gift" (vv. 23–24).

How important is the local church in the process of dealing with temptation and sin? Although in Matthew 5 the church had not yet been established, we learn that God's Son places a high value on relationships between believers. The context of Matthew 5 is one of worship. You remember, as you are worshiping, that your brother has something against you. Jesus does not say that you are to wait until your brother is led by the Holy Spirit to come and talk with you. Rather, Jesus teaches that the burden is on you to do something about what you have remembered.

Jesus commands three steps to take when you remember that you have offended another: The first step (believe it or not) is to *interrupt your worship*—leave your gift at the altar. Most of us think that worshiping God is far more important than harmony between humans. But God cares so much about relationships in the Body that He commands worship to be interrupted so that problems can be worked out.

The second step which must be followed is to *take a trip*—go find your brother. The assumption is that your brother is not with you in worship. You are to take the initiative in pursuing reconciliation. Making that effort to reconcile then leads to the third step.

The third step is to come back and *offer your gift*. The circle is complete. What had been interrupted (for a very good reason) now is resumed and completed.

Matthew 5 is crystal clear that God wants relationships between believers to be reconciled. He gives us verbs of action: Stop! Think! Leave your gift! Interrupt your worship! Go! Be reconciled! Come back and finish your worship!

Matthew 18: When You've Been Sinned *Against*

Jesus teaches us the following in Matthew 18:

> If your brother sins against you, go and show him his fault, just between the two of you. If he listens to you, you have won your brother over. But if he will not listen, take one or two others along, so that "every matter may be established by the testimony of two or three witnesses." If he refuses to listen to them, tell it to the church; and if he refuses to listen even to the church, treat him as you would a pagan or a tax collector.
>
> I tell you the truth, whatever you bind on earth will be bound in heaven, and whatever you loose on earth will be loosed in heaven.
>
> Again, I tell you that if two of you on earth agree about anything you ask for, it will be done for you by my Father in heaven. For where two or three come together in my name, there am I with them. (18:15–20)

In a mere six verses, Jesus provides specific instructions which, if followed, would create havoc for every church in the world! But we would be the better for it. Obeying Matthew 18 would not make life easier for our congregations, but the issue really is not comfort, but obedience, right?

Note that the context has to do with a brother who sins against you.[3] Some have suggested that if the sin is not directly against *you*, then you don't have to get involved. But Galatians 6 says, "Brothers, if someone is caught in a sin, you who are spiritual should restore him gently. But watch yourself, or you also may be tempted. Carry each other's burdens, and in this way you will fulfill the law of Christ" (vv. 1–2).

It is interesting that in Matthew 5 you are the offender and in Matthew 18 you are the one sinned against. But in both contexts *you* are to go to your brother to work things out. In both situations you and I are to take the initiative in seeking reconciliation.

Before we go into the details of Matthew 18, let's look at the context of the whole chapter and the overall tone of the verses. Matthew 18 covers several issues, all related to sin and forgiveness. It deals with the disciples' question concerning who is the greatest in the kingdom of heaven, addressing the sin of pride and the importance of humility (vv. 1–4). It calls us to welcome children and not to cause them to sin (vv. 5–6). It stresses the seriousness of sin by advising us to amputate body parts that cause us to sin (vv. 7–9).

In this chapter, Jesus also tells the parable of the lost sheep (vv. 10–14), answers Peter's question about how many times he should forgive his brother, and tells the parable of the unmerciful servant (vv. 21–35). And, of course, there is the section we are dealing with: what to do when a brother sins against you (vv. 15–20). The words *sin* and *forgive* are used frequently in this chapter.

So Matthew 18 has a great deal to do with sin, forgiveness, humbling oneself, avoiding eternal judgment, seeking the lost, repentance, etc. The text is not just about church discipline, although that is one aspect of it. Matthew 18 is really a treatise on sin.

What is the overall tone of the verses in Matthew 18? The text teaches humility, warns against being a stumbling block and against things that cause us to sin. His warning against looking down on children and the parable of the lost sheep shows that God's heart is that none of these little ones be lost. Our hearts ought to be the same!

This is what leads up to the section on the brother who sins against you. We are given four specific steps to follow in seeking to win our brother over to repentance. We move from "just between the two of you" to "one or two others" to "the church." Beyond those three stages lies excommunication or expulsion (vv. 15–17).

Jesus then says that what we bind and loose on earth is bound and loosed in heaven (v. 18), that what we agree upon on earth moves the Father in heaven (v. 19), and makes that oft-quoted statement, "For where two or three come together in my name, there am I with them" (v. 20). Set in the context of church discipline, this shows the importance of the fellowship of believers.

But the chapter is not finished. Peter asks Jesus how often he should forgive a brother who sins against him. Jesus responds with the story of the unmerciful servant who was forgiven a great debt by the king, but refused to forgive a fellow servant who owed him a relatively small debt. The king finds out and turns the unmerciful servant over to the jailers to be tortured, "until he should pay back all he owed" (v. 34). Jesus concludes this parable by saying, "This is how my heavenly Father will treat each of you unless you forgive your brother from your heart" (v. 35). The joy of having one's massive debt canceled is lost because the offer is retracted when the debtor refuses to extend forgiveness to another.

Down to the Details

Let's now examine the details of Matthew 18:15–20. Even though there is some debate regarding the expression "against you" in verse 15, we are going to assume that the sin or offense in question is against another individual Christian who needs to get involved in confronting and restoring the erring brother. For the sake of our discussion, we will use the second person pronoun ("you") as we move our way through the text.

The specifics of the sin which has been committed against you are not given. Presumably, it is a sin serious enough that it cannot be thought of as mere opinion or a trivial matter since Jesus' instructions eventuate in the *expulsion* of that brother who does not repent.

Step One: One and Done

Notice who takes the initiative—if *you* have been sinned against, *you* must begin the process of confrontation and restoration. You can't merely pray privately that the Holy Spirit will bring the offender to his senses and that *he* will come to you to confess. *You* are to go and show.

What is the issue at hand? You are to "show him his fault," as the NIV puts it. However, the specific words "his fault" are not in the original Greek. The text actually says "expose him" (or perhaps "expose it"), and "his fault" is simply implied. It is an interesting combination of words: "expose him . . . between you and him alone."

How do other translations deal with verse 15? Some translations also add the words "his fault"; others, including the NASB, translate it "reprove him." This verb "reprove" has the idea of putting to shame, to cross-examine, to accuse, to bring convincing proof. This sounds very much like a legal matter. You have some convincing to do.

Notice that this first step is an effort to keep the issue quiet, to keep to the bare minimum the number of parties involved: "just between the two of you." Is it not the case that we often make public that which ought to remain private and we keep private what ought to become public? We know from the antics of daytime talk shows that fractured people seem to need little incentive to air the most intimate and torturous aspects of their lives before audiences numbering in the millions. Marital confrontations which cry out for in-depth counseling degenerate into fist-fights before live audiences. And on the opposite end of the spectrum, in our churches we maintain our personal privacy to the point of shutting out any intervention or help. Then the crisis comes and it is often too late.

This first step involves the offender, the offended one and the Lord. One party does the talking; the other party potentially does the listening; and the possible result is "you have won your brother over." In a postmodern culture which doesn't care for terms like "win" and "lose," there is much at stake in this two-person conversation.

What we really have in Matthew 18:15–17 is a series of "if/then" statements, and the first two are *positive*:

IF . . .	THEN . . .
"your brother sins against you . . ."	"go and show him his fault, just between the two of you."
"he listens to you . . ."	"you have won your brother over."

Step Two: Can I Get a Witness?

If the "one and done" approach is not successful, the confronting Christian is not to give up. If your testimony alone
is not enough, what would you do in a courtroom? You would
say, "Your Honor, if it pleases the court, I would like to call
so-and-so and so-and-so as witnesses." And the judge says,
"You may proceed."

Step two involves witnesses: "But if he will not listen,
take one or two others along" (v. 16). Why the need for
witnesses? Apparently the offender's refusal to listen expresses
a disbelief in the charges. Could it be that the offender responds, "What? I didn't do that!"[5]

"But if he will not listen" indicates the very real possibility that personal confrontation will not work. The offender
may choose not to listen, which in this context means not
responding, not repenting, not reconciling. But the offended
one is still obligated to seek reconciliation with his brother.
Long-standing rifts between believers are not to be the norm
in the church. God wants matters settled!

Why are one or two witnesses brought in? So that the
truth is known to all, and the offender has to acknowledge
his sin. Godly peer pressure of a legal nature is the focus: "So
a matter must be established by the testimony of two or three
witnesses." This is a quotation from Deuteronomy 19:15.
That same chapter in Deuteronomy also includes a call for a
"thorough investigation" if a witness is suspected of lying. If
it is proven that the witness gave false testimony, the punishment is severe. This should be a strong reminder to us to be
sure we have our facts straight (and we aren't just listening to
rumor) before we bring others into the situation.

Step Three: Tell It to the Church

If this second step, bringing one or two reliable witnesses to provide evidence, is met with resistance, you are to "tell it to the church" (v. 17). Does this mean the church as a whole, or the spiritual leaders of the church? Answering this question is a bit difficult, for Matthew uses the term "church" only twice in his Gospel—here and in 16:18, where he says to Peter, "And I tell you that you are Peter, and on this rock I will build my *church*, and the gates of Hades will not overcome it."

I suggest that Jesus meant the leaders of the church, who will provide spiritual guidance in the matter and inform the congregation only to the degree they think is necessary. Why do I think this? Because throughout this process, the intent always is to keep the matter between as few people as possible. It is interesting that Jesus never says at any point, "Well, then, just drop the matter." No, it has to be seen through to a conclusion—and the offender does not control the conclusion. He controls only his reaction to the church's conclusion.

The gravity of the situation has reached a decision point. This appearance before "the church" provides the last opportunity for the offender to "come clean." What if he says, "Get out of my face! I will live as I please!"?

"If he refuses to listen *even* to the church . . .", we read. This should be an unthinkable situation! How can one turn his back on God's appointed method of spiritual guidance? Such disrespect for the church is simply disrespect for God Himself. What then can the church do?

We are told: "Treat him as you would a pagan or a tax

collector" (v. 17). The term "pagan" is used four times in the Gospel of Matthew. In 5:47 Jesus asks, "If you greet only your brothers, what are you doing more than others? Do not even *pagans* do that?" In 6:7 Jesus says, "And when you pray, do not keep on babbling like *pagans*, for they think they will be heard because of their many words." In that same context the Lord Jesus says the believer is not to worry about food or clothing, "For the *pagans* run after all these things, and your heavenly Father knows that you need them" (6:32). We then have our reference in Matthew 18: "If he refuses to listen to them, tell it to the church; and if he refuses to listen even to the church, treat him as you would a *pagan* or a tax collector" (v. 17).

How is the unrepentant believer to be treated like a pagan? He is to be seen as someone who is not a "brother" (5:47), someone whose prayers are like babbling (6:7), and someone who anxiously runs after what the heavenly Father willingly provides for His children (6:32). To treat the unrepentant believer as a pagan, in Matthew's context, means to reach out to him as a genuinely lost person.

How did the Lord Jesus treat pagans and tax collectors? Jesus actually called a *tax collector* to become one of His followers (9:9), and even has dinner at Matthew's home. We read that "many *tax collectors and 'sinners'* came and ate with him and his disciples" (9:10). Jesus calls Himself "a friend of *tax collectors and 'sinners'*" in 11:19. The last reference in Matthew's Gospel to tax collectors comes in 21:31–32, where Jesus said to the religious leaders of Israel,

> I tell you the truth, the *tax collectors* and the prostitutes are entering the kingdom of God ahead of you. For John came to you to show you the way of righteousness, and you did not

believe him, but the *tax collectors* and the prostitutes did. And even after you saw this, you did not repent and believe him.

To treat an unrepentant believer as a tax collector, according to Jesus, means to invite him to become a fully-devoted follower of the Lord Jesus (9:9), to spend time with him over a meal (9:10), and to become his friend (11:19). Tax collectors, according to Jesus, were those who were entering the kingdom of God before the religious leaders of Israel because they believed John's message about the way of righteousness (21:31).

So when we read in Matthew 18:17, "treat him as you would a pagan or a tax collector," I suggest Jesus is saying to no longer treat him as a brother in Christ, but as a lost person who needs to be saved. Jesus is *not* saying that he should be shunned. That's what Israel's religious leaders did with pagans and tax collectors—and were soundly rebuked by Jesus for their lack of love.

Imagine a brother in Christ who has been caught in a sin. He is confronted by another brother, either one who was sinned against, or one who has uncovered the sin. His response might be to say, "SIN? What sin? I haven't sinned!" The confronting brother then gathers witnesses. To their testimony the erring brother says, "Get lost! I'll do as I please!" The two or three confronters then bring the matter before the church. The offender is obviously aware of this third step. He either doesn't show up for the church meeting or he tells the church leadership to take a long walk off a short pier.

What's a church to do? The church has options. It is not helpless at this point. It now moves from treating him as an erring believer who needs to repent and be restored, to an unbeliever who needs to be saved. And the church body is unified at this point. There is no second guessing of the leadership. Every member begins to pray for the one acting like a pagan and each individual looks for opportunities to share the message of salvation with him.

Binding and Loosing

What is the impact of such a united, God-honoring action on the part of the local church? The Bible could not put it in stronger terms. Jesus says, "I tell you the truth, whatever you bind on earth will be bound in heaven, and whatever you loose on earth will be loosed in heaven." (v. 18). What is meant by this binding and loosing language?

In this same Gospel, in fact, two chapters earlier, Jesus uses the same words in the context of the predicted establishment of the church. Jesus says to Simon Peter,

> "And I tell you that you are Peter, and on this rock I will build my church, and the gates of Hades will not overcome it. I will give you the keys of the kingdom of heaven; whatever you bind on earth will be bound in heaven, and whatever you loose on earth will be loosed in heaven." Then he warned his disciples not to tell anyone that he was the Christ. (Matt. 16:18–20)

There is only one difference between these two passages: the pronoun in the Matthew 16 passage ("you") *is singular* (referring to Peter), but in Matthew 18 the pronoun ("you") is plural. What Jesus said personally to Simon Peter in Matthew 16 is now said to the church as a whole when it is exercising church discipline.

This idea of "binding and loosing" has been made much

of in "spiritual warfare" circles,[7] but here in our text, Matthew 18, there has been nothing said about Satan and demons.[8] It seems patently clear that the issue in Matthew 18 is not demonic involvement, but human stubbornness.

The translation of Matthew 18:18 is very important. The verse literally reads, "Whatever you bind upon the earth will have been bound in heaven, and whatever you loose upon the earth will have been loosed in heaven." A very interesting question is, If the binding and loosing here has to do with local church discipline, does it mean heaven responds to the decision the church has made, or is the church declaring publicly a decision which has already been reached in heaven? While this is a thorny question, I would suggest that Jesus' promised presence (v. 20) at the least assures us that heaven gives its full blessing upon the church which seeks to lovingly and carefully follow God's Word in this critical issue of church discipline.

Jesus says in the very next verse, "Again, I tell you that if two of you on earth agree about anything you ask for, it will be done for you by my Father in heaven" (v. 19). The context is still the context of church discipline. We again have the earth/heaven relationship (as we saw in v. 18). Note the two expressions: "you on earth" and "my Father in heaven."

Jesus then says, "For where two or three come together in my name, there am I with them." (v. 20). Two questions occur to me as I think about this verse. The first is, Who are the "two or three"? Well, we've already had a reference to "one or two others" and "two or three witnesses" (v. 16). It seems most reasonable that the verse is not referring to Christians in general, but the witnesses who come to give testimony for the purpose of restoring a fallen brother.

The second question concerns the expression "in my name." Where else does Jesus use that expression? In Matthew 18:5 Jesus speaks of welcoming little children "in my name" to come to Him. Others will misuse His name, Jesus says, and will come "in my name" claiming to be the Christ (Matt. 24:5). Mark 9:39 speaks of those who do a miracle in Christ's name. In that same chapter we read of those who give a cup of water in His name (v. 41). We learn of those who will drive out demons in Christ's name in Mark 16:17. Jesus promises to do whatever His followers request in His name (John 14:13–14). In that same chapter Jesus promises the Holy Spirit "whom the Father will send in my name" (John 14:26).

It seems reasonable that in Matthew 18:20, "For where two or three come together in my name, there am I with them," the emphasis is on His *authority*. Such a gathering has the full authority of the Son of God as it meets. What is being done in following the steps of church discipline is not merely a human matter; there is the full approval and support of the Son of God upon those who carry out His prescription.

First Corinthians 5 and the Sadness of Expulsion

Our third and final text, First Corinthians 5, goes into greater detail concerning this issue of church discipline. We have seen from Matthew 5 that the restoration of believers is important enough to interrupt one's worship. And we have observed the specific steps of Matthew 18 in seeking to bring a sinning believer to repentance.[9]

Paul gives additional teaching on this critical subject of dealing with sin among God's people. There are ramifications that go beyond the immediate parties in a discipline situation. We read in First Corinthians 5:1–2,

> It is actually reported that there is sexual immorality among you, and of a kind that does not occur even among pagans: A man has his father's wife. And you are proud! Shouldn't you rather have been filled with grief and have put out of your fellowship the man who did this?

Some have said that we cannot control how we feel about things. Well, here the Corinthians were feeling the wrong emotions about this man's sin. Instead of being grieved—and doing something about it—they were proud! What makes us think that our feelings are morally neutral? Every aspect of who we are has been tainted by sin—including our emotions. It is *wrong* to feel pride about a brother in Christ who is shacking up with his step-mother. Wrong, wrong, wrong!

We must renounce the myth of morally-neutral emotions. How we feel often determines how we think and how we act. Ecclesiastes 3:4 says there is "a time to weep and a time to laugh." We can have our emotions wrong and we can have our timing wrong. How we react emotionally shows what's in our hearts. Some emotions are always sin (such as lust, murder, envy, etc.); other emotions can be either good or bad (anger, jealousy, pride). God might not express His wrath toward us for our *initial* emotional reactions to things, but He does warn us of on-going, perpetual, life-dominating, twisted emotions which take our hearts from Him.

As an example, one thinks of God's rebuke of Jonah several times when his responses seem inappropriate to the situation. We read in chapter 1, "The captain went to him and said, 'How can you sleep? Get up and call on your god! Maybe he will take notice of us, and we will not perish.'" (v. 6). Jonah should have felt panic because of the storm; instead, he was sound asleep. Later, Jonah also gets inappropriately angry:

> But Jonah was greatly displeased and became angry. He prayed to the LORD, "O LORD, is this not what I said when I was still at home? That is why I was so quick to flee to Tarshish. I knew that you are a gracious and compassionate God, slow to anger and abounding in love, a God who relents from sending calamity. Now, O LORD, take away my life, for it is better for me to die than to live."
>
> But the LORD replied, "*Have you any right to be angry?*" . . .
>
> When the sun rose, God provided a scorching east wind, and the sun blazed on Jonah's head so that he grew faint. He wanted to die, and said, "It would be better for me to die than to live."
>
> But God said to Jonah, "*Do you have a right to be angry about the vine?*" (4:1–4, 8–9)

On the other hand, there is such a thing as appropriate anger, such as when the Lord Jesus was grieved at the hardness of the hearts of the Pharisees: "He looked around at them in anger and, deeply distressed at their stubborn hearts, said to the man, 'Stretch out your hand'" (Mark 3:5).[10]

Is there a difference between a feeling and an emotion? My suggestion is that feelings come on us suddenly, while emotions we may allow to grow and to take up permanent residence. Feelings are fleeting; emotions can enmesh us. We make choices with our emotions. Emotions are feelings that are allowed to control us and our responses. God rebukes not our feelings but our emotions. This may be similar to temptation and sin. Temptation is not wrong; sin is. Jesus was overwhelmed by feelings in the garden, at the death of

Lazarus, and on other occasions, but He did not allow His feelings to deter Him from doing the Father's will.

There should have been a godly outrage at this man's behavior! The Corinthians were *wrong* to feel pride about his conduct. Paul appeals to the Corinthians' conscience, asking them, "Shouldn't you rather have been filled with grief?" Their emotional response to this man's sin was wrong—and the Corinthians should have felt guilty because of it.

When we declare our emotions protected territory, we make excuses for not feeling the way God feels about sin. Our feelings are not the Switzerland of our lives; they do not possess a neutrality which makes them off-limits to criticism. We are emotional creatures who are responsible for how we react emotionally and how we remain emotionally.

Note that Paul not only condemns their emotional response to this man's sin. He also says that they should have "put out of your fellowship the man who did this." Right emotions lead to right actions. Wrong emotions (in this case, pride) led to wrong action/inaction (tolerating this sinning believer in their congregation).

Decisive Steps in Discipline

In verses 3–5 Paul assures the Corinthians that they have his full support for carrying out judgment on this sinning believer. His physical presence is not required; he is with them "in spirit."

Paul even outlines for them the steps which they should take: (1) "When you are assembled in the name of our Lord Jesus" (an official meeting of the Body); (2) "and I am with you in spirit" (you know I am in support of your actions);

(3) "and the power of our Lord Jesus is present" (perhaps Paul is thinking back to Jesus' promise of His presence "where two or three come together in my name," Matt. 18:20); (4) "hand this man over to Satan."

What does this expression, "hand this man over to Satan," mean? It is used in only one other place in Scripture: "Among them are Hymenaeus and Alexander, whom I have handed over to Satan to be taught not to blaspheme" (1 Tim. 1:20).

What does it mean to be handed over to Satan? From First Corinthians 5:5, we learn the purpose of such an action is "so that the sinful nature may be destroyed and his spirit saved on the day of the Lord." How is "handing over to Satan" conducive to the sinful nature's being destroyed? I don't believe the Bible teaches the eradication of the sin nature until we are with the Lord in heaven. Perhaps the idea of the sinful nature being destroyed is that it is rendered ineffective. In other words, that the unrepentant believer will come to his senses, confess his sin and be restored to God's people.

It appears that the expression "handing this man over to Satan" is equivalent to:

(1) "put out of fellowship" (v. 2);
(2) "pass judgment on the one who did this" (v. 3);
(3) "get rid of the old yeast" (v. 7);
(4) "let us keep the Festival, not with the old yeast" (v. 8);
(5) "you must not associate with anyone who calls him self a brother but is sexually immoral" (v. 11);
(6) "with such a man do not even eat" (v. 11);
(7) "are you not to judge those inside?" (v. 12);
(8) "Expel the wicked man from among you" (v. 13).

So what is involved in "handing over to Satan"? Putting out of fellowship, passing judgment on, not associating with, not eating with, judging those inside, and expulsion. Figuratively, it involves getting rid of the old yeast.

There is not a hint of demoniac involvement here. The idea seems to be that expulsion from the church means being cast into the world where the devil is the "prince of the power of the air" (Eph. 2:2 KJV). If this unrepentant believer is going to act like a pagan, then he needs to be with pagans and to be cut off from pretending that all is right with his soul and with his fellow-believers.

In verses 6–8 Paul uses the metaphor of yeast to describe the effect of false teaching and wrong attitudes. He states a basic culinary fact: "a little yeast works through the whole batch of dough." (v. 6). Once yeast has begun to spread, it cannot be separated out.

The Corinthians had forgotten the spreading effect of unconfessed sin. They thought a little sin could be tolerated and kept "in house." Paul tells them bluntly: "Get rid of the old yeast!" He wants the Corinthian church to be a new batch of dough without yeast. The old yeast symbolizes malice and wickedness, and God demands worship that is marked by sincerity and truth.

A Convenient Confusion

Paul then moves on and reminds them of what he had written to them on an earlier occasion. His previous words were clear: "Don't associate with sexually immoral people" (v. 9). However, the Corinthians misunderstood what he meant. They thought he meant "the people of this world."

Paul agrees that the people of this world are often unsavory. But if those people had been the audience he had in mind, "in that case you would have to leave this world" (v. 10).

Paul does not deny the sinfulness of the people of this world. In fact, he lists several of their sins: immorality, greed, swindling, idolatry. Our job is not to sugarcoat the evil of our world. Nor is our job to modify the behavior of lost people.[11] Our job is to share Jesus with them. In Paul's mind it is unthinkable that any believer would leave this world.

"But now I am writing you . . ." Paul feels a necessity to write again his instructions. He says, "you must not associate with anyone who calls himself a brother but is . . .". This is a radical thought. We Christians hardly ever think that we should disassociate with other believers. We are certainly not to shun each other because of our struggles (Rom. 12:15) or because of our economic status (James 2). It is only in the case of willful, blatant, premeditated, sinful hypocrisy that we are not to associate with another believer.

Paul then gives several examples of the kind of sin that might have a death-grip on a believer: sexual immorality, greed, idolatry, slander, drunkenness, swindling. Note that the two lists are very similar:

The sins of unbelievers (v. 10):

> IMMORAL
>   GREEDY
>   SWINDLERS
>   IDOLATERS

The sins of believers (v. 11):

SEXUALLY IMMORAL
GREEDY
IDOLATRY
SLANDERER
DRUNKARD
SWINDLER

Paul adds to the list of sins when he thinks of sinning Christians, perhaps indicating God's high standards for His people. Paul has clearly said, "do not associate with" (v. 9); now he says "with such a man do not even eat" (v. 11). Physical disassociation is not a suggestion for believers, but a command. Notice the verse says, "do not *even* eat." The implication is, "With such a man do not even *continue* to eat." That seems to imply to me, "Don't let it be business as usual with this believer." Things are *not* normal; it's not "all good"; we can't just ignore the unrepented sin and think it will go away.

An Expulsion Mandate

Paul then asks an interesting question: "What business is it of mine to judge those outside the church?" (v. 12). He makes it quite personal. He doesn't ask, "What business is it of *yours* to judge those outside the church?" We Christians are experts when it comes to judging the world. Perhaps the Corinthians had wanted Paul to confirm their anti-world attitude.

He then clearly declares, "Are you not to judge those inside?" (v. 12). I often hear people quote Jesus' statement in

Matthew 7:1, "Do not judge, or you too will be judged," interpreting it to mean that we are not to make moral judgments at all concerning another person. That is not the thrust of Jesus' teachings in Matthew 7. His injunction is against hypocrisy. We *are* to judge; we are to judge those in the family of God.

But if we don't judge those in the world, will those in the world get away scot-free? No! Paul reminds the Corinthians, "God will judge those outside" (v. 13). Judging those outside the church is not the church's responsibility. What is the church's responsibility? "Expel the wicked man from among you" (v. 13). Paul is obviously paraphrasing the repeated expression in Deuteronomy, "purge (or expel) the evil from among you" (Deut. 17:7, 19:19, 21:21, etc.), which almost always referred to a sin punishable by *death*.

However, when Paul says "expel the wicked man from among you," he certainly does not mean execution.[12] It is also interesting to note that in each of the Deuteronomy passages the "you" is singular (that is, the instructions are given to Moses as Israel's leader), while the "you" in First Corinthians 5:13 is plural—that is, the directions are given to the church as a whole.

Satan's Double Victory

The Corinthians' confusion over Paul's instructions actually led to a double victory for Satan. They had misunderstood Paul when he wrote them, "you must not associate with sexually immoral people." They thought he had meant the people of this world, so they isolated themselves from lost people who needed the gospel. He actually meant, "you must not associate with anyone who calls himself a brother but is sexually immoral." So, they tolerated a sinning believer in their congregation.

By their misunderstanding Paul's instructions, they made two serious errors. They ruined evangelism because they isolated themselves from unbelievers. And they destroyed discipleship because they tolerated an unrepentant believer in their congregation.

Two simple charts may help us see the damage done by their misunderstanding:

Chart A:

Their Misunderstanding of Paul
Isolation: From Unbelievers ..... *ruined evangelism*
Toleration: Of unrepentant believers .... *destroyed discipleship*

How can a church win lost people to the Lord if that church is convinced it should isolate itself *from* lost people? Where, then, is friendship evangelism? Where will that church practice being "a friend of publicans and sinners" as modeled by the Lord Jesus (Matt. 11:19)? Like the Corinthians, we can isolate ourselves from exactly the wrong group of people.

With Paul's corrective in First Corinthians 5, the chart would look like this:

Chart B:

Their Corrected Understanding of Paul

Toleration: Of Unbelievers;
   Being a friend of sinners;
      Not attempting to change
         their behavior .... promotes evangelism

Isolation: From unrepentant   believers .... develops discipleship

In Chart B we see that the church tolerates the sin of *unbelievers* without seeking to make them act like Christians.[13] This is not to say that the church condones sinful behavior. It is simply making the point that our number one priority is not the behavior modification of lost people.[14]

We also see in Chart B that unrepentant *believers* will be dealt with by the church. Christians who want to live like the devil will be turned over to the devil! The church is not impotent here. It is to draw the line and say, "If you want to live like a pagan, if you refuse to submit to the loving discipline of this local church, then you are no longer a part of our congregation." With tears this church will exclude that individual from fellowship, not out of anger, but out of grief that sin has taken such a hold of this person. And this church's attitude will be: "Whenever you wish to turn from your sin, we will work with you. Call us anytime, 24 hours a day, and we will meet with you for the purpose of repentance and restoration. But we will not treat you as if things are fine or as if your hard-heartedness does not matter."

✓ Practical Action Points

1. Ask yourself if there is any believer with whom you need to meet to reconcile. Whether you are the offender (Matt. 5) or the offended one (Matt. 18), make sure that you are doing everything in your power to "live at peace with everyone" (Rom. 12:18).

2. Share this material with the spiritual leadership of your local church. What is the process in place to deal with unrepentant sin in the congregation? Are there examples of church discipline that have gone poorly in your congregation? Are there examples of church discipline that have gone well?

3. How do you treat those who have been put under church discipline?[15] Do you see them as lost individuals who need to be saved? Do you love them enough to say to them, "I will meet with you anytime to help you come back to the Lord and His people"?

4. How might your church work more closely with other churches who seek to exercise church discipline in the power of the Lord? Do your spiritual leaders interview church transfers to see if they are leaving their previous church on good terms? Does your church respect the judgments of other churches in matters of discipline? How might we show unanimity in this matter of church discipline with the wider Body of Christ?

5. Carved in wood over the door of a church in Ohio are these words: "Enter at your own risk." Are our churches sufficiently "dangerous"? What I mean is, we should consider issuing a warning (perhaps better thought of as a promise) to potential new members something like the following: "If you join this church, we will not leave you alone. We will fight sin in your life! Positively, we will work hard at discipling you, putting you both in a relationship where you can be mentored and help you find a relationship where you can mentor someone else. Where we believe we need to lovingly intervene in your life because of sin, we will do so in the power of the Spirit."

9

Chapter Nine

Some Specific Strategies for Dealing with Temptation and Sin

Our lives for Christ are not just a life or death matter.
They are a matter of eternal life and eternal death. (Bill Hybels)

I could not help but think how desperate we are
for time away with God to heal from the harshness of this
world and to gain the courage to soften up again. (Beth Moore)

Therefore, dear friends, since you already know this,
be on your guard so that you may not be carried away
by the error of lawless men and fall from your secure position.
But grow in the grace and knowledge of our Lord and Savior
Jesus Christ. To him be glory both now and forever! Amen.
(2 Pet. 3:17–18)

So, if you think you are standing firm, be careful
that you don't fall! (1 Cor. 10:12)

I have a confession to make. *Beth Moore really ticks me off.*
She is the best-selling author of many books, Bible study
series, Christian DVDs, radio broadcasts, websites, Congres-

sional legislation, peace treaties between developing nations, and so on. (Actually, she hasn't written any legislation or peace treaties, but she ticks me off anyway.)

She has positively impacted more women for eternity than I ever will (oh, that pesky thing called gender) and will probably produce a best-selling DVD entitled something like "When Temptation Strikes!" just a week before this book sees the light of day. She's covered the Old Testament story of Daniel, the Gospel of John, and the Ascent Psalms in her studies, and is probably gearing up to take on the entire Pentateuch or perhaps a "Light-Hearted Look at the Apocrypha" next.

To make matters worse, my wife made me go into a Christian bookstore the other day to purchase Beth's latest study series for a women's group. I got the last "kit" in the store, and it cost $149 for the DVD, a leader's guide and one participant's manual. Trying to cheer myself up, I asked if they carried any books by "Larry Dixon," and they said . . . well, you can guess what they said. You see why Beth Moore ticks me off?

Actually, I need to come clean. I have the highest regard for Beth Moore. Her studies have changed my wife's life— and she wasn't all that bad to begin with! I asked my wife why she likes Beth Moore so much, and she said, "Because she's humble. She never goes into detail about her sin to sensationalize. She makes Bible study fun, even though it's hard work. She gets you passionate about studying the Word and living for the Lord."

"But . . ." I started to say.

"*And,*" my wife continued, "she shows the Word's power to break the strongholds of the devil. She offers freedom in

Christ, rather than a list of things to do. Her focus is on having a vital relationship with the Lord. All I can say is, read Beth Moore!" I then asked my wife what she liked about me and she said, "You're kinda cute, I guess."

Beth Moore does say some things very, very well. For example:

> I have discovered that if Satan can't get to me with destruction, he will try to get to me with distraction. We have only one turn on this green earth. We will never get to do this again. We cannot do a hundred things to the glory of God, but we can certainly do a few. What you and I need is focus. Day in and day out. Eyes on the goal.[1]

Those two tools of the Evil One—destruction and distraction—keep us from wholeness in Christ and focusing on His Word for our strength against temptation and sin. We've talked about Satan's M.O. in Chapter 3. He hates each child of God with an intensity lit by the flames of hell. We saw in Chapter 4 that we ourselves are often our own worst enemies. We got into specifics with the so-called Seven Deadly Sins in Chapter 5. After analyzing David's fall and his confession in Chapter 6, we focused on the need to break the hold of unholy habits in Chapter 7. Although not intended to be depressing, Chapter 8 concluded with an unrepentant sinner being expelled from a local church—which is enough to make anyone feel down.

Before we conclude this book with the wonderful subject of heaven and no more temptation or sin (or further "study series" by Beth Moore—just kidding!), we want to concentrate on our need to personally strategize against temptation and sin in our lives. This chapter considers three subjects:

personal spiritual growth, the importance of relationships, and professional help (for you, not for me).

Personal Spiritual Growth

For the men who are still reading this book (despite the many references to Beth Moore), I want to point out a basic fact: We are not living in our father's generation. Back then, if a man wanted pornography, he had to order it by mail in a plain brown wrapper and hope that the mailman (the previous generation's term for a letter carrier) would not tell his wife on him. Today's male knows that hard-core porn is just two mouse clicks away.[2] Unless a man resolves by God's grace to avoid those two clicks, he will be drawn into a world which will rot him from the inside out.

We—both men and women—must strengthen ourselves against temptation. How does one develop such moral muscle? I'm not attempting here to provide seven magic keys to spiritual maturity or five easy rules of righteousness, but simply to suggest some practical steps that help me resist temptation and avoid sin.

1. I must remind myself not to trifle with temptation.

Just like children, we may tend to get as close to the edge of evil as we can, not realizing that we might slip (or be shoved by the Evil One) over the precipice. Jesus commanded His disciples to "Watch and pray so that you will not fall into temptation. The spirit is willing, but the body is weak" (Matt. 26:41). When we do not watch and pray, we get preyed upon.

2. I must take responsibility for strengthening myself in the Word of God.

Jesus used the Word of God to withstand the attacks of the devil in Matthew 4, and we must do the same. Psalm 119 says,

> Let me understand the teaching of your precepts;
> then I will meditate on your wonders.
> My soul is weary with sorrow;
> strengthen me according to your word.
> Keep me from deceitful ways;
> be gracious to me through your law. (vv. 27–29)

"Strengthen me according to your word," says the Psalmist. How dare we enter a new day thinking we are strong in ourselves to withstand the "flaming arrows" of the Evil One (Eph. 6:16)? Recognizing my own weaknesses is the first step to finding help from the Savior. We are told by James (who seems to be quoting Proverbs 3),

> "God opposes the proud but gives grace to the humble." Submit yourselves, then, to God. Resist the devil, and he will flee from you. Come near to God and he will come near to you. Wash your hands, you sinners, and purify your hearts, you double-minded. . . . Humble yourselves before the Lord, and he will lift you up. (4:6–8, 10)

First Peter 5 also quotes Proverbs 3 and says, "All of you, clothe yourselves with humility toward one another, because, 'God opposes the proud but gives grace to the humble.' Humble yourselves, therefore, under God's mighty hand, that he may lift you up in due time" (vv. 5–6).

3. I must seek to maintain a tender heart before the Lord.

My good friend, Dr. Lindsay Hislop, preached a great sermon on what he called the four hearts. He talked about "a rebellious heart," one that denies sin and responsibility. He spoke of "the careless heart," one that casually shrugs off sin and goes on. He taught us about "the fearful heart," one which wallows in sin and failure. He then encouraged us to ask God for "a sensitive heart," one which confesses quickly and gets going again in fellowship with God.

King Josiah illustrates a tender or sensitive heart:

> *"Self is a STEALTH enemy! We need to choose our mirror carefully. If our mirror is the Word of God (James 1:23), then we don't look nearly as good as we think we do!" (Businessman)*

Because your heart was responsive [tender, KJV] and you humbled yourself before God when you heard what he spoke against this place and its people, and because you humbled yourself before me and tore your robes and wept in my presence, I have heard you, declares the LORD. (2 Chron. 34:27)

4. I must not think that I am facing temptation or sin alone.

When I was a kid, I loved the old "Lone Ranger" television program. Sure, it was in black and white, and the hero didn't always treat his "trusty sidekick" Tonto as he should have, but it was an exciting part of my young life. At the end of each episode, as I recall, the Lone Ranger would leap onto his valiant horse Silver who would beautifully rear up, and the show would conclude with the Lone Ranger saying, "Hi, Yo, Silver! Awaaaay!"

It was a great TV show, but it's no way to live the Christian life. We can't be Lone Rangers. We can't act as if we do not need the body of Christ, a topic we'll return to in a moment. But first, let's take a look at a familiar passage: "No temptation has seized you except what is common to man. And God is faithful; he will not let you be tempted beyond what you can bear. But when you are tempted, he will also provide a way out so that you can stand up under it" (1 Cor. 10:13).

The first thing we notice from this passage is that temptation is a *common experience* for the follower of Christ. You and I are not unique in facing temptation. (The Christian who says he is not facing temptation will probably lie about other things as well!) Incidentally, Paul refers to a temptation that "seizes" you. Sometimes we chase temptation, catch it, and grieve when we have fallen into sin. The promises of First Corinthians 10:13 are for believers who get *seized* by temptation,[3] not for those who *seek out* temptation.

Second, we not only have a common experience, but we also have *a faithful Protector*. The faithfulness of God causes Him not to let you or me be tempted beyond what we can bear. I understand that to mean that God will never put us in a situation where we must sin. James 1:13 reminds us that "When tempted, no one should say, 'God is tempting me.' For God cannot be tempted by evil, nor does he tempt anyone."

Third, there will be for us *an offered exit*. The last sentence of First Corinthians 10:13 is a wonderful promise, but the wording is somewhat puzzling. He will provide "a way out" so that you can "stand up under it." "A way out" sounds like we can get away from the temptation. The words "stand up under it" sound like we still have to endure the temptation without giving in to sin. I believe the point is that we may not be able to escape the temptation, but we can certainly escape the sin.

So in terms of personal spiritual growth, I must not trifle with temptation. I must, however, take responsibility for becoming strong in the Word of God, which includes a biblical humility. It is also critical that I seek to maintain a tender heart before the Lord, recognizing that I am not facing temptation or sin alone. This brings us to our second major subject.

The Importance of Relationships

A contemporary television commercial shows a typical family of four, each engaged in their own activities. The son is in his room reading, the daughter is talking on her cell phone, the dad is playing a football video game on his desktop. Then the mother drives up in the family's new minivan and shouts out, "Hey, let's all go for a ride!" You can see the bored reactions of each family member, but they reluctantly go.

As the mom begins driving down the road, the family starts to talk with one another, play games with each other, and enjoy each other's company. At the end of the commercial, the teenaged daughter says to her brother, "You know, you're not so bad, Billy."

He says, "My name is Bobby."

"I knew that," the sister replies.

How pathetic! It takes a new minivan to get families to relate to each other? What will it take for us in the church to relate to one another?

God puts a premium on strong relationships between believers. We saw in the previous chapter that a conflict between Christians is enough for God to call a halt to worship so that reconciliation can take place. Paul stressed to the Galatians the importance of looking out for each other: "Brothers, if someone is caught in a sin, you who are spiritual should restore him gently. But watch yourself, or you also may be tempted. Carry each other's burdens, and in this way you will fulfill the law of Christ" (6:1–2).

Watchman Nee tells the story of bathing with some other brothers in a river in China. One brother got a cramp in his leg and was sinking fast.

> I motioned to another brother, who was an expert swimmer, to hasten to his rescue. But to my astonishment he made no move. Growing desperate I cried out, "Don't you see the man is drowning?" and the other brothers, about as agitated as I was, shouted vigorously too. But our good swimmer still did not move. Calm and collected, he remained just where he was, apparently postponing the unwelcome task. Meantime the voice of the poor drowning brother grew fainter and his efforts feebler. In my heart I said: "I hate that man! Think of his letting a brother drown before his very eyes and not going to the rescue!"
>
> But when the man was actually sinking, with a few swift strokes the swimmer was at his side, and both were soon safely ashore. Nevertheless, when I got an opportunity, I aired my views. "I have never seen any Christian who loved his life quite as much as you do," I said. "Think of the distress you would have saved that brother if you had considered yourself a little less and him a little more." But the swimmer, I soon discovered, knew his business better than I did. "Had I gone earlier," he said, "he would have clutched me so fast that both of

us would have gone under. A drowning man cannot be saved until he is utterly exhausted and ceases to make the slightest effort to save himself."[4]

We need our fellow believers, and sometimes only a sense of desperation will cause us to cry out for help. Sometimes others can't help us until we give up trying to do it on our own.

May I suggest that each of us needs to develop a serious relationship with three kinds of people? We each need a Paul, a Barnabas, and a Timothy in our lives. We each need someone who can spiritually mentor us, a Paul. We each need a peer, a Barnabas, someone with whom we can serve the Lord. And we also each need a Timothy, someone whom we can mentor or disciple.[5] These three relationships—a mentor who has wisdom, a peer who understands what I'm going through, and a mentoree who can benefit from my walk with Christ—are not stages that the Christian grows through, but connections or relationships that he or she makes which may be lifelong.

Let me speak of one other relationship which can be of great help to the believer in resisting temptation and turning away from sin. That is a relationship with God the Holy Spirit. You might be thinking, "I'm to have a relationship with the Holy Spirit?" Yes, but I'm not suggesting you must speak in tongues, or experience miracles on a daily basis.

If the Holy Spirit is a Person (and the Bible clearly declares His personality),[6] then we can relate to Him on a personal level. We can speak with Him (I believe the Bible allows, but does not command, prayer to the Holy Spirit) and ask for His various ministries in our lives (convicting us and others of sin,[7] illuminating our minds as we study the Scriptures, guiding us, reminding us of our place in God's family, etc.). Because the Holy Spirit is divine, He knows my struggles (He is omniscient), He can empower me against temptation (He is omnipotent), and He can assure me of His sustaining presence (He is omnipresent).

One need only consider Acts 5:1–11 to see that the way we treat the Holy Spirit is very important. Ananias and Sapphira, apparently wanting to be like Barnabas, sold a piece of property and donated the money to the apostles to assist poor believers. But they lied about their gift and kept back part of the money for themselves. They were not required to sell their property or to give all the proceeds to the apostles, but they were expected to tell the truth. Peter confronts Ananias, accuses him of lying to the Holy Spirit, and watches as God strikes him dead on the spot! The youth group comes and buries him. Three hours later Sapphira comes in, is confronted by Peter, and lies as well. Peter says to her, "Hark! I hear the footsteps of the youth group coming up the sidewalk. And they are coming for *you*!" She is also struck dead.

The point of Acts 5 is not that God will strike us dead if we don't give Him all our money. The point is that God hates hypocrisy—and can act in great judgment when we lie to the Spirit of God.[8] The preacher Vance Havner once said, "Aren't you glad God does not act that way in judgment today? If He did, every church would need a morgue in its basement!"

Professional Help

The third subject which we want to consider in strategizing against temptation and sin is the issue of professional help: pastors, counselors, psychologists and psychiatrists. They have their place, though we should be discerning about the kind of professional advice we receive. One of my favorite stories about counseling is the following:

> *"Sin? Sure it exists. I'm sinning less and at the same time enjoying freedom and liberty more. I don't fret and stew and worry about sin anymore. Christ in God took all my sins upon Himself 2000 years ago on the cross, so I can now be free to serve Him and not have to worry about whether I sinned when I stepped on that ant on the sidewalk yesterday." (Internet chess friend)*

A pastor was counseling a couple who had marital problems. The woman came in first and said all the horrible things she could about her husband. The pastor said to her, "You know, you're right!" The assistant pastor was there, and watched the woman leave. The next day her husband came in and said all kinds of bad things about his wife. When he had finished the pastor said to him, "You know you are right. You are absolutely right!" After the husband left, the assistant pastor said to the pastor, "What kind of marital counseling is that? You told both of those people that they were right!" The pastor answered and said, "You know, you're right. You're absolutely right!"[9]

I believe there is much confusion today in Christian circles about the need for professional counselors, psychologists and psychiatrists. There is no question that a great deal of the literature in some of these fields comes from a secular viewpoint. Let me be perfectly candid: I have not always appreciated the discipline of counseling and have been extremely wary of (to put it bluntly) the anti-God perspective of many leaders in this area. Whether it is Freud who declared religion to be a neurosis or some contemporary psychiatrists who advocate adultery as a treatment plan for marital problems (!), there is much nonsense and dangerous material in non-Christian sources.

However, I affirm in no uncertain terms the concept of general revelation, which means that although all the Bible is true, all truth is not in the Bible. Before you start to stone me, let me explain. God has given us much truth outside the Scriptures which we can learn and use for His glory. The Bible is not a repair manual for my car, nor does it explain how to remove a kidney. I would be greatly upset if I took my car in to my mechanic and found him bending over his Bible to figure out how to replace the timing belt. I would be even more upset (if the anesthesia had not yet kicked in) if I saw my surgeon consulting the Old Testament for instructions on how to do surgery.

In the same way, much truth about human personality can be learned through the sciences and through counseling techniques—even some that have anti-Christian advocates. I help teach a course entitled "The Integration of Psychology and Theology," and although I believe that the Word of God is

> *"To me as a psychiatrist, I can see how the mind can easily project and concretize our own fears, images, and impulses into the stories of Satan, devils, and demons. There is no scientific proof that these beings are real or not real either, so I leave that fact up to future research."*
> *(A non-Christian psychiatrist in Colorado)*

our final authority in matters of faith, morals and values, I think we can learn much from counseling, psychology and, yes, even psychiatry. There. I've stuck my neck out. Please put down your rocks.

Ideally, the church and professional counseling can work hand in hand. For example, although a young teen with *anorexea nervosa* may need serious intervention from a professional counselor, the loving relationships offered in a Christian congregation may do much to bring about healing and hope. On the flip side, an alcoholic or drug addict may need more help to kick his habit than a typical church can give; professional counseling or therapy, by God's grace, may uncover the roots of the addiction. I highly recommend Larry Crabb's excellent book *Connecting*, described as a "groundbreaking work [which] shows readers how to build intimate, healing connections with others . . . where God's power to heal souls is quickened and released through individuals' compassionate, authentic relationships with [others]."[10]

On the Couch

To get the perspective of counseling professionals, I interviewed two of my colleagues at Columbia International University, Dr. Allan McKechnie and Dr. Mark Bolte. Al is the director of pastoral counseling and spiritual formation, and Mark is the acting director of our MA in counseling program. They both have a heart for broken people.

Al, you've said that many people are afraid to trust the church to do counseling, fearing a lack of confidentiality or wisdom to deal with their particular problem.

Al: Yes, but small groups in our churches often reduce need for counseling because there can be a lot of confession and intimacy where a person can tell his or her story. But so much gets hidden. We don't give each other much permission in our churches to share our struggles. We find it's much easier to attack someone for being sinful than to take that failure apart and figure out what led to the collapse.

What about the issue of temptation?

Al: I don't believe there's temptation without vulnerability to temptation. The stronger we are in Christ, the less vulnerable we are. A good Christian counselor can unpack (but not excuse) sin, perhaps explaining why something is more tempting, more seductive, than it normally would be. Nothing in our past makes us sin. But the church often does not know what to look for, that appetite, that warped theology. A counselor can bring that out into the open.

Mark: Adam and Eve's fall in the Garden was really about not trusting God to be the ultimate satisfaction of man's longings. We seek to manage the outcome of our lives, doubting God's goodness, just like the serpent challenged Eve. The core of our sin nature is self-management. I have this felt need and I figure out how I can protect myself and meet that need.

That sounds a bit like Larry Crabb's approach in his book *Connecting*.

Mark: Yes. I agree with Crabb that each of us adopts certain patterns of self-protection, trying to make life "work" on our own. Part of our difficulty, especially in the church, is that we redefine sin as a list of behaviors, instead of the disposition of our heart. Counseling seeks to shift from the external to the internal—the state of our heart. Relationships which provide safety, trust and grace create an atmosphere which allows who we are to come to the surface. It is then that His grace and truth can begin to have its redeeming effect on our core self-serving strategies.

How does the church fit in?

Al: The church is an environment where things can come out. But the church sometimes does not know what to do when it is out. There may be a medical issue; the person may be on drugs; there could be a psychological syndrome as part of the problem. Psychology is good at digging things up; the light of Christ is where the healing comes from. When each does what it is supposed to do, that can lead to real health.[11]

How do churches sometimes fail to help?

Al: The church often gets rid of the person immediately and will not do the hard work that the Scripture requires it to do for sanctification, reconciliation, restoration and redemption. Either the church doesn't know how or doesn't want to. A climate of gossip and suspicion can develop in a church, instead of Christ's mercy.

Mark: The church is often too superficial. . . . It is not a culture that invites depth or fosters truth, intimacy or safety. Often the emphasis is on doing right or thinking right, or a combination of both. A church person might think, "Here are this community's rules to keep if I want to be accepted. If I keep these rules, there will be connection, security, esteem. I'm going to keep my heart issues, the things that are not on that list, private." This Christian is not free to share the riskier parts of himself or herself. We either define the need incorrectly, teaching people how to measure up, or we say, "No matter what you do, your heart is depraved. All you do is tainted by sin; it is hopeless." We are far from teaching the victorious Christian life. But this is so sad. God gives us the supernatural power to do what we can't do on our own.

Al: "All Scripture is God-breathed and is useful for teaching, rebuking, correcting and training in righteousness, so that the man of God may be thoroughly equipped for every good work" (2 Tim. 3:16–17). These verses speak of how we often have a skewed perception of reality. . . . We fail to teach the whole counsel of God, and what we ignore today becomes tomorrow's heresy. We might have the doctrine followed by the rebuking, but we don't hang around to correct. A lot of correcting takes place in counseling, not in the church. We ask questions like, "How are you thinking? How are you rehearsing things in your mind? How are you behaving?" We teach people to live differently.

Are you saying that we often teach truth in our church, but fail to show how it can be lived out?

Al: Yes. How do we teach people to practice patience? As John Ortberg says, teach people to get in the longest line in the supermarket, to go the speed limit. The church doesn't teach patience. The teaching of these skills has been relegated to consultants and counselors, which is really sad. . . . A new habit will replace an old habit if it is done twenty-one times in twenty-one days. We need to help people replace old behaviors, old ways of reacting.

How can churches and counselors learn to respect each other?

Al: We ball out sinners in our churches, then what? Counselors end up doing the training. We're taking up ground that belongs to the church. So many clients tell counselors about the damage churches have done to them. Most churches don't like counselors because they think we excuse sin and turn people away from Christ. All a pastor has to have is one positive experience of a member with a counselor, in drawing that person to Christ and helping them mature, and they're sold!

Mark, how do your counseling students relate to the local church?

Mark: My vision . . . is that our counseling grads will be the new evangelists of our age. In their counseling ministry they will be strategically entering the most hidden, secret places of people's hearts and bringing to bear God's truth and grace.

We only begin to grow when we're in relationship with one another. Some people need . . . to address their relational wounds. A brief discipleship relationship may not be appropriate for that. Here a Christian counselor can help. It seems to me that today's church is much more positive toward the values of counseling. The church is hungry for authenticity. With the shift from modernity to post-modernism, many are saying, "Prove it to my experience!" Counseling is *centered* on experience. Therefore, counselors can speak to issues of the heart. Most of my students are developing a strong appetite for grace. They realize, as Josh McDowell says, "It's relationships that engender belief." Or as Crabb put it, "Nothing changes us more deeply than to look bad in the presence of love."

Any other thoughts about how we can strengthen our churches?

Mark: In our churches we often preach or teach a too-superficial strategy of change. We don't address the core fears. Consequently, people are not able to make those changes. It's like trying to tell a child to do something that they are not programmed developmentally to do. We need in our churches to appreciate where people are developmentally. Change is not just a matter of willpower. Our people need to be open to grace to receive something they lack within themselves.

Don't counselors often euphemize sin, call it something less offensive?

Al: It seems to me there are two ways to be told of sin. The first is simply to be *told*: "You've sinned! You've done something wrong! Now STOP IT!" The second way is to bring that person to where they discover that for themselves. We're talking internal versus external. I often ask a client, "What did this mistake, this poor choice, cost you?" The term doesn't matter. Don't get me wrong. "Sin" is an important word—but sometimes we hide behind that word and go no further. We treat sin as a stain that temporarily soils our clothes, so we throw them in the laundry and come back when they're done. I don't mind euphemisms as long as a person gets to the core of what's happened to them and how it hurts their relationship with God and others. Picture a young woman who is very bitter against men. . . . I can confront her in her sin, but what if it comes out, not as an excuse, that what created that vulnerability was her sexual abuse by her father, uncle, whatever? At some point she needs to become aware that the sin that was done against her created sin in her. But I'm not going to start there. If she comes in broken and hurt, and her coping is to sinfully use anger as a way to feel strong and vengeful, the last thing she needs is for someone to say, "You're a sinner too. It's your fault." But we will end up there. . . . And that may take three months to get to. But that is a life-changing discovery that I can help her find for herself. I can take this approach—or I can be just one more male who tells her, "You're no good." I think it's up to counseling to teach the church about the slow process of change.

What counseling approaches or models should be used in a Christian context?

Al: Our counseling model must sit on top of our theology. In fact, I change models depending on the client, how they learn, the type of issue they have, our type of relationship. I have about seven or eight models I use. It is dangerous when our model becomes our pseudo-theology. We really have to have our Bible and our theology nailed down. Some recent studies suggest that one's model is irrelevant; it's the personality of the individual counselor that counts. The model is certainly not as important as your theological underpinning and the personal transformation you bring into the room. Biblically, that person has to be closer to Christ or accepted Christ by the time you're done. . . . The Lord Jesus handled different people in different ways. The bottom line is that people without Christ are unfulfilled. Some people may have better coping strategies than others so that unfulfilledness doesn't bother them as much and some people might be wealthier than others to delay the onset of discouragement. But without Christ, they are headed for an eternal existence separated from God. I must bring them closer so the Holy Spirit can do powerful things in their lives.

What thoughts do you have about the devil and our sin?

Al: The devil wants us to curse God with our lives. He can't get at God directly, so he attacks God's children. We can give the devil so much power that we lose control. We can be turned over to Satan. We can lose God's protective powers. So Satan can be as powerful as we let him. Or we say the devil made me do it. In North American spirituality Satan and hell are not now in vogue. The message we hear is, "You can do this. Pull yourself up by your bootstraps and God will bless you." Jay Adams is right: We're in hand-to-hand combat with Satan in the counseling session, and he's invested twenty to thirty years of his work in somebody's life. I always assume Satan's involvement. He's always involved. But I prefer a "truth encounter" to a "power encounter." We must recognize where our vulnerabilities to temptation have come from (family systems, etc.), but we must not overestimate him and underestimate Christ.

Any thoughts about the Seven Deadly Sins?

Al: There may well be increased vulnerability to certain sins because of family background, learned behavior or genetic predisposition. We underestimate sin. And this present generation often refuses to address issues, so we get angry or insulate ourselves from intimate relationships. Satan catches us off-guard because he starts the process of temptation perhaps hundreds of years before we are on the scene. I think Satan will set up one generation just to get to the next generation.

What factors cause someone to fall into one of the Seven Deadly Sins?

Mark: Well, there are two primary motivators: We are either driven out of love or out of fear. Fear enslaves, but love sets us free. God's motivation for all He does is love, and the chief evidence of His image in us is love. The danger of looking at any list of sin behaviors is that we fail to appreciate what's going on behind that behavior at a deep, core level.

How would that concept apply to the sin of sloth, for example?

Mark: There might be fear behind sloth. That is, I don't want to provide proof to others that I really don't have what it takes. . . . So to protect myself from hurt, I won't take risks; I'll simply stay on the sofa. I won't run the risk of playing the game and failing. Or conversely, what if I succeed? If I show I'm good at this, then others' expectations of me are raised . . . setting me up for a larger failure.

Any parting thoughts, gentlemen?

Mark: We started our discussion talking about Larry Crabb. In his book *Inside/Out*, he emphasizes that God designed us with significant interpersonal needs. The needs are not the problem, but how we go about meeting those needs.

Al: One question remains paramount in my mind. . . . The question is: What scares me about heaven? I fear standing before God and He says, "This is what I planned for you. I wanted to use you. But you insisted in staying in your own comfort." I don't want that kind of life.

I also interviewed Dr. David Henderson, a psychiatrist with the Meier Clinics in Dallas, Texas. He is a committed (no pun intended) Christian psychiatrist, and I believe he has much to offer suffering, broken individuals.

Dave, perhaps you can remind us what a psychiatrist is.

Dave: Of course. A psychiatrist is a medical doctor . . . who special-
         izes in the evaluation, diagnosis and treatment of mental dis-
         orders. There are many medications that we can prescribe to
         help individuals suffering from mental illness.

But do we need medications—or truth?

Dave: I can understand people's hesitation to take medications for
         something that seems, and often is, closely related to the spirit-
         ual realm. However, all suffering, be it physical, emotional or
         mental, is a direct result of the Fall. Adam and Eve in the
         Garden of Eden did not know heart disease, cancer, diabetes
         or . . . depression, anxiety or psychosis. Why? Because sin had
         no influence in their world. But notice what happens after
         they sin for the first time: Pain enters the picture. God says to
         the woman, "I will sharpen the pain of your pregnancy, and
         in pain you will give birth" [Gen. 3:16, NLT]. And to the man
         He says, "All your life you will struggle to scratch a living
         from [the ground]. . . . By the sweat of your brow will you
         have food to eat until you return to the ground from which
         you were made" [Gen. 3:17, 19, NLT]. The NIV describes
         Adam's work as "painful toil." Now God was not just talking
         about physical pain. . . . It goes way beyond that. It's the
         frustration of working at something and never seeming to
         make headway. It's the fear of knowing that if I don't keep
         this job, I might not have enough money to feed and clothe
         my family. It's the anguish a mother feels when the child she
         bore turns around and spits in her face. Add on several thou-
         sand years of man's cruelty to man and you have the ingredi-
         ents for severe mental and emotional suffering. Now, if physi-
         cal, emotional and mental pain are all a result of the Fall, why
         is it that we tend to glorify the medical treatment of one and
         demonize the medical treatment of the other? Most people
         would not question the necessity of seeing a cardiologist for a
         heart attack, but we often cringe at the thought of seeing a
         psychiatrist for disorders of the brain, a physical organ essen-

tial to the regulation of our thoughts and emotions. For those who are doubtful, let me give you a few examples. We know from scientific study that one-sided brain damage (through a stroke, let's say) can alter a patient's normal emotional responses. . . . Patients will cry or have sudden mood swings for no apparent reason. Depression is the most common emotional disturbance after a stroke and can be successfully treated with medications. Likewise, damage to the frontal lobes of the brain (from a car accident, let's say) can change a patient's personality or disinhibit them to do things they would not do otherwise.

Can you give me another example?

Dave: Of course. Another example of the physical nature of mental illness are the effects of chemicals on the human mind. Anyone that lived through the 1960s will remember the popularity of hallucinogens for "spiritual enlightenment." Drugs like LSD have the ability to alter a person's sensory perceptions to the point that they can see, hear, taste and smell things that are not real. Even chronic alcoholics who are in withdrawal have been known to hallucinate. With long-term use, these chemicals can permanently destroy the brain's ability to function, known as substance-induced persisting dementia. These effects are not just caused by drugs of abuse, however. One of the side effects of beta blockers, commonly prescribed medications for heart disease and high blood pressure, is depression. Other drugs . . . used to treat cramps or . . . hypothyroidism, can precipitate mania. All of these are examples proving that mental illness has a physical component. If disease, injuries and drugs can affect the mind and emotions, then it stands to reason that medications can be used to treat such disturbances.

But apart from prescribing medications, of what value are psychiatrists?

Dave: Not only are psychiatrists trained in the biological treatment of disease through the use of medications, but we are also trained in the psychology of human behavior, namely, why do we humans do what we do? All of us are sinners. "All have sinned and fall short of the glory of God" as the Bible says. But why does John struggle with pornography and not alcoholism? Why does Harry have a problem with lying but not stealing? Why does Sally like to gossip but not cheat? What happened to Jessica that makes it so difficult for her to trust others? How did Fred become such an angry person? We all know how difficult it can be at times to recognize our own sins. All of us have said at one time or another, "Here I go again." By studying human behavior, recognizing patterns in people's lives, and helping them to implement strategies for change, we can equip individuals with yet another tool to use when facing temptation.

But if intimacy and relationships are one major factor of helping others, how is a dispassionate, "objective" counselor or psychiatrist able to help another human being?

Dave: Well, first, I don't think it's necessary for a psychiatrist to be dispassionate. I think we are as passionate about helping people as any other profession of medicine. And objectivity, though we strive for it, can be very difficult to achieve. I think this is why a person needs to be careful when seeking therapy from a psychiatrist with a secular worldview. However, the patient-physician relationship provides some unique benefits that no other relationship can. To begin, this is not a friendship. I in no way believe that the patient-physician relationship should be a substitute for intimate, meaningful friendships. In any relationship there is a give and take aspect, but this relationship has clearly established boundaries. The therapist's job is to focus on the patient's problems and not his or her own. How many of us would go to a family practitioner for a cold and endure listening to him the entire time, rattling off the symptoms of his recent kidney infection? In this sense, the relationship is very one-sided. The only time that a therapist might discuss something personal with a patient is if they deemed it to be therapeutic for the patient. Likewise, the relationship should remain within the context of the session. Prolonged interaction outside of that professional context is considered unethical. Second, the patient-physician relationship is an opportunity for people seeking help with emotional problems to learn about themselves in a safe, confidential environment free of consequences. The only time a physician is required to break confidentiality is when patients are in danger of hurting themselves or someone else. In the session we can explore painful emotions and thoughts such as anger, sorrow, fear, even hatred, lust or contempt without the often painful consequences that might arise in a real relationship. In a sense, it allows someone with mental or emotion problems the opportunity to practice how to think, feel and behave before stepping out into the real world where the consequences of misplaced or poorly handled emotions can have serious consequences.

So how do you view suffering as a Christian psychiatrist?

Dave: Suffering is a part of life. Unlike some of my colleagues, I believe that we will never find the "magic pill." The ultimate cure to all pain and suffering will only come with Christ when He returns to take us home to be with Him. As a physician my job is to relieve suffering where I can, but it is not something we should seek to completely avoid or remove. God can use suffering in our lives to draw us closer to Him, and as I've said before, I don't believe that that suffering is limited to physical pain.

How, then, do you keep the secular sciences from overrunning your biblical convictions?

Dave: Well, first it's important for me to discern theory from fact. There are a lot of secular theories out there that are touted as fact, but when they are in direct contrast to what the Bible teaches, you can be sure that they are lies. For the believer the Bible supercedes all knowledge, and so every truth must be tested by its teachings. Therefore, it is important for me, as it is for all believers, to be firmly grounded in the Word of God. Second, I have to remain teachable. Scientific discovery has done wonders for mankind, but sometimes Christians have a natural tendency to be skeptical. Remember that many Christians were opposed to the view that the world was round, claiming Scripture as their authority, when in reality the Scriptures do not teach that the world is flat. I think we need to be careful about falling into this same trap today. Often we take dogmatic stands on things that have no scriptural basis. That being said, I read scientific studies critically, both in terms of content and methods, and I pray that the Holy Spirit will give me wisdom in the moment as difficult decisions arise.

✓ Practical Action Points

1. Read Appendix "A" for my confession of a recent sin. Write out a similar story of a recent sin of yours. Analyze what happened, where you made choices, where the Evil One might have been involved, your steps in making things right, etc.

2. With which of our four suggested steps in personal growth do you most struggle?

3. Do you have a Paul, a Barnabas and a Timothy in your life? Begin to pray that God will bring those three individuals into your life.

4. Do you know a Christian counselor, psychologist or psychiatrist? If so, commit yourself to praying for that brother or sister on a daily basis.

10

Chapter Ten

Finally—When Temptation and Sin Are No More

When I get to heaven I shall see three wonders there.
The first wonder will be to see many people there whom I did not
expect to see; the second wonder will be to miss many people whom
I did expect to see; and the third and greatest wonder of all
will be to find myself there. (John Newton)

Listen, I tell you a mystery: We will not all sleep,
but we will all be changed —in a flash, in the
twinkling of an eye, at the last trumpet. For the trumpet
will sound, the dead will be raised imperishable, and we will be
changed. For the perishable must clothe itself with the imperish-
able, and the mortal with immortality. When the perishable has
been clothed with the imperishable, and the mortal with
immortality, then the saying that is written will come true:
"Death has been swallowed up in victory." "Where, O death, is
your victory? Where, O death, is your sting?" The sting of death is
sin, and the power of sin is the law. But thanks be to God! He
gives us the victory through our Lord Jesus Christ.
(1 Cor. 15:51–57)

Four preachers were in the same town speaking at differ
ent Bible conferences. When they realized they were staying at the same hotel, they got together for some fellowship.
Very quickly their conversation turned to the Second Coming of the Lord. The first said, "He's coming back for *us*!
What could be better than that?" And they were all excited
about that fact.

The second preacher said, "That's true, but I've got something even better. We read in First John 3 that 'we shall see
him as he is.' Wow! What could be better than that?" And
they rejoiced in that truth.

The third said, "Hey, I've got something even better than
that! We also read in that first epistle of John that 'we shall be
like Him.' That's incredible. Our sin will be gone. No more
pain or suffering. What could possibly be greater than that?"
And they all praised God for the truth of sin being no more.

The fourth preacher, who had been quiet while the others had spoken, finally said, "I know what could be better
than that." The other three preachers looked at one another,
thinking they had covered all of the truths of First John 3,
wondering what their friend would contribute. "What each
of you said was wonderful. He's coming back—for us! And
we shall see Him as He is—amazing! And we shall be like
Him—incredible! What could possibly be greater than those
truths?" He paused for a moment. "It will be forever!"

What *will* heaven be like? More specifically, what do we
know will be the case when we see the Lord? What do the
Scriptures teach about heaven, our sins, and our present responsibility before we get to glory?

Before we dive into three New Testament texts which discuss the believer and the culmination of human history, we

must challenge two myths, certainly held by the world, and frequently, perhaps unconsciously, considered by believers.

Two Major Myth-stakes[1]

The late science-fiction writer Isaac Asimov, who wrote over 500 books, and whose science fiction story "Nightfall" was voted the best science-fiction short story ever written,[2] once said, "I don't believe in an afterlife, so I don't have to spend my whole life fearing hell, or fearing heaven even more. For whatever the tortures of hell, I think the boredom of heaven would be even worse."

I must point out (and I say this with great sorrow) that he knows better now. If our understanding of Scripture is correct, and he died without a saving knowledge of the Lord Jesus Christ, Mr. Asimov is presently in a place of weeping and wailing and gnashing of teeth, a place of great darkness and absolute aloneness, a place of punishment which will never end.[3] He is forever separated from fellowship with God or His people. He is beyond the point of fearing hell—he is *in* hell!

We Christians must stop waffling on this crucial issue. Everybody is going to live somewhere for all eternity. People without Christ go to hell forever.

Asimov grew up with a father who accused him of being a *folyack*, Yiddish for sluggard. He made it his goal for over fifty years to get up every day at 6 a.m. and write until 10 p.m. He once said, "I am still showing my father I'm not a *folyack*."[4] How enormously sad. He spent his life trying to please his earthly father, forgetting the Father who is in heaven.

But it is actually the second half of Mr. Asimov's quote that troubles me the most, for I'm afraid it expresses the unspoken fear of many Christians. Mr. Asimov says, "For whatever the tortures of hell, I think the boredom of heaven would be even worse." Wow, he must have met some excruciatingly boring believers in his 72 years on the earth!

The first myth-stake which we must eliminate from our thinking is that heaven will be boring. What a small view of God one must have to conclude that the place where He dwells would be anything other than absolute joy, excitement and "life to the full"!

> *"We Christians walk around convincing ourselves that heaven will be just like one of our church meetings —only longerrrrr." (A theology professor)*

Satan began his propaganda crusade against God in the Garden when he convinced Eve that God was holding out on them, that He was not all that good. He continues his campaign of lies, I would suggest, on the believer in Christ. He realizes that although he cannot reclaim a holy child of God for himself, he can undermine that child's hope of heaven.

The Bible teaches that all the effects of the Fall will be reversed, there will be a new heavens and a new earth, and sin will be no more (see Rev. 21:27). How could we have such a poor view of eternity? Scripture clearly lays out, at the very least, five truths about heaven. First, heaven will be a place of joy and happiness. Jesus will say to the faithful servant: "Enter into your Master's *happiness*" (Matt. 25:23). C.S. Lewis said, "The serious business of heaven is joy,"[5] and the central feature of that joy, I would suggest, is not heaven's furniture but heaven's focus: the Lord Jesus

Christ. "In commanding us to glorify him," Lewis says, "God is inviting us to enjoy him."[6] The Message renders Luke 15:8–10 as "that's the kind of party God's angels throw every time one lost soul turns to God." If angels throw parties over sinners when they repent, what is going to happen when all those redeemed sinners are finally home?

Second, heaven will be a place of usefulness. Jesus says to that faithful servant in Matthew 25:21, "You have been faithful with a few things; I will put you in charge of many things." We will have responsibilities, meaningful work, exciting challenges in heaven. Weary work, not work itself, was the result of the Fall in the Garden. We will not be sitting around on clouds waiting for harp lessons.

Third, heaven will be a place of rest. We read in Hebrews 3:11 of God saying, "So I declared on oath in my anger, 'They shall never enter my rest.'" Revelation 14 promises that those who die in the Lord "will rest from their labor" (v. 13) and says that for the wicked "there is no rest day or night" (v. 11). We will forever be with the One who said, "Come to me, all you who are weary and burdened, and I will give you rest. Take my yoke upon you and learn from me, for I am gentle and humble in heart, and you will find rest for your souls" (Matt. 11:28–29).

Fourth, heaven is described as the place of life itself. Jesus says in John 3:16, "For God so loved the world that he gave his one and only Son, that whoever believes in him shall not perish but have eternal *life*." We read in Matthew 18:9, "And if your eye causes you to sin, gouge it out and throw it away. It is better for you to enter *life* with one eye than to have two eyes and be thrown into the fire of hell." In Matthew 19:17 we read of Jesus saying, "If you want to enter *life*, obey the commandments." Only those whose names are written in the Lamb's book of *life* will enter heaven, says Revelation 21:27. In fact, "Nothing impure will ever enter it, nor will anyone who does what is shameful or deceitful," we are told.

Fifth, heaven will be a place of permanence and eternal reality. Paul writes, "We fix our eyes not on what is seen, but on what is unseen. For what is seen is temporary, but what is unseen is eternal" (2 Cor. 4:18). C.S. Lewis reminds us that "All that is not eternal is eternally out of date."[7]

Eyewitness Testimony

Much, much more could be said about the Scriptures' teaching on heaven, but let's hear from someone who has been there, the Apostle Paul. He describes having been "caught up to the third heaven . . . caught up to paradise" (2 Cor. 12:2, 4).[8] The experience happened to him fourteen years previously, and he does not say why he waited so long to speak of it.

How does Paul describe his experience? He puts it under the category of "visions and revelations from the Lord" (2 Cor. 12:1). He may be saying that being caught up to paradise was just one of several experiences he had, or he may be saying that he received visions and revelations while being caught up. He does say later in verse 7 that he received a thorn in the flesh to keep him from being conceited "because of these surpassingly great revelations."

At the very least, the *sights* of heaven overwhelmed Paul. Visually speaking, this does not sound to me like heaven will be a boring place! He also says that "he heard inexpressible things, things that man is not permitted to tell" (v. 4). I wonder what Paul heard? At any rate, he knows that he is not permitted to tell what he heard. There are sounds and words and music and conversations and perhaps secrets that await us in heaven. Auditorally speaking, that doesn't sound like heaven will be boring to me!

Reasons for Our Boredom

So why have we thought of heaven as boring? Four possible reasons come to mind. First, we may think of heaven as boring because we've become satisfied with the things of earth. Rick Warren says, "You will never feel completely satisfied on earth, because you were made for more."⁹ Throughout his writings C.S. Lewis talks about the "inconsolable longing," that wandering toward the source of this joy, toward one's real home, toward heaven.

Second, we may think of heaven as boring because we have not used our imaginations and engaged our minds with the Scriptures. It is written, "'No eye has seen, no ear has heard, no mind has conceived what God has prepared for those who love him'—but God has revealed it to us by his Spirit" (1 Cor. 2:9–10).

Third, we suffer from a low view of God Himself. If heaven is the presence of God and God is not boring, how dare we think heaven boring? A low view of heaven is, at root, a low view of God.

Fourth, we conceive of heaven in a limited way, instead of thinking of its sheer variety. Gary Thomas in his *Sacred Pathways* reminds us that there are nine ways people draw near to God:

- Naturalists, those most inspired to love God out-of-doors;
- Sensates, those who love God with their senses and appreciate beautiful worship services that involve the five senses;
- Traditionalists, those who feel closer to God through rituals, liturgies, symbols and unchanging structures;
- Ascetics, those who prefer to love God in solitude and simplicity;
- Activists, those who love God through confronting evil, battling injustice, and working to make the world a better place;
- Caregivers, those who love God by loving others and meeting their needs;
- Enthusiasts, those who love God through celebration;
- Contemplatives, those who love God through adoration;
- Intellectuals, those who love God by studying God with their minds.[10]

Heaven sounds boring when we think it will be an eternity only of Intellectuals ("and I'm a Sensate"), or we will only worship God as Enthusiasts ("and I'm a Contemplative")!

The Second Myth-Stake

Not only do Christians sometimes fear that heaven will be boring, but many are convinced (and I know this sounds terribly irreverent) that somehow sin is a necessity, that goodness can only be appreciated in contrast with badness, that evil equals excitement. If in heaven we will only be able to choose the good, will that "limitation" make us less human?

John Hick suggests that if there were no evil we would not be able to make moral choices and therefore be incapable of moral growth and development. One Catholic writer says,

> Religions with a linear concept of time tend to see the defeat of evil as taking place at the end of time; religions with a cyclical concept of time tend to see evil as inevitable at the end of each cycle. If we could solve the problem of suffering we would have solved the riddle of life itself. For Christians suffering remains a mystery, but a mystery into which God has also entered and in which we can find God.[11]

I would beg to disagree with his second sentence. I don't believe that solving the problem of suffering would mean solving the riddle of life itself. Life, as originally brought into existence by the Creator, did not necessitate the presence of evil. Evil is constantly portrayed in the Scriptures as an enemy, an invader (Gen. 3; Rom. 5).

May I suggest, without becoming too philosophical, that we have succumbed to a kind of dualism: the idea that God and Satan are equal but opposing powers and that good and evil are both eternal. Another writer in considering the thought of C.S. Lewis says,

"The church doesn't want to appear to be imperfect, because of ridicule and shame . . . and so the heart of the matter is never really uncovered. Where can the hidden things come to light and be healed without the fear of rejection? Where are the folks with the goods to get God's kids healed, delivered and set free?" (Christian recording artist)

> For Lewis, the Devil was definitely not eternal. Real but not everlasting. This accords with the New Testament view

of evil and the Devil as an influence of power whose days are definitely numbered. In short, evil for all its terror is within time but not of eternity.[12]

Although this topic is an interesting one to pursue,[13] what do we learn from the Word of God? We learn that one day death and sin will be abolished. The "perishable" will be clothed with the "imperishable," "the mortal" with "immortality." Death will be swallowed up in victory, says the Apostle Paul (1 Cor. 15:54). The Apostle John writes,

> And I heard a loud voice from the throne saying, "Now the dwelling of God is with men, and he will live with them. They will be his people, and God himself will be with them and be their God. He will wipe every tear from their eyes. There will be no more death or mourning or crying or pain, for the old order of things has passed away." (Rev. 21:3–4)

We read in that same chapter that "Nothing impure will ever enter it, nor will anyone who does what is shameful or deceitful, but only those whose names are written in the Lamb's book of life" (v. 27).

Adam and Eve did not need to sin in order to have choice. Evil was not necessary in creation. God did not leave out an essential element of what it means to be truly human by creating a world free from evil. Adam and Eve's rebellion against God in the Garden did not add anything to their existence that God had unlovingly withheld. The absence of evil in heaven does not mean that man will be less than he was originally created to be. We will finally become all that God intended for us in creation. We will never again be inflicted with jealousy, pettiness, unrighteous anger, envy, laziness or any other sin. The "Seven Deadly Sins" will be no more.

I want to look at three Scripture passages to help us gain some sense of what eternity will be like with no more temptation and no more sin. These passages will also help us consider what kind of people we ought to be right now as we anticipate that future.

Ephesians 4 and Perfection

In Ephesians 4:11–16 we are again reminded of our goal in becoming like Christ. Although this text does not directly mention heaven, Paul is speaking of that point at which believers will "[attain] to the whole measure of the fullness of Christ" (v. 13). This process will not be complete until we reach heaven.

What we learn in Ephesians 4 is that God has put together a program for perfecting His saints. His leadership structure for the local church is described in verse 11: He gave "some to be apostles, some to be prophets, some to be evangelists, and some to be pastors and teachers."

> *"The church that doesn't want to grow is saying to the world, 'You can go to hell!'"*
> *(Rick Warren)*

Why has God given these leaders to the church? There are various reasons given in Scripture for such leaders, but here in Ephesians 4 it is in order to "prepare God's people for works of service" (v. 12). Such leaders are not given to do all the work themselves. The myth of the omni-competent pastor, who has all spiritual gifts and can do all the ministry in a local church, leads to what is called the "clergyman's coronary"!

The emphasis in this text is *not* on their specific *functions* in the church, but on their *leadership* in bringing God's people to maturity.[14] As God's people serve, the body of Christ is built up. God's people serving out of their God-given gifts will build up the body. What is the goal of that building up? Verse 13 tells us: "until we reach unity in the faith and in the knowledge of the Son of God and become mature, attaining to the whole measure of the fullness of Christ." We are certainly to strive for unity, knowledge and maturity now, but its fullness will not be achieved until we see the Lord.

The immediate, practical consequence of being built up is *doctrinal stability*, so that "we will no longer be infants," tossed by the waves and blown by the wind. A child who wanders too far out into the surf will get pounded by the current. What is "current" in our culture does the same to us. God does not want tossed and blown children. The allure of some new gust of wind must not overcome the believer and keep him or her in doctrinal infancy. The world of ideas and concepts is not populated solely by well-intentioned, orthodox teachers. It is not too much to say that, "There be [theological] pirates out there!" And those false teachers will employ all their cunning and craftiness in order to deceive God's people (v. 14).

What is the alternative to being doctrinally infantile, personally deceived and biblically unstable? We are told in the next verse of Ephesians 4: "Instead, speaking the truth in love, we will in all things grow up into him who is the Head, that is, Christ" (v. 15). Teaching others the truth that is in Christ contributes to our growth. And somehow our growth is connected to our life in the Head, the Lord Jesus: "From him the whole body, joined and held together by every supporting ligament, grows and builds itself up in love, as each part does its work" (v. 16).

"Every supporting ligament" may perhaps be describing the individual believer. A ligament is a tough band of tissue that holds the bones and organs in place. Ligaments are very important to the body (after all, who wants an organ to fall out of place?). I became painfully aware of the importance of ligaments (and tendons) several years ago when I had an athletic "mishap."

I was playing pick-up basketball with a few other teachers when I went up for my signature three-point jump shot. It is normally a thing of beauty, shot in the old-fashioned manner of one hand on each side of the basketball. I remember leaping, and then feeling as if a baseball bat had been applied to the back of my left ankle. I collapsed to the gym floor, looking around for someone to blame. I saw a young man kicking a soccer ball in the gym and I yelled, "Hey! Why did you kick that ball into me?!" But it became painfully obvious that no one had hit me—I had done the damage to myself.

I dragged myself to the men's locker room, took a shower, and taught my afternoon class on crutches, almost fainting a couple of times (cue the violin music). I drove myself home still not knowing how badly I was injured. At the time my wife Linda was substitute teaching at a rural school down from our house, so I picked up my son and told him to run into the school to tell Mom that I was going to drive myself to the hospital about 20 minutes away to get checked out. When he came out of the school, I said, "What did your Mom say?"

"She said you're always getting hurt! You're too old to play basketball!"

With those words of comfort, I drove myself to the hospital. When the doctor saw me, he gently touched the back of my ankle with his thumb and forefinger and said, "Well, I guess we'll be doing surgery tonight."

"I don't remember using the 'S' word!" I protested. "What do you mean 'we'll do surgery tonight'?"

"Well, you've completely torn your Achilles' tendon. It has to be sown back together!"

This was obviously a doctor who had flunked "Bedside Manners 101."

After surgery—the surgeon said it was like sewing two mops together—they put on a full leg cast, from the tips of my toes to my hip. They cast the injured ankle with the toes forcibly pointing downward so that the repaired Achilles could begin healing. They didn't tell me what I would have to endure one week later.

After cutting off the full leg cast, the surgeon said, "I'm going to have to straighten out your ankle which will break some scar tissue, so the healing can continue." Before I had the chance to say, " You're going to do *what?!* " he grabbed my ankle and started pointing my toes upward, putting pressure right on the spot where the two mops had been sewed together.

I screamed! I have never felt such pain in my entire life. My wife, normally a very caring and spiritual person, started laughing! "Why are you laughing?" I asked.

"Now you know what labor is like," she said.

I replied (in between screams), "At least you got a baby out of it!" Now the doctor and nurses were laughing.

After six months of rehab, I was as good as new. I learned a lot from my injury, not the least of which is that you know you are getting old when body parts start exploding with no warning. And I no longer take my "supporting ligaments" for granted.

There will come a day when temptation and sin will be no more. Ephesians 4 teaches us that on that day we will attain perfect unity in the faith, full maturity, and the realized goal of fullness in Christ. Until then, we should be striving *now* to play our part in being "supporting ligaments," building up the body of Christ and being built up ourselves.

Second Peter 3 and the Destruction of All Things

Our second passage, Second Peter 3:10–14, is much more direct in its treatment of the end of this world as we know it:

> But the day of the Lord will come like a thief. The heavens will disappear with a roar; the elements will be destroyed by fire, and the earth and everything in it will be laid bare. Since everything will be destroyed in this way, what kind of people ought you to be? You ought to live holy and godly lives as you look forward to the day of God and speed its coming. That day will bring about the destruction of the heavens by fire, and the elements will melt in the heat. But in keeping with his promise we are looking forward to a new heaven and a new earth, the home of righteousness. So then, dear friends, since you are looking forward to this, make every effort to be found spotless, blameless and at peace with him.

Here Peter is discussing the "Day of the Lord," a rich concept throughout Scripture.[15] We learn that the Day of the Lord will humble the proud (Isa. 2:12) and will come "like destruction from the Almighty . . . a cruel day with wrath and fierce anger" (Isa. 13:6, 9). It is described as "a day of vengeance" (Jer. 46:10), a "great" and "dreadful" time when the "sun will be turned to darkness, and the moon to blood" (Joel 2:11, 31).

The prophet Amos says, "Woe to you who long for the day of the LORD! Why do you long for the day of the LORD? That day will be darkness, not light" (5:18). Other minor prophets speak of that Day; Malachi, for example, states that the Lord will send Elijah the prophet before the coming of the great and dreadful day of the LORD (4:5).

The day of the Lord will come as "a thief in the night," Paul says (1 Thess. 5:2), a fact which Peter reiterates in Second Peter 3. Peter's focus in this passage is on the destruction of the physical realm: The heavens will "disappear with a roar; the elements will be destroyed by fire, and the earth and everything in it will be laid bare" (v. 10). Later in verse 12 we read of "the destruction of the heavens by fire, and the elements will melt in the heat."[16]

Peter does not give us this information for speculative purposes. He immediately follows up his predictions about universal destruction with personal challenges about present, individual holiness. In light of creation's destruction, Peter asks, "what kind of people ought you to be?" Then he answers his own question by saying, "You ought to live holy and godly lives" (v. 11). This world's destruction should not lead the believer into complacency or inactivity, but into a pursuit of holiness and godliness.

Many would say that we should not look forward to God's destroying judgment upon this world, but Peter disagrees. He refers to our "looking forward to" three times in this text: "as you look forward to the day of God and speed its coming" (v. 12); "we are looking forward to a new heaven and a new earth" (v. 13); "since you are looking forward to this . . ." (v. 14). We are not longing for destruction but for holiness, for righteousness. The personal application of the anticipation of this future event is: "Make every effort to be found spotless, blameless and at peace with him" (v. 14).

When I was a young teenager I remember visiting preachers coming to our church who spoke on the Second Coming. One, in fact, had a multi-media presentation. Don't misunderstand me—"multi-media" in the early 1960s was not high-tech; it merely meant he used something other than just his voice to present his sermon. (We only had "Power-Point" back then when the preacher pointed his finger at you and said "Repent!" or "Confess!" or "Hey, you! Stop falling asleep in my service!")

This one particular visiting preacher brought with him a massive, multi-colored banner which stretched from one side of the platform to the other. The banner had the title "From Eternity to Eternity" and was very professionally done. It portrayed biblical history from creation to the final state of heaven and hell. I remember this preacher explaining biblical prophecy, the dispensations and the "clear biblical teaching about the pretribulational coming of the Lord." While others were impressed with his speculations, I recall being somewhat troubled with his sermons. (To be quite honest, it seemed to me that his *message* was going to last "from eternity to eternity"!) To my teenage mind, his sermons seemed to have little *present* application.[17]

Peter does not mince words when he speaks of the end times. He drives home the point that the future destruction of the heavens and earth should lead to present, practical change in God's people. We should be pursuing holiness, godliness, spotlessness, blamelessness and peace with Him right *now*!

Face to Face?

The Bible is quite clear that upon death or the Lord Jesus' Second Coming we will see the Lord. This momentous event—what could be greater?—is traditionally called "the beatific vision." Beatific is an old word which means "showing or producing exalted joy or blessedness." For the believer in Jesus Christ, what could produce more joy or blessedness than seeing the Lord Jesus face to face?

I went online and looked up the term "beatific vision." To my amazement I discovered the following banner advertisement: "Shop at Amazon.com for low prices on beatific visions. Free Super Saver Shipping on qualified orders over $25!" I know Amazon carries millions of books, but I never knew they also sold beatific visions—with free shipping, no less!

The Bible says much about seeing the Lord face to face. For example, we are told that the Lord "would speak to Moses face to face, as a man speaks with his friend" (Exod. 33:11). In Genesis 32 Jacob wrestled with a "man" that he later realized was an angel. Afterward, he named the place where they wrestled *Peniel*, which means "face of God," because "I saw God face to face, and yet my life was spared" (v. 30).

Believers are promised in First Corinthians 13:12, "For now we see through a glass, darkly; but then face to face: now I know in part; but then shall I know even as also I am known" (KJV). Revelation 22:4 says, "And they shall see his face; and his name shall be in their foreheads" (KJV). Second Corinthians 3:18 says, "But we all, with open face beholding as in a glass the glory of the Lord, are changed into the same image from glory to glory, even as by the Spirit of the Lord" (KJV).

First John 3 and the Beatific Vision

In our third passage, John is led by the Spirit of God to give some details as to what that day will be like when we see the Lord Jesus face to face. In chapter 3 we read,

> How great is the love the Father has lavished on us, that we should be called children of God! And that is what we are! The reason the world does not know us is that it did not know him. Dear friends, now we are children of God, and what we will be has not yet been made known. But we know that when he appears, we shall be like him, for we shall see him as he is. Everyone who has this hope in him purifies himself, just as he is pure. (vv. 1–3)

This key passage on eternity begins with a consideration of God's love. John speaks of the Father's love being "lavished" on us. Not only are we *called* the children of God— we actually *are* the children of God! That reality of presently being the children of God causes John to think about the future. And he becomes very specific about the future. The future John contemplates is *our* future—what we will be like. He first admits that all information has not been given to us as to what we will be like (v. 2). John does not dwell on what we do not know. He quickly moves to what we do know.

What *do* we know? We know first that He will "appear" (v. 2). He is returning for His children. This is a given in Scripture. It is not in doubt because of its delay. Our foolish speculations about Christ's Second Coming unfortunately undermine confidence in the *fact* of His return. When our predictions don't come true, some are tempted to believe that His promise is not true.

The first consequence of John's assurance that Christ will

come back for us is that "we shall be like Him" (v. 2). What does it mean to be like Him? All that we learn in the Gospels about the character of the Lord Jesus will be true of us. To be like Him is to be completely pleasing to the Father. It is to be in complete conformity with His holiness. To be like Him is to reflect His glory. It means that the process described in Second Corinthians 3:17–18 will be completed: "Now the Lord is the Spirit, and where the Spirit of the Lord is, there is freedom. And we, who with unveiled faces all reflect the Lord's glory, are being transformed into his likeness with ever-increasing glory, which comes from the Lord, who is the Spirit."

What brings about our being like Him? John says "we shall be like him, for we shall see him as he is" (v. 2). The veil of sin over our eyes will be taken away. Our misconceptions will vanish. Our perception will catch up to reality. We will fall on our faces in awe. I can imagine us saying, "Isn't He something?" No more will we attempt to make God in our image. Our efforts—even unintended ones—at making Christ to be what we want Him to be will be over. The stark reality, the unvarnished truth of the Person of Christ, will be before our eyes. And it will change us.

This text is not dealing with all people. This text is the private experience of the redeemed as they see their Lord face to face. Whatever remains of the process of becoming like the Lord Jesus (what theologians call "sanctification") will be completed at that moment. "We shall be like him . . ." The job will be finished by the Son of God as He appears before His saved ones. After all, He promised to complete that work in us. We read in Philippians 1:6, "being confident of this, that he who began a good work in you will carry it on to completion until the day of Christ Jesus."

What should be our present response to that future certainty? Should we, His people, simply take it easy and glide to glory? One of my wife's favorite hymns as a child has the stanza:

> Must I be carried to the skies
> On flow'ry beds of ease,
> While others fought to win the prize
> And sailed through bloody seas?

John leaves no doubt in his discussion of this wonderful future event: "Everyone who has this hope in him purifies himself, just as he is pure" (v. 3). That future, yet certain, event of seeing Christ must have an impact on believers in the here and now. It must result in a commitment to purity with our Lord as our standard. Discussion of prophecy without a resultant practice of purity is purposeless! Paul gives us this challenge: "Since we have these promises, dear friends, let us purify ourselves from everything that contaminates body and spirit, perfecting holiness out of reverence for God" (2 Cor. 7:1).

We can look forward to the day when we will see Him as He is and be like Him. This world is not our final home. We are to pursue holiness as we anticipate His return for us.

One day after theology class a young man entered my office. "Dr. Dixon," he said, "I think I've reached that point."

"What point would that be, Derrick?" I asked.

"Well, you talked today about sinless perfectionism. I think I've reached that point of no longer sinning. I believe that I have complete victory over sin in my life. Because of Christ, of course," he added.

"Of course," I said, trying to think fast as to how to respond. I looked behind him and noticed a young lady in the hallway. "Who is this?" I asked Derrick.

"Oh, this is my fiancée, Debbie."

"Hi, Debbie," I said. "Nice to meet you."

"Nice to meet you, Dr. Dixon," Debbie said. Debbie seemed to look a bit stressed. Finally, she said, "Dr. Dixon, Derrick says he thinks he has reached sinless perfection, right?"

"Yes, that's what he said," I answered.

"Well, Dr. Dixon, I don't know how to say this. But would you like his sins listed alphabetically or chronologically?" You should have seen the look on Derrick's face as he sheepishly left my office.

Although there are some believers who teach sinless perfectionism, I believe only Christ can finish the job He has started in us. And that will be completed when we see Him.

✓ Practical Action Points

1. We must recognize and deal with the two myths of heaven being boring and evil being necessary. Read a good study on heaven (like Randy Alcorn's *Heaven*) and discuss it with other believers.

2. Discuss with other Christians what you imagine heaven will be like. Don't be afraid to use your sanctified imagination. Think about such matters as worship, fellowship, food, discovery, adventure, work, etc.

3. Have an in-depth conversation with an older believer who is thinking much about "going home." What are they looking forward to? What thoughts do they have about the end of temptation and sin?

Appendix

My Sin

The morning started out innocently enough. We were on vacation, enjoying a beautiful resort right on the beach! I was working on this book, thoroughly immersed in the process of writing and thinking through the issues of temptation and sin.

Then it happened. I sinned. I didn't plan on it happening. I had not set out that day to give in. When it was all over and I had time to think about what I had done, I realized how subtle temptation and sin are.

You may laugh at the sin I'm going to describe to you. "It was nothing!" you might say. (Or you might say, "My goodness, you've been thinking about temptation and sin way too much!")

Here's my account of what happened. My wife and I sell used books on Amazon.com as a part-time hobby. We're not major book dealers (that fact becomes important in a few moments), but we enjoy buying books at thrift stores and re-selling them on the Internet.

When we drove up to the "Litter Box," a thrift store whose

profits help abandoned pets, I did not realize how quickly my sinful nature would take over my mind, my behavior and my person.

Most guys I know, for reasons unexplainable, do not want a woman to tell them how to drive, how fast to go, or where to park the car. And even though I have a great relationship with my wife of thirty-seven years, when she told me where to park in front of this thrift store, I know I shouldn't have gotten upset inside, but I did. A little bit.

Then we entered the "Litter Box," a very organized, clean, *non-profit* (this point becomes important later in the story) thrift store. My wife and I headed directly to the book section and both of us began pulling various books from the shelves to consider whether we ought to buy them. We had not realized that the books were meticulously organized and sorted according to subject matter—and that the middle-aged woman who had done a world-class job of organizing those books was standing there—and was still busy at work sorting out her books.

She came up to me, looked at the thirty or so books that we had unceremoniously pulled from their proper slots and had piled on a table, and asked with a sneer, "You are going to buy all these books, right?"

I said, "Well, I'm going to think about buying some of them." (I thought to myself, "How dare she ask me if I'm going to buy these books!") What I was actually going to do was write down the ISBN numbers of the books, go back to our vacation condo and look them up on Amazon to see if they were worth anything, then return the next day to buy the ones that were valuable.

"You're going to *think* about buying *some* of these?!" she asked indignantly. "I had all these books perfectly shelved according to subject matter!"

I responded, "What? You don't want me to buy these books? I thought that's why they're here!"

Her face contorted into an angry, irritated look. (It reminded me of the Wicked Witch of the East in "The Wizard of Oz" just before the house fell on her.) "But why can't you pull each one out of its space, look it over, decide whether you want to buy it or not, then replace it if you're not going to buy it?" I could see that she was getting steamed. All I could think of was, *Why is this woman in my face? I'll bet she tells her husband where to park as well!*

The bell rang, ending Round One, and we momentarily took a break in our conversation. She went around another book case and I began furiously writing down ISBN numbers. But then she returned for Round Two. She got in my face again and said, "You know, this is a non-profit humane society thrift store. I'll bet you're a book dealer, aren't you? You're out to make money, aren't you?" She said those last words as if I was in the same category as someone who would sell children to slave traders in Thailand.

"Well, I'm not exactly a book dealer" (I didn't mean to lie; I guess I was thinking that my *primary* occupation is not a "book dealer"), I said with a strong voice. "And what's that got to do with? Don't you *want* to sell these books?!" (I'm certain I asked these two questions in the most pastoral tone possible.)

She went to get the manager as I continued to write the ISBN numbers down even more quickly. The manager, a nice lady by the name of "Bobbi," immediately took my side, and said to the Gestapo book lady, "We don't have these kinds of confrontations with our customers, Ethyl. The customer is *always* right." "Ethyl" slinked away to go harass some other innocent thrift store patron.

Bobbi calmly said to me, "You know, she's a new volunteer here. However, she has worked very hard to shelve these books. Were you intending on purchasing all of these?"

"I'm not sure," I said somewhat shaken. "My plan is to look up these ISBN numbers on the Internet, then return and buy the books that I can re-sell."

"That's fine," Bobbi said. "It would have been good if you could have . . . uh, never mind," she said. "How about I get you a box to put these books in and I'll put them aside for you. Then you can either come back tomorrow or call me to let me know if you want to buy some of them."

"That would be great, Bobbi," I said. I was glad to get out of that store.

After looking up the ISBN numbers, I did the brave thing and sent my wife back the next day to purchase the books we wanted. But, lest you think I'm a complete coward, I did call Bobbi and apologize to her for my part in the little tiff in her store.

An Analysis of My Sin

As I said earlier, this may seem like a trivial matter, a silly sin to discuss. However, as I reflect on how I conducted myself, I believe I blew it in several significant ways. What might be viewed as "a little tiff" was, I think, something much more.

First, I was irritated when I entered the store, foolishly angry at my wife for telling me where to park. The last thing

I needed was another woman to get in my face and tell me what to do! My heart and mind were not prepared to represent Christ as I entered the "Litter Box."

Second, I completely ignored the biblical teaching that "A gentle answer turns away wrath, but a harsh word stirs up anger" (Prov. 15:1). The New Living Translation reads: "A gentle answer deflects anger, but harsh words make tempers flare." Talk about tempers flaring! My wife told me later she was afraid that we would come to blows. I thought I had been fairly calm.

Instead of responding in kindness and gentleness, I stood my ground, stood up for my rights, and unleashed a firestorm—in that lady and in me! My wife actually whispered to me when the conversation started, "Let it go!" (I don't remember hearing that.) How could I have handled that situation better?

When she "got in my face" and rebuked me for messing up her well-organized shelves, I should have honestly said, "I am so sorry. I've never seen such a well-organized book section in a thrift store! Would it help if I promise to re-shelve each of these books after I've written down their ISBN numbers?"

To be perfectly honest, I'm not sure that would have satisfied her (she was ticked that we had taken out so many books from their spaces), but I know that it would have been a far better way for me to respond to the situation. There is only one person's responses over which I have some measure of control, and that person is me.

Even though the manager said that the customer is always right, I was wrong in how I responded, wrong in how I defended my "rights," and wrong in my heart. I don't know how, or if, Satan was involved in my conduct in that store. I believe he has been a student of human behavior for thousands of years. He—or more likely one of his minions—has studied my personality and my reactions all my life. If he was at all involved in engineering or encouraging the conditions of my sin that day, it is because he knows my weaknesses and my desperate need to submit myself to the Lord at every moment of my life. Thank God for the opportunity for repentance and forgiveness!

Endnotes

Introduction

1. Cited by Philip Yancey, *Soul Survivor* (New York: Doubleday, 2001), p. 58.

Chapter 1: Shh! We're Going to Talk about the "S" Word!

1. I'm reminded of this statement by Elisabeth Elliot: "We can stand a lot of honesty that concerns other people. But we are marvelously uncritical and generous when it comes right down to the nitty-gritty of our private lives" (Elizabeth Elliot, *All That Was Ever Ours* [Grand Rapids: Revell, 1988]).

2. John Updike, introduction to F.J. Sheed, ed., *Soundings in Satanism* (New York: Sheed and Ward, 1972), pp. vii-viii.

3. Sanhedrin 98a.

4. Quoted in Raphael Patai, *The Messiah Texts* (Detroit: Wayne State University Press, 1989), p. 31.

5. Online at http://www.hadavar.org/additional-obj-9.html. Accessed January 25, 2007.

6. Online at http://www.chaim.org/leper.htm. Accessed December 31, 2007.

Chapter 2: Getting Our Terms Straight

1. For a discussion of Jesus' doctrine of everlasting conscious punishment, see my book *The Other Side of the Good News: Contemporary Challenges to Jesus' Teaching on Hell* (Ross-shire, UK: Christian Focus, 2003).

2.   "The Cross of Christ: The Atonement and Men Today," online at http://wwwdrsamstheology.com/theology/theological_studies.pdf, p. 151. Accessed January 9, 2008.

Chapter 3: Our Enemy's M.O.

1.   Philip Schaff, ed., *The Nicene and Post-Nicene Fathers of the Christian Church* (Grand Rapids: Eerdmans, 1979), vol. XI, p. 10; vol. X, p. 84.

2.   It is interesting to note that the verb "destroy" could be translated "loose" or "set free." The meaning of the verse would then be quite different. Jesus came to "loose" or "set free" the works of the devil. I really like the Wycliffe translation which says, "In this thing the Son of God appeared, that he undoes the works of the devil." This could certainly be a correct translation of the Greek verb that is used here. This same word translated "destroy" or "loose" or "set free" is used in Luke 13:15-16: "The Lord answered him, 'You hypocrites! Doesn't each of you on the Sabbath untie his ox or donkey from the stall and lead it out to give it water? Then should not this woman, a daughter of Abraham, whom Satan has kept bound for eighteen long years be set free on the Sabbath day from what bound her?'" If First John 3:8 does not refer to the destruction of the devil's works (but their un-loosing), we have Hebrews 2:14 which says, "Since the children have flesh and blood, he too shared in their humanity so that by his death he might destroy him who holds the power of death—that is, the devil . . ." The term used here in Hebrews 2:14 is not the same verb as First John 3:8, but carries with it the idea of "rendering ineffective, to put an end to."

3.   We will examine First John 2:15–17 more in-depth in our next chapter.

4.   It is interesting that Matthew and Luke present different orders of the three temptations of Jesus. Matthew has the order: stones into bread, jump from the temple, and worship Satan. Luke has stones into bread, worship Satan, and jump from the temple. Mark 1 only says, "At once the Spirit sent him out into the desert, and he was in the desert forty days, being tempted by Satan. He was with the wild animals, and angels attended him" (vv. 12–13).

5.   It is fascinating that in light of Satan appearing to Adam and Eve as a serpent in Genesis 3, in this very Psalm we read in verse 13: "You will tread upon the lion and cobra, The young lion and the serpent you will trample down."

6.   We do read in Malachi 3:10, "Bring the whole tithe into the storehouse, that there may be food in my house. Test me in this," says the LORD Almighty, "and see if I will not throw open the floodgates of heaven and pour out so much blessing that you will not have room enough for it." This is obviously a positive challenge for Israel to take God at His word.

7.   Rick Warren writes, "The most important decision you can make today is to settle this issue of what will be the ultimate authority for your life. Decide that regardless of culture, tradition, reason, or emotion, you choose the Bible as your final authority." (*The Purpose-Driven Life* [Grand Rapids: Zondervan, 2002], p. 187).

8.   Contrasts:

      a. Satan appeals to Adam and Eve in a perfect environment where all their needs were being met, where no sin had yet invaded their world. He appeals to the Lord Jesus in His period of physical weakness in the environment of a fallen world.

      b. Satan appeals to Adam and Eve to sow doubt about God's goodness, intimating that God was holding out on them. With Jesus, Satan challenges Jesus to prove that He is the Son of God, to test the Father by acting independently of Him, by putting Himself in harm's way, by taking the kingdoms of the world.

      c. Satan's approach to Adam and Eve is "Did God say?" Jesus' response to his taunts was "God *said*!"

      d. Satan uses *deceit* ("more crafty than any of the wild animals the Lord God had made," Gen. 3:1) to go after Adam and Eve. He uses *direct confrontation* to challenge Christ.

      e. Adam and Eve are not "led by the Spirit" to be tempted by Satan in the Garden as Jesus was in His trial (Matt. 4:1).

      f. Eve had Adam who should have helped her turn from Satan's temptation. Jesus "only" had the Father!

g. In its effects, Adam and Eve's transgression was followed by severe consequences (a damaged relationship between Adam and Eve, banishment from the Garden, an angel with a flaming sword to guard the way to the tree of life, etc.). Jesus' episode concluded with the devil departing and angels ministering to the Lord Jesus.

Chapter 4: The Other Two-Thirds of Our Enemies

1. C.S. Lewis, *The World's Last Night and Other Essays* (New York: Harcourt Brace Jovanovich, 1960), "The Weight of Glory" (ch. 1, pp. 3–4). Somewhere St. Augustine said, "We move spiritually not by our feet, but by our desires."

2. The book, *The Evangelical Universalist* (Cascade Books, 2006), written by Gregory MacDonald (a pseudonym), pulls out all the stops to argue that everyone without exception will ultimately be saved. This book, I would suggest, is one example of a hope or desire which clearly conflicts with God's Word.

3. Looking at James 1:14–15 carefully, this text sounds very much like a sexual assault. In fact, it sounds like *self-rape!* Sometimes we are, quite literally, our own worst enemies.

4. Online at http://www.safefamilies.org/sfStats.php.

5. Online at htp://thegoodnewsonline.net/atf.php?sid=549. Accessed July 21, 2008.

6. Wheaton, IL: Crossway Books, March 3, 2003.

7. We read of David looking upon Bathsheba in Second Samuel 11:2 that "the woman was very beautiful to look upon."

8. Garrison Keillor, *Lake Wobegon Days* (New York: Viking Penguin, 1985), p. 111.

9. C.S. Lewis, *Screwtape Letters & Screwtape Proposes a Toast* (New York: Macmillan, 1961), p. 132.

10. It seems to me that "eating [Jesus'] flesh" in John 6 is not a reference to the Lord's Supper, but to an intimate faith relationship with Him.

11.   That leaves 64 uses by Paul of the "flesh" in the rest of his epistles for you to study if you wish. Using a concordance or biblegateway.com will help in this important study.

12.   C.S. Lewis, *Mere Christianity* (New York: Macmillan, 1974).

Chapter 5: Seven Deadly Mistakes We Make about the Seven Deadly Sins

1.   Chapter 8 of this book deals in-depth with First Corinthians 5.

2.   See discussion in Chapter 4.

3.   Late-night comedian Conan O'Brien says, "A new study shows that three-quarters of all Americans are overweight. In fact, it is so bad that three-quarters of all Americans are nine-tenths of all Americans." ("Late Night with Conan O'Brien," NBC).

4.   Leroy Thompson, Sr., *Money Cometh! To the Body of Christ* (Tulsa, OK: Harrison House, 1999).

5.   James Emery White suggests six faces of sloth: laziness (not doing our work heartily unto the Lord, Col. 3:23–24), tolerance (intellectual or moral laziness, the opposite of discrimination or discernment), apathy (just "driving by" someone in need, see Luke 10:33–34), procrastination (knowing what we need to do but never quite bringing ourselves to do it), activity (staying busy but not focusing on what is really important), and circumstance (using circumstances as an excuse to be lazy) (*Long Night's Journey Into Day*, WaterBrook Press; 2002).

6.   http://www2.hawaii.edu/~lady/snapshots/peggy-lee.html. Accessed January 10, 2008.

7.   C.S. Lewis, *Mere Christianity*, p. 120.

8.   Eugene Peterson, *Subversive Spirituality* (Grand Rapids: Eerdmans, 1997), p. 237.

9.   *Selected Works of Jonathan Edwards* (London: Banner of Truth Trust, 1959), vol. 2, Sermons, pp. 183–199.

10.   Some of the following material was adapted from my *The Other Side of the Good News*, pp. 21ff.

11.   J.I. Packer, *Knowing God* (Downers Grove: InterVarsity Press, 1973), p. 136.

12.   Ibid., p. 142.

13.   The punishment may seem a bit harsh. But we read in First Corinthians 10:4 that the children of Israel from the Old Testament who wandered with Moses in the wilderness "drank the same 'spiritual drink' from the rock that accompanied them and the rock was Christ." Is it possible that this "rock" mentioned in the Old Testament was a theophany of Christ? At any rate, Moses' wrath forfeits his entrance into the Promised Land. Deuteronomy 32:15, 18 indicates that there was more to Moses' action that just anger.

14.   Please see our discussion of God's hatred in Chapter 2.

15.   For a true confession, see Appendix A.

16.   C.S. Lewis, *Mere Christianity*, p. 109.

17.   Joan Rivers, *Bouncing Back: I've Survived Everything . . . and I Mean Everything . . . and You Can Too!* (New York: Harper Torch, 1998).

18.   Rick Warren, *The Purpose-Driven Life*, p. 33.

19.   *The Christian Century*, Sept. 28, 1977, p. 836.

20.   *Today in the Word*, September 10, 1992.

21.   Online at http://books.google.com/books?id=fPsuAAAAMAAJ& q=A+brazen+girl+possessed+of+seven+devils&dq=A+brazen+ girl+possessed+of+seven+devils&pgis=1

Chapter 6: Coming Clean

1.   In his final words David mentions Uriah as the last of his thirty-seven brave men (2 Sam. 23:39; cf. 1 Chron. 11:41). When wicked king Abijah's reign is described, we have this statement about David: "He [Abijah] committed all the sins his father had done before him; his heart was not fully devoted to the Lord his God, as the heart of David his forefather had been. Nevertheless, for David's sake the Lord his God gave him a lamp in Jerusalem by raising up a son to succeed him and by making Jerusalem strong. For David had done what was right in the eyes of the Lord and had not failed to keep any of the Lord's

commands all the days of his life—except in the case of Uriah the Hittite" (1 Kings 15). [There are a number of references to "Uriah the priest."]. The last reference in the Scriptures to Uriah is in the genealogy of the Lord Jesus recorded in Matthew 1. There we read, "David was the father of Solomon, whose mother had been Uriah's wife . . ." (v. 6).

2.   Online at http://bible.gen.nz/amos/hebrew/mem/maskil.htm. Accessed January 10, 2008.

3.   Online at http://www.maskilrecords.com/History1.html. Accessed January 10, 2008.

4.   Speaking of "counting" our sins, missionary Gerry DeRenzo gives the following illustration: "Let's say that I have one bad thought, say one bad word, and commit one bad deed per day. That's over 1000 sins a year! And I'm over 55 years old. If we give me my first 10 years free, that's 45,000 sins!"

5.   Sisters, OR: Multnomah Books, 2001.

6.   C.S. Lewis, *The Lion, the Witch, and the Wardrobe* (New York: Macmillan, 1950), pp. 75–76.

7.   J. Sidlow Baxter suggests that the inscriptions may actually be footnotes to the preceding psalm, not titles of the psalms to which they are attached. (*Explore the Book*, p. 93). In *An Introduction to the Old Testament*, Raymond B. Dillard and Tremper Longman, III, conclude: "The best solution is to regard the titles as early reliable tradition concerning the authorship and setting of the psalms. The titles, however, should not be taken as original or canonical" p. 215).

8.   We need to be careful about shame. Sometimes shame is nothing more than surprised pride about our failure. Perhaps a better term than "shame" is "sorrow" over sin.

9.   A recent sermon I heard reminded me that Satan is a 24/7 accuser of believers (Rev. 12:10), but his "ministry" of accusation is more than sufficiently overcome by Christ's constant intercession for us (Heb. 7:25).

10.   In a fascinating book, Earl Jabay makes the point that we begin life in the "tyranny of self-deification," seeking to set up ourselves as Num-

ber One, rather than God Himself (*The Kingdom of Self: A Fresh, Penetrating Analysis of Your Greatest Predicament* [Plainfield, NJ: Logos International, 1974], p. 16).

11. *Memoirs of Jonathan Edwards* as found in his *Works*, vol. 1, pp. xlvi–xlviii. Online at http://www.aomin.org/sovereign.html. Accessed on January 9, 2008.

Chapter 7: Breaking the Hold of Unholy Habits

1. We read in Romans 8:29, "For those God foreknew he also predestined to be conformed to the likeness of his Son, that he might be the firstborn among many brothers" We also read in Philippians 3:10, "I want to know Christ and the power of his resurrection and the fellowship of sharing in his sufferings, becoming like him in his death."

2. On New Year's eve we worshiped at an African-American church. We were overwhelmed by the love and deep spirituality of the congregation. However, like many white churches, there were a number of pregnant but unwed women there, families abandoned by the fathers, etc. My point is that true spirituality involves giving our *bodies* to the Lord.

3. Bruce K. Waltke, *Finding the Will of God: A Pagan Notion?* (Grand Rapids: Eerdmans, 1995).

4. C.S. Lewis, *Mere Christianity* (New York: HarperCollins, 2001), p. 189.

5. We can *inhabit* a practice, can't we?

6. *USA Today*, 11/14/2007, p. 3D.

7. We are not denying the component of a chemical dependency, for example, in alcoholism.

8. Larry Crabb's *Inside Out* (NavPress, 1998) has sold over 400,000 copies and is an excellent study on internal change for the believer in Christ.

9. http://thinkexist.com/quotes/charles_r._swindoll/. Accessed January 9, 2008.

10. A.W. Tozer, *That Incredible Christian*, quoted in *Gems from Tozer* (Weston-super-Mare, London: Send the Light Trust, 1969), p. 39.

11. http://inthemidstofit.blogspot.com/2006/04/favorite-quotes.html

12. We today are hardly "friends of publicans and sinners" (Matt. 11) as the Lord Jesus was. Often we engage in blackmail-type relationships with unbelievers ("Look. I'll give you six months. And if you don't trust Christ by then, well, I'll just have to move on . . ."). I've written some about our need to be friends of sinners in my *DocWALK: Putting into Practice What You Say You Believe*, Chapter 8 (Ross-shire, UK: Christian Focus Publications, 2005).

13. Rick Warren, *The Purpose-Driven Life*, p. 51.

14. Ibid., p. 127.

15. http://quotations.about.com/cs/inspirationquotes/a/Habits1.htm. Accessed January 9, 2008.

Chapter 8: What's the Church Got to Do with It?

1. Lewis B. Smedes, *Shame and Grace: Healing the Hurts We Don't Deserve* (San Francisco: HarperSanFrancisco/Zondervan, 1993), quoted in Erwin W. Lutzer's *Why Good People Do Bad Things* (Nashville: Word, 2001), p. 70.

2. Admittedly, these three texts deal with the hard task of excommunication. A study of the church's *positive* role in helping us resist temptation and sin is touched on in our next chapter.

3. There is some debate here. Some manuscripts do not have the expression "against you" in verse 15.

4. Note that these "two or three" correspond with the second level of intervention in this text. Therefore, the primary force of Christ's promised presence pertains to the context of church discipline.

5. This might be evidence that the textual variant "against you" might not be original. In other words, if the offender says *to the one he sinned against* "I did not do that," that seems patently absurd. He is denying his offense before the one he actually offended! Perhaps the confronter is not the direct offendee.

6. Note: Deuteronomy says *two or three* witnesses. Matthew 18 is specifying only *one or two*. Deuteronomy may be including the offendee.

7. Those who focus on spiritual warfare, the idea that we are to daily battle demonic forces, talk about "binding" Satan and demons. There are several passages which relate to this subject, such as Jude 6 which speaks of demons "bound with everlasting chains for judgment on the great Day." We also read about Satan being bound for a thousand years in Revelation 20:2. Matthew 12:29 asks, "How can anyone enter a strong man's house and carry off his possessions unless he first ties up the strong man?" For this perspective, see K. Neill Foster's *Binding and Loosing: Exercising Authority over the Dark Powers* (Camp Hill, PA: Christian Publications, 1998). For a fine, small text which challenges some of the spiritual warfare writers' assumptions, see Chuck Lowe's *Territorial Spirits and World Evangelisation?* (Ross-shire, UK: Christian Focus Publications, 1998).

8. True, we do read in 1 Timothy 1:20, "Among them are Hymenaeus and Alexander, whom I have handed over to Satan to be taught not to blaspheme." However, this does not seem to be binding demons, but somehow *using them* to accomplish God's purposes.

9. I believe that Matthew 18's steps have been followed and have been unsuccessful in the case of the man discussed in First Corinthians 5.

10. See our discussion of this text in Chapter 5.

11. I'm reminded of the statement by Bill Hybels that our job is not the behavior modification of unbelievers. Our job is to introduce them to the Lord Jesus. Behavior modification is the job of the Lord Jesus! Someone has written:

    Be ye fishers of men.
      You catch them—
        He'll clean them.

12. Although execution *is* the verdict in at least five of the six situations in Deuteronomy.

13. In fact, when we try to get unbelievers to behave like Christians, to give up their sinful habits, are we not mis-communicating the gospel? Are we not encouraging them to clean up their lives so that God will love and forgive them?

14. I am not making the case for Christians to have no moral impact on their culture. Jesus is clear that we are to be the salt and light of the world (Matt. 5:13–14) and should have a preserving, flavoring and illuminating influence in the circumstances in which the Lord places us in this world.

15. It is fascinating that this same individual is the reason Paul writes in Second Corinthians 2:6–11: "The punishment inflicted on him by the majority is sufficient for him. Now instead, you ought to forgive and comfort him, so that he will not be overwhelmed by excessive sorrow. I urge you, therefore, to reaffirm your love for him. The reason I wrote you was to see if you would stand the test and be obedient in everything. If you forgive anyone, I also forgive him. And what I have forgiven—if there was anything to forgive—I have forgiven in the sight of Christ for your sake, in order that Satan might not outwit us. For we are not unaware of his schemes." In First Corinthians the issue was their failure to discipline this man. In Second Corinthians 3:11 the issue is their failure to *forgive* this man. Our discussion of this verse should be seen in this context.

Chapter 9: Some Specific Strategies for Dealing with Temptation and Sin

1. Beth Moore, *Believing God* (Nashville: LifeWay Press, 2002), p. 79.

2. A friend of mine has the address of every web site that he visits on his computer automatically emailed to several friends to hold him accountable for where he surfs.

3. Compare Galatians 6:1, which speaks of someone "caught" in a sin.

4. Watchman Nee, *The Normal Christian Life* (Fort Washington, PA: Christian Literature Crusade, 1977), pp. 167–68.

5. One of my colleagues tells me that *Connecting: The Mentoring Relationships You Need To Succeed In Life* by Paul D. Stanley and J. Robert Clinton (Navpress Publishing Group, 1992) is well worth reading in this area. Also Don Howell, Jr.'s study *Servants of the Servant: A Biblical Theology of Leadership* (Wipf & Stock Publishers, 2003) is also highly regarded on this subject.

6.   See my book *DocTALK: A Fairly Serious Study of All That Theological Stuff* (Ross-shire, UK: Christian Focus Publications, 2002) for the chapter on the Holy Spirit.

7.   We are not to play the Holy Spirit's role in convicting others of sin. However, they will often be convicted when they see our example or hear us preach the truth. In Acts 2:36–37 we read, "Therefore let all the house of Israel know assuredly, that God hath made the same Jesus, whom ye have crucified, both Lord and Christ. Now when they heard this, they were pricked in their heart, and said unto Peter and to the rest of the apostles, Men and brethren, what shall we do?" (KJV).

8.   I believe the situation in Acts 5 is unique in the sense that this was the beginning time of the church—and God would not tolerate such deception.

9.   Many thanks to preacher Stephen Brown for this story.

10.   Review on Amazon.com. Accessed January 16, 2008.

11.   Dr. Henry Cloud says in his book *Changes That Heal: How to Understand Your Past to Insure a Healthier Future* (Grand Rapids: Zondervan, 1992): "If anything comes through the message of this book, it is that the body of Christ is the only place in which we grow" (p. 10).

Chapter 10: Finally—When Temptation And Sin Are No More

1.   I call these "myth-stakes" because of the serious nature of these false beliefs. They are more than mistakes, for a number of other biblical truths are compromised when these two errors are embraced.

2.   He also wrote "I, Robot" in 1950, which became a hit movie starring Will Smith in 2004.

3.   Please see my *The Other Side of the Good News* for an in-depth study of the fate of the lost.

4.   Online at http://rudysbooks.com/asimovobit.html. Accessed January 11, 2008.

5.   C.S. Lewis, *Letters to Malcolm, Chiefly on Prayer* (New York: Harvest Books, 1973), ch. 17.

6.   Quoted in Rick Warren, *The Purpose-Driven Life*, p. 55.

7.   Quoted in Rick Warren, *The Purpose-Driven Life*, p. 50. Apparently the original source is Lewis' *The Four Loves*.

8.   See also my discussion of this passage in my book *Heaven: Thinking Now about Forever* (Camp Hill, PA: Christian Publications, 2002).

9.   Rick Warren, *The Purpose-Driven Life*, p. 50.

10.   Cited in Rick Warren, *The Purpose-Driven Life*, p. 103.

11.   "Is Evil Necessary?" Dominic Walker. Paper given to the Spirituality Special Interest Group of the Royal College of Psychiatrists. http://www.catholicdoctors.org.uk/CMQ/May_2002/is_evil_necessary.htm

12.   http://www.liverpool.anglican.org/people/bishops/jamesspeeches/0307%20C%20S%20Lewis%20Summer%20Institute.htm

13.   See Thomas Ice and Timothy Demy, *What The Bible Says about Heaven & Eternity* (Grand Rapids: Kregel, 2000).

14.   Many theologians believe the local church *offices* of apostle and prophet have passed away.

15.   The following references are from the King James Version of the Bible.

16.   Randy Alcorn in his book *Heaven* discusses the question: Will the heavens and the earth be destroyed—or renewed?

17.   Eugene Peterson has written: "There is a great market for religious experience in our world; there is little enthusiasm for the patient acquisition of virtue, little inclination to sign up for a long apprenticeship in what earlier generations of Christians called holiness" (*A Long Obedience in the Same Direction*, [Downers Grove, IL: Intervarsity Press, 2000]).

This book was produced by CLC Publications. We hope it has been life-changing and has given you a fresh experience of God through the work of the Holy Spirit. CLC Publications is an outreach of CLC Ministries International, a global literature mission with work in over 50 countries. If you would like to know more about us or are interested in opportunities to serve with a faith mission, we invite you to contact us at:

CLC Ministries International
P.O. Box 1449
Fort Washington, PA 19034

Phone: (215) 542-1242
E-mail: orders@clcpublications.com
Website: www.clcpublications.com

DO YOU LOVE GOOD CHRISTIAN BOOKS?
Do you have a heart for worldwide missions?

You can receive a FREE subscription to
CLC's newsletter on global literature missions.
Order by e-mail at:

clcheartbeat@clcusa.org
or fill in the coupon below and mail to:

P.O. Box 1449
Fort Washington, PA 19034

FREE HEARTBEAT SUBSCRIPTION!

Name: _____

Address: _____

_

_____

READ THE REMARKABLE STORY OF

the founding of
CLC INTERNATIONAL

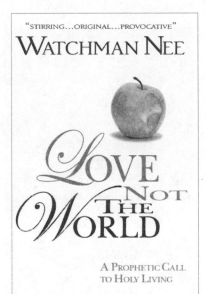

Love Not the World

Watchman Nee

A provocative look at a world where the natural tendency is away from God and toward Satan. How can the Christian live and work in these worldly systems and not be "of the world"? A classic from this great teacher!

Trade paper • 118 pages
ISBN: 978-0-87508-787-0

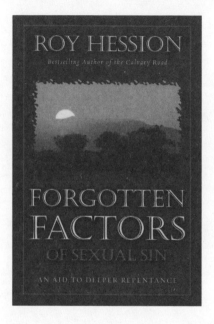

Forgotten Factors of Sexual Sin

Roy Hession

This book on temptation and sexual sins specifically addresses the factors that need to be dealt with when people who succumb try to get their lives together again.

Trade paper • 107 pages
ISBN: 978-0-87508-823-5

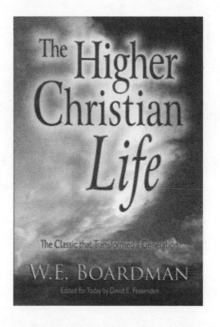

The Higher Christian Life
W.E. Boardman

Warning: This book, which sparked a revival on two continents in the 1800s, could change your whole viewpoint on the Christian life. Are you ready to be challenged and changed? Now edited for today's reader.

Trade paper • 164 pages
ISBN: 978-0-87508-894-5